Executed
for Ireland

The back of a Holy picture where Paddy Moran wrote a message for his girlfriend on the eve of his execution.

EXECUTED FOR IRELAND

THE PATRICK MORAN STORY

MAY MORAN

MERCIER PRESS
IRISH PUBLISHER – IRISH STORY

MERCIER PRESS

Cork

www.mercierpress.ie

Trade enquiries to CMD BookSource,
55a Spruce Avenue, Stillorgan Industrial Park,
Blackrock, County Dublin

© May Moran, 2010

ISBN: 978 1 85635 661 9

10 9 8 7 6 5 4 3 2 1

A CIP record for this title is available from the British Library

Printed and bound in the EU.

CONTENTS

Introduction

During the period 1916–1922, when Ireland, which had been governed until then by Great Britain, fought to become an independent state, many lives were lost on both the Irish and the British sides. Some men went down fighting, others were assassinated, and towards the end of that war, ten men, members of the Irish Republican Army, were hanged. Their remains were buried in the grounds of Mountjoy Jail, Dublin, by the prison authorities and there they lay for more than eighty years. On 14 October 2001, the remains of nine of those ten men were reburied in Glasnevin cemetery, Dublin, and the tenth was reburied in Ballylanders, County Limerick, all with full state honours.

Two of the ten, Paddy Moran and Thomas Whelan, were accused of complicity in the assassination of British military officers on Sunday, 21 November 1920. On that Sunday morning twelve British army personnel, some of them secret service agents, and two cadets were killed by members of the Irish Republican Army, in an operation directed by Michael Collins. Later on that same fateful day, the Dublin Castle authorities sent a military force allegedly to search for arms in Croke Park, Dublin, where a Gaelic Football match between Dublin and Tipperary was being played. On the arrival of the British forces during the match, shots were fired, resulting in fourteen civilians being killed and seventy injured. It is little wonder that the day has become known as Bloody Sunday.

Paddy Moran from Crossna, Boyle, County Roscommon, and Thomas Whelan from Sky Road, Clifden, County Galway, were the only men executed for their alleged part in the killing of the secret service agents on that Sunday morning and both protested their innocence of the crimes for which they were hanged on 14 March 1921.

Paddy Moran's sister, B (Bridget), was his last surviving sibling and she died in her 103rd year in the last days of 1997, leaving me a little brown case which contained my uncle's last letters home, the daily papers that reported on his trial and other memorabilia. The case had always lodged on the top of the wardrobe in her bedroom. I knew it was there and I knew that it contained material belonging to my uncle, but I never saw what was inside. When I opened it, I was fascinated by its contents and by his story. I realised that I had no real picture of what his life had been like, and only a very hazy idea of what had happened to him. Moran Park in Dun Laoghaire and a seat in Blackrock Catholic Church, County Dublin, are dedicated to him, while a plaque in Banba Hall, now the Hugh Lane Gallery, bears his name and he gets a mention in some published works; nevertheless very little is known about the man who was Paddy Moran.

The contents of the case started me on a journey of discovery of the true story of this uncle, whose name had been revered but seldom mentioned in my childhood. It was a journey that was emotional, revealing, informative and at times traumatic. I felt I had to walk in his footsteps and I did that by going to all the places that I knew he frequented. I walked down George's Street, Dun Laoghaire, around Blackrock, Phibsboro, Parnell Square and O'Connell Street, Dublin, and thought of him treading the same streets. I visited Kilmainham Gaol and saw the grim cell where he spent several weeks. Later, when I visited Mountjoy Jail, I saw the execution chamber and thought how it must feel to step onto that platform and wait for an executioner to pull the lever.

Research into Paddy's story took me to the Public Record Office in Kew, London, now the British National Archives, to the

National Library in Dublin, the UCD Archives, the Bureau of Military History in Cathal Brugha Barracks, the Allen Library, the House of Commons and to the National Archives in Bishop Street, Dublin, which coincidentally, is housed in the building that Paddy occupied in Easter week 1916, Jacob's Factory.

The story of Paddy Moran's life as handed down in our family was a truly heroic one in which he was unjustly hanged by the British for a crime which he did not commit. During the course of my research, I discovered that this was not the full story. While Uncle Paddy was indeed innocent of the crime for which he was hanged, he was in fact involved in another mission on that fateful morning of Bloody Sunday, 21 November 1920. He was part of the action at the Gresham Hotel where two suspected British agents were killed. At this point, I wondered if I should continue writing. The Moran family had always believed that Paddy was an innocent victim. I discussed the matter with family members and only then discovered that some of them did know about Paddy's involvement in the Gresham. A wish to record the truth motivated me to continue.

This book will endeavour to tell his story and to assess his contribution to one of the most important periods in Irish history.

CHAPTER 1

WHO WAS PADDY MORAN?

Amongst the wild March days my birthday came,
Near Patrick's Day — and I would often blame
Him, that for Ireland little he had done,
Or long before this day the fight were won.
But now I think that I perhaps was wrong,
That he, instead, was forming all along
Battalions radiant of our martyred race,
And one by one he calls them to their place
In Heaven. Soon I, too, shall join that band
Of some battalion, maybe, take command;
At roll-call meet again lost comrades true,
And if some day I mobilise you, too,
Flinch not, but face with pride, as I do now
The road where Ireland calls. I've kept my vow,
And from beyond I'll watch her victory.
Slán Leat, comrade-in-arms, and pray for me.[1]

Paddy Moran was born in March 1888, in Crossna, a small townland in the parish of Ardcarne, Boyle, County Roscommon.[2] It is a picturesque little place nestling in the hills overlooking Lough Key, with a view across a countryside that spans the Plains of Boyle over to Carrick-on-Shannon, across Sliabh an Iarainn, over the Arigna mountains, the Ox mountains and finally over to Queen Maeve's grave on Knocknarea, County Sligo.

Born to Bartholomew and Brigid Moran (née Sheeran) Paddy was the third child in a family of eleven children – six boys and five girls. Paddy's grandfather, John Moran, constructed the house in which Paddy was born, a small thatched cottage typical of its time. John's wife, Mary Regan, was born by the shores of Lough Arrow, a few miles away. Together they set up home across the road from John's family home and their new house was severely tested within its first year. The sod and thatch roof was in place, but still settling, on the night of the 'Big Wind', 6 January 1839. Neighbouring men were called in to secure it with ropes and were fortified with poitín while they did so! That house was the Moran family home until 1960, when a new bungalow was built beside it.

John and Mary's family of six, three boys and three girls, were all born before or during the famine years and, although they lived on a small farm, they seem to have fared reasonably well during that period, because John also ran a carting business, one of the first in the area. He is said to have transported the massive stone steps of Boyle courthouse from a quarry in Arigna. John's three daughters became teachers, his eldest son, also John, inherited a farm in nearby Dereenadouglas, and his youngest son, Thomas, went into an apprenticeship in Ballyfarnon and then into the drapery business in Dublin. Bartholomew, Paddy's father, was the third eldest child in the family and he inherited the family home and farm.

Paddy attended the local school in Crossna where, in his first years, his teacher was Miss Lane. When he heard of her death, he recalled that she was 'sweet with the rod'.[3] Some of the boys, when they were finished their infant schooling, went on to the adjacent school in Cartron, probably because Mr Conway, the teacher, was well regarded locally. Mr Conway was a local man who had a reputation for his knowledge of Irish history and for his ability to enliven it for his students. Paddy Moran listened attentively to those lessons and after one class he exclaimed, 'When I grow up

I'll fight for Ireland.' One student remarked that to be shot was not so bad, but hanging was an awful death. 'Ah no,' said Paddy, 'don't say that; was hanging not mostly the Irish patriot's death? Think of Robert Emmet.'[4]

Like most young boys of the time, he left school as a teenager, and went to work in Doyle's grocery shop in Cootehall, a few miles from his home but still in Ardcarne parish. From there, he went on to serve his time as a grocer's assistant in Paddy O'Rourke's grocery shop in Main Street, Boyle.[5]

His time in Boyle had a profound impact on shaping his social consciousness. His route home took him past the demesne wall that surrounded Rockingham Estate, a large estate comprising about 2,000 acres of the best land in the area and owned by the King Harmon family. Lord Lorton, the late landlord of Rockingham, had a reputation for evicting Catholic tenants and replacing them with Protestant tenants.[6] Paddy contrasted the lifestyle inside the estate with that of his family and neighbours outside. The gentry had plenty to eat, they were involved in pursuits like hunting and horse-racing, and held grand balls for the upper classes from the surrounding areas. In contrast, those outside were struggling to eke out a living for themselves and their families on their smallholdings.

When he had finished his apprenticeship in Boyle, Paddy obtained a position in Patrick Maguire's of 49 Main Street, Mohill. In August 1910, while at home on holiday, he received a letter from Patrick Maguire telling him not to return, as business was very quiet. It included a statement of account, a cheque for £21.11.10½ and a note saying that his belongings were being sent by train to Boyle.[7] The cheque was the balance due to him from his £40 salary for the year. Business may have been quiet, but by 1911 Patrick Maguire had four assistants and an apprentice employed – perhaps he could not afford a trained assistant.[8]

In September 1910, Paddy went to Dublin.[9] He tried for a

position in John Doyle's pub, the well-known landmark 'Doyle's Corner' on Dublin's northside, but there was no vacancy, so he went to Athy, County Kildare, and worked for a little over a year in S.J. Glynn's grocery shop. During his time there he was a member of the local Catholic Young Men's Society (CYMS) and he played an active part in local amateur theatricals. He played football for the local Geraldine Football Club and one of his playing colleagues was Golly Germaine.[10] Sometime later he returned to Dublin and took up a position in Doyle's. When he joined the National Health Insurance in July 1912, Doyle's, Phibsboro, was named as his place of work.

As well as joining the National Health Insurance scheme in 1912, a Protection and Provident Benefit Society for assistants employed in the licensed grocery trade in Dublin, Paddy also became an active trade unionist and joined the Grocers' and Vintners' Assistants' Association.

In 2001, John Douglas, General Secretary of the Mandate Union, the union that now represents the Grocers, Vintners and Allied Trades, painted a picture of what life was like in Dublin at that time: 'Dublin was, in the early part of the twentieth century, very different to now. Families lived in tenement slums, workers experienced harsh working hours, low wages and poor conditions. The fledgling trade union movement was under severe attack from employers. There were riots in O'Connell Street; workers in Wexford were locked out for weeks on end. All this culminated in the Great Dublin Lockout of 1913 led by James Connolly and Jim Larkin and no doubt with the involvement of Paddy Moran.'

The 1913 Lockout came about because employers resisted attempts to unionise unskilled labour and sacked workers who refused to sign an undertaking not to join the Irish Transport and General Workers Union (IGTWU), established by Jim Larkin, mainly for unskilled workers. More than a quarter of the male population in Dublin were unskilled labourers and they were living in poverty because of the lack of employment. The average wage was about 18 shillings a week, but for many it was as low as 15 or 16 shillings. When the Employers' Federation dismissed 100 workers because they refused to sign the undertaking not to join the union 'Larkin called out the tramway workers paralysing the transport system during Horse Show week, one of the social highlights of the year'.[11] The employers locked the men out and a series of strikes by different groups ensued. By September 1913, there were about 20,000 either on strike or locked out, a situation that quickly became untenable for the men and their families who were starving. 'By early 1914 the men were returning to work on the best terms they could get.'[12]

Although it was regarded as a failure, it is estimated that the strike campaign of 1913 raised wage levels for the unskilled by about twenty to twenty-five per cent. Larkin's greatest achievement was, perhaps, that he persuaded the unskilled workers to show solidarity, by refusing to take on the jobs of those on strike or to handle goods belonging to strike-bound employers.[13]

In 1915 Mr Glynn, the proprietor of the shop in Athy where Paddy had worked, wrote to him, asking him to consider returning to work with him. It is in that letter that we find the first mention of his involvement in politics and the Gaelic League:

Our Joe of late has a tendency to be careless about the business and I fear the tendency to get tired of constant work may lead him in [a] wrong direction. I find it hard to keep him from boozers' company; he is well inclined but very easily led astray so I have decided to make a change in my assistants. We could find no men since O'Brien left for the army, so I tried girls but they are all an utter failure. I've had a couple and one was worse than the other so I'm parting with her and won't try girls again. Would you be willing to come to us, your political and other opinions coincide with our own and they will help keep Joe straight, in line with the right side. Especially in the temptation to drink your example would do infinitely more good than our exhortations to keep out of boozers' company. The Gaelic League wants a bit of energetic organisation as it is at sixes and sevens and you are just the man to get them together again. Other reasons too might induce you to renew country life! If you consider this offer let me know your terms; I may say that at present trade being under the average owing to the war I could not afford to pay a big salary, but I actually would improve it as trade improved and you would certainly improve it very much. You know my infirmity handicaps me terribly and Joe [is] not working as he ought so it is urgent. The business wants an industrious working man who would take the interest you always did. There are other things to be said but space does not allow. If you have strong reasons for declining, do you know of a good substitute whom I can trust to work right and do me justice? If disengaged so much the better but it will do after notice say end of December or at any time.

With much regard from Mrs Glynn and self,

Faithfully yours, S.J. Glynn

Need I say if you come you'd be one of ourselves.[14]

He did not return to Athy in 1915 and I don't know whether he was able to help Mr Glynn to find a suitable employee, male or female!

Paddy was a gentle youth, whose natural, unassuming manner and quiet, natural reserve were his most striking characteristics.[15] Those who knew him well regarded him as a loyal friend with a good sense of humour, a great organiser and a lover of life and family. He had a cheery personality and often sang or whistled as he went about the neighbourhood. Once when his mother wanted him to do something for her, she found him sitting on her kitchen table entertaining his siblings with 'The Whistling Gypsy'.[16]

He was a keen sportsman and an early recruit to the GAA. He played football for the Grocers Assistants' and Marlborough

Rangers Gaelic Football teams in Dublin. Marlborough Rangers was associated with Marlborough Street National School and existed from the early years of the twentieth century until the 1930s, fielding football and hurling teams.[17] A medal with the inscription 'County Dublin Football League, Patrick Moran, Junior League Runners up, Marlborough Rangers 1914–1915' is part of the family collection. The Emeralds team won that league final but Marlborough Rangers lodged an objection because two players on the Emeralds were ineligible to play, having played at senior level in that season. The county board committee rejected the appeal and Marlborough Rangers appealed to the Leinster council.[18] It upheld the appeal, but the county committee in turn appealed to the appeals board against that Leinster council decision. The argument rumbled on and was raised at the annual Dublin county board convention held on 17 October 1915. Paddy Moran and C.J. Walsh were delegates for Marlborough Rangers. A motion in the name of the club was proposed by C.J. Walsh: 'That in the opinion of this convention, the county board has misinterpreted the rules of the organisation in so far as it has reinstated Senior Championship players of last season to Junior League status within the same season, and that it be an instruction to the incoming county board not to follow this precedent pending a definite pronouncement on the question by the next All-Ireland Convention.' There was heated discussion on the motion after Walsh accused the committee of 'rigging', but finally an amendment was added: 'That it be an instruction to the incoming committee to re-open the case of the Emeralds' players concerned in the objection by Marlborough Rangers'.[19] The new committee decided that the players in question did not mislead the committee and the reinstatements granted remained effective.[20] Emeralds team therefore kept their title of Junior League winner.

Paddy Moran started a new football club in 1918 in Dun Laoghaire called 'Dunleary Commercials'. It won the Intermediate

Football Championship in 1920 and finished runner-up in the Junior Football League in that same year.

Paddy may also have played for University College Dublin on the Sigerson Cup team in February 1920, although he never studied there. UCD beat University College Cork 1–7 to 1–4. Dónal Mac an Ailin compared the P. Moran pictured with that team, in the *Freeman's Journal* on 20 February 1920, with Paddy's photograph in the Grocers' Assistants team of 1913 and concluded that it was the same man.[21] It would not have been unusual at the time for players who were not students to play on a university team. According to an often-repeated anecdote, one player on the Cork University team, when asked what he was studying, replied, 'sums'![22] Dónal suggested that Paddy's association with players like Mick Mullins, Frank Burke and other Volunteers was the most likely reason for his inclusion, if he did play. I would contend that it was probably his good friend Dan O'Carroll, who was a Professor of Mathematics and Irish in Belvedere College and had studied at UCD, who recruited him. Dan played with him on the Marlborough Rangers Football Team and was a member of the same Volunteer company as Paddy. Dan O'Carroll emigrated to Australia in late 1923 because of ill health and he died there on Christmas Day in 1924. His father Jeremiah wrote to Paddy's father thanking him for his letter of sympathy and went on:

How he could talk for hours on the merits of Paddy: there was none to equal him. A mutual friend of both wrote me from Dublin that Dan lost all interest in life after Paddy's death.

I had a small picture here of Paddy and another of Martin Savage, both in uniform. I got both enlarged in one and hung it in the parlour and I think nothing would have given him such genuine pleasure.

When Paddy and he used get letters from you and me they'd sit down and compare advices and he told me anyone would think we sat at the same table and copied what each wrote.[23]

18

Paddy was anxious to pass on the football skills he learned in Dublin to the youth in Crossna. On his frequent visits home he was often found in Fryre's field training them in the skills of catching the ball in the air and kicking it from the hand, skills that were new to them.[24] The Crossna men were not new to football. The club first fielded a football team in the County Championship in 1889. However, by 1900 there was no club in Crossna and none in County Roscommon. By 1914 Crossna had reformed the club and during the 1920s and 1930s there was great rivalry between the two clubs in the parish, Crossna and Cootehall. In 1941 the two clubs amalgamated to form St Michael's.[25] Paddy Moran was honoured in his native area in 1956 and 1957 when St Michael's and a neighbouring team, St Ronan's, joined together to form a senior team called Paddy Morans.[26]

Fishing was another pastime of his and when at home he liked nothing better than to join his neighbours on their fishing trips to the nearby Feorish river. His cheery personality made him a favourite companion to the seasoned fishermen. On one occasion, in 1914, he brought home a fishing net thinking that it would be an advance on the 'line and rod'. He and his brother Tom set off on their bicycles. Charlie Bruen, a neighbour, accompanied by his dog, rode alongside them on a jennet, full of expectation for what the new net might deliver. The trip proved fruitless and the following poem was written by Paddy:

THE FISH THAT WEREN'T CAUGHT

Come all ye dryland fishermen and listen to my song.
There aren't many verses so I won't detain you long.
I'll sing you of a stirring scene that's writ down in my log,
The heroes are the Morans, Bruen, his jennet and his dog.

The fish in all the rivers and the lakes for miles around
Had heard a net was landed somewhere above the ground
For weeks they did not eat or drink – some swam off to the bog
To escape from the Morans, Bruen, his jennet and his dog.

One morning in the 7th month just at the break of day
A mist hung o'er the valleys as Bruen rode down the bray
The net and sinks were ready with a bag to bring the prog
And for slaughter went the Morans, Bruen, his jennet and his dog.

The clatter of the jennet's hoofs, the rattle of the bikes
I'm sure that peaceful rugged road had never heard the likes.
And Larry frightened from his wits looked out and said 'begob'.
What's up! With the Morans, Bruen, his jennet and his dog?

The bridge at Tim's was held by goats, it seemed no one could pass.
While further on at Carty's lay a roarin' big jack ass.
When Charlie got the order, charge, they fled and killed a frog
And forward went the Morans, Bruen, his jennet and his dog.

People said the Ulster Volunteers were surely on the move
And that they weren't bluffing this day they meant to prove
But as they left their warm beds and gazed out thro' the fog.
They saw but the Morans, Bruen, his jennet and his dog.

Then as the sun was rising, on the river bank they stood
And each man swore to fill the net he'd do the best he could
They beat the river up and down the result alas! My God!
There was nothing for the Morans, Bruen, his jennet and his dog.

Martin Sheeran and McLoughlin were there to have their laugh
And laugh you think they didn't, they didn't no, not half
But Charlie said going up the field 'If I'd me line and rod,
I'd load both the Morans, Bruen, his jennet and his dog.'[27]

Paddy wrote the poem on the flyleaf of a book that his sister Annie won at a Feis in Boyle in July 1912. The book, *Gill's Irish Reciter*, was awarded to her for 'Superior Merit in Stáir' (History).[28]

In Dublin, much of Paddy's time was taken up with his work, his involvement in the Volunteers, the Gaelic League and the Gaelic Athletic Association, and his involvement in the trade union movement, but he also made time for socialising. The McAllister Gaelic Athletic Club held a dance in the Grand Restaurant, O'Connell Street, on Saturday 25 April 1914 and a dance card that he kept shows that he had promised six of the twenty dances to the cardholder.

It is not clear when and where Paddy became involved in the Sinn Féin organisation, but he was a member of the GAA and the Gaelic League, and like many others who shared these interests it is possible that he was an early recruit to Sinn Féin. 'In the decade before 1914–1918 World War there was in Dublin a kind of natural graduation, which led to participation in the Easter Rising of 1916, for lads of the more advanced national views. One usually began by playing Gaelic football or hurling, from that the next step was to the Gaelic League, from that to the Sinn Féin movement and later to the Irish Volunteer Movement.'[29] Pádraic Pearse, one of the leaders of the 1916 Rising, wrote in 1914: 'The Gaelic League will be recognised in history as the most revolutionary influence that has ever come to Ireland'.[30]

In Ireland, in 1912, political debate was centred on the 1911 Act granting a measure of Home Rule for Ireland. The measure was largely supported by John Redmond and the Irish Parliamentary Party, as well as by Sinn Féin, who declared that 'no measure which gave the Irish people genuine, even if partial control of their own affairs ought to be opposed.'[31] Nationalists, north and south, saw it as a stepping stone to greater independence and by and large welcomed it. However, there was complete opposition from the unionist community and the Ulster Volunteer Force was formed in 1913 to defend the unionist position against Home Rule.

At this point in the south of Ireland the only militant force in existence was the Irish Republican Brotherhood (IRB), a secret organisation formed in the nineteenth century to work towards an Irish Republic. Paddy was a member of the IRB and Seán Farrelly, a publican and also a member of that organisation, who ran a business at the corner of St Stephen's Green, said that he proposed him for membership.[32] All IRB members took a solemn oath: 'In the presence of God, I _____ do solemnly swear that I will do my utmost to establish the national independence of Ireland, that I will bear true allegiance to the Supreme Council of the IRB and government of the Irish Republic, that I will implicitly obey the constitution of the IRB and all my superior officers, and preserve inviolable secrets of the organisation. So help me God.'[33]

Gradually, probably as a result of the influence of the IRB, it was felt that nationalist Ireland should unite and organise to defend itself just as the unionists were doing. A proposal to establish a National Volunteer Movement was made by Professor Eoin Mac Néill in an article in the Gaelic League magazine and a meeting was subsequently held on 14 November 1913 in Wynne's Hotel in Abbey Street, Dublin, for the formation of such a movement.[34] Following that a general meeting was held in the Rotunda Rink on 25 November 1913. All shades of political opinion were represented and the Volunteers were formally established. The enrolment form stated: 'I, the undersigned, desire to be enrolled in the Irish Volunteers founded to secure and maintain the rights and liberties common to all the people of Ireland without the distinction of creed, class or politics.'[35] Approximately 4,000 men enrolled at that meeting and Paddy Moran was probably one of those.

Fifteen companies of Volunteers were formed in Dublin city, and arrangements were made for the organisation of companies throughout Ireland. The members were grouped according to the locality of their homes; the companies were split into sections and the sections into groups of 100 men, each under a captain. The provisional committee issued instructions to organisers to invite all organisations of a nationalist tendency to join the Volunteers and to ensure that all sections of Irishmen were represented on committees. 'The organisation was a democratic one. Any Volunteer might be elected onto the committee, which appointed officers and made all arrangements. Later the companies were organised into battalions and the battalions into brigades.'[36]

Large numbers of those who joined the Volunteers in the beginning were followers of John Redmond and the Irish Parliamentary Party, who wished to achieve independence by constitutional means and were prepared to wait for Home Rule to become a reality. However, many others were members of the IRB, who were prepared to fight for independence. Tensions developed quickly within the newly formed movement between these two groups. To make matters more difficult, the British government was dragging its feet on the implementation of Home Rule and, when the bill was finally placed on the Statute Book on 18 September 1914, a Suspensory Act was also passed, with a promise of reactivating Home Rule after the end of the First World War which had broken out a month earlier. At this point Redmond urged the National Volunteers to enlist in the British army and to fight for Britain. Several thousand Irishmen took his advice and joined the British army. This caused a split in the movement in August 1914 and led to the formation of the Irish Volunteers as distinct from the National Volunteers, the latter continuing to support John Redmond and the Irish Parliamentary Party.

Paddy Moran sided with the Irish Volunteers, joined D Company, 2nd Battalion, Dublin 2 Brigade, and was elected adjutant of the company, with Séamus Kavanagh its captain. The 2nd Battalion operated in the North Liffey and East O'Connell Street area.[37] D Company was specially organised for those who were working in the bar and grocery trades and who, because of the nature of their work, were unable to meet at normal times. They drilled at Fr Matthew Park, Fairview, on Sunday mornings at 11 a.m. and met also at the Foresters Hall in Parnell Square.[38] Their area of operation extended from the Parnell Monument, up North Frederick Street, Blessington Street, Berkeley Road and by the tram line to 'Dunphy's Corner', Phibsboro Road, and from there northwards to the canal, on to Summerhill Bridge and back towards the Parnell Monument at the bottom of Parnell Square.[39]

Around this time in Paddy's native Crossna, a new curate, Fr Michael O'Flanagan, was appointed by the Bishop of Elphin and a long association began between Fr O'Flanagan and the Moran family. Fr O'Flanagan had been the curate in Cliffoney, County Sligo, for about fifteen months before his appointment to Crossna, and while there he was involved in a dispute with the Congested Districts Board (CDB), on behalf of some of his parishioners, about the withdrawal of turbary rights. The CDB was established in 1891 to develop the west of Ireland and, by 1909, it had a budget of £250,000, which it used to purchase land, carry out drainage, and construct roads and fences, as well as promoting the development of cottage industries. When the war broke out in 1914, the CDB ceased to purchase land for distribution and it refused to distribute land in its possession unless the applicant established his fitness for it by joining or getting his sons to join the British army. The CDB had acquired the Hippesley and Sullivan estates and only tenants of the board could acquire a turf-bank on these lands, a right that had previously been enjoyed by many of Fr O'Flanagan's parishioners. He asked how his parishioners could be expected 'to allow their children shiver in the cold next winter while you retain the bogs for prospective tenants'.[40] Fr O'Flanagan encouraged those who wanted a turf-bank to assemble at his house on 30 June 1915, and to go with him to Cloonercoo bog to cut turf. An injunction against Fr O'Flanagan and some of his followers was granted to the Congested Districts Board in the High Court in August 1915, but, during the hearing, the board agreed that it was reasonable to sell turf-plots to more than its own tenants.[41]

The annual police report for the year 1915 describes the occurrence:

> Some slight trouble arose in August in connection with a dispute about a bog. The Reverend M. O'Flanagan, CC, having been refused an allotment of bog on land in the possession of the Congested Districts Board, called a meeting of his parishioners and went with them to the bog and cut turf. The Congested Districts Board then obtained an injunction against Fr O'Flanagan and his followers restraining them from further interference. Later on, in October, Fr O'Flanagan was transferred to another curacy [Crossna], and thereupon the people of Cliffoney locked up the church against Fr O'Flanagan's replacement, Fr McHugh, who subsequently forced the door and entered the building. On leaving the church he was 'groaned' by the people, who again locked and guarded it. Fr McHugh made no further attempt to enter the church, which remained closed until Christmas Day, when the dispute was ended by the people giving up the key to the parish priest.[42]

In that same year, 1915, the vice-president of the Board of Agriculture addressed a public meeting in Sligo, to encourage farmers to grow more tillage. Fr O'Flanagan argued that the meeting should reject the proposal unless it was accompanied by radical provisions for land reform.[43] He was a man who was not afraid to speak out and to act against injustice.

Shortly after this meeting Fr O'Flanagan was transferred to Crossna and when he met Paddy Moran he met a kindred spirit. When a company of Volunteers was formed in Crossna in 1916, Paddy Moran and Fr O'Flanagan managed to procure arms for them. Sixteen shotguns and some ammunition were hidden in a trunk brought by train to Carrick-on-Shannon by Fr O'Flanagan.

He got off at Carrick-on-Shannon, rather than Boyle, because Boyle was a garrison town and it was more likely that the large trunk would be spotted there and its contents revealed. His caution proved wise. When Batty Moran, Paddy's brother, brought the empty trunk back to Boyle to be returned to Paddy in Dublin, he was stopped by the police and questioned. He explained that the trunk had been sent down with old clothes that 'we needed and he did not'.[44] His questioner was satisfied with this simple explanation.

Where did these arms come from? Paddy Moran was at this time adjutant of D Company and in that capacity he might have had little difficulty in procuring arms. However, it is well known that the Volunteers at the time did not have a large supply of arms, so it seems strange that he managed to send sixteen guns to Crossna. My father spoke about Paddy being part of a delegation to Germany, but it is not clear if this was a mission to procure arms. The fact that Paddy was able to send sixteen shotguns to Crossna suggests that he was in a position of influence within the Volunteers. (One of the guns he sent to Crossna is still a treasured possession of the family.)

However, the men of Crossna did not get an opportunity to use the guns. My father Tom's statement to the Military Service Pensions Board in 1937 states that in Easter week 1916 he was 'acting under orders of my superior officer' and that he had his men 'standing to, awaiting orders', but the action went no further than that.[45]

The gun that has survived from the cache sent to Crossna.

CHAPTER 2

THE 1916 RISING

The Irish Republican Brotherhood saw Britain's involvement in the First World War as an opportunity to rebel against her occupation of Ireland and secretly made preparations for such a rebellion. Many of the Volunteers who broke away from John Redmond when he advised participation in the war, were also members of the IRB. However, only a few of those who were not IRB members were taken into the confidence of the IRB leaders. James Connolly, the leader of the Citizen Army, who had been making preparations for his own rebellion at Liberty Hall, the headquarters of the Irish Transport and General Workers Union of which he was president, was one of these.[1]

Pádraic Pearse issued orders on 3 April 1916 for three days' 'march' throughout Ireland to begin on Easter Sunday, 23 April 1916. Eoin Mac Néill, who was chairman of the Volunteer executive, was not privy to the plans. When he discovered what was planned, he summoned the Volunteer headquarters staff and demanded that they give no order outside the routine to the Volunteers without his endorsement. However, Connolly, Pearse and the IRB continued with their original plans. Mac Néill discovered this and issued countermanding orders through the national press on Easter Sunday.[2] The rank and file members of the Volunteers read or heard of Mac Néill's countermanding orders and obeyed them. The result was that nothing happened in many parts of the country during Easter week. Even in Dublin, where most of the activity did take place, there was a great deal of confusion. The Easter Sunday march was called off and many Volunteers received no orders to re-assemble or march on Easter Monday. Volunteer Pádraig Ó Ceallaigh decided to go to the Fairyhouse Races on Easter Monday and when he was returning home by train he heard about the fighting in Dublin. He presented himself at the General Post Office (GPO) and was told to join the garrison in Jacob's Biscuit Factory.[3]

Paddy Moran and Hugh Maguire, both members of D Company, received orders from Captain Tom Hunter to march on Easter Sunday, to carry with them whatever arms they had and to bring provisions for forty-eight hours. On Easter Sunday morning Thomas MacDonagh, then O/C of Dublin Brigade, instructed the men to parade that evening in St Stephen's Green at 5.15 p.m. However, a message was sent to the men in the early afternoon to say that the parade was cancelled. Despite being informed of this, Hugh Maguire proceeded to St Stephen's Green to see what was happening. There he met Paddy Moran, his adjutant at that time. As they walked down Grafton Street towards the centre of the city they met a large group of the Citizen Army led by James Connolly and Countess Markievicz marching up towards the Green. When that group had passed, Paddy Moran said, 'If those parades had not been cancelled, you and I would be walking in an independent Ireland by this time tomorrow.'[4]

Volunteer Matthew Connolly, in his witness statement, confirms that the Citizen Army, headed by James Connolly, Michael Mallin and Countess Markievicz, made a tour of the principal city streets at three o'clock and returned to Liberty Hall at five o'clock. When James Connolly addressed his troops on their return he told them that they were no longer the Citizen Army, they were now merged with the Irish Volunteers, under the title 'The Irish Republican Army'.[5]

At the bottom of Grafton Street, Hugh Maguire and Paddy were told that their headquarters at Fr Matthew Park was being raided by the Dublin Metropolitan Police. Maguire recalled: 'Moran asked me if I had a gun on me and I said I had a .22 revolver. He said he had one also and that we would go to Fr Matthew Park. We went there but found no excitement whatsoever. We came back into the city to Parnell Park, where we parted company about 8 p.m. on that Easter Sunday night.'[6]

Some Volunteers received orders by word of mouth to reassemble on Easter Monday; others arrived by chance and joined in the action. The companies gathered at different places in the city. Thomas MacDonagh gathered his troops in St Stephen's Green. Paddy Moran, as adjutant of D Company, was probably in St Stephen's Green on Easter Monday to hear MacDonagh give an outline of the plans for the Rising. Some of D Company were posted in the College of Surgeons, some in the GPO and some in Jacob's Biscuit Factory – Paddy ended up in Jacob's.[7] However, he left no record of his time in Jacob's and so we must rely on the testimony of other Volunteers to provide us with a picture of what Easter week must have been like for him.

Volunteer William Slater arrived at St Stephen's Green to see Volunteers from different companies getting into line under their respective commanders. Volunteers from other battalions who did not know where to report, and who were in uniform and had ammunition, were told to fall in.[8] Séamus Pouch, a member of Na Fianna, describes how he and a few others went to Volunteer headquarters in Dawson Street on Easter Monday morning only to find it closed. On their way back to St Stephen's Green they met Gerry Holohan who told them to parade with the nearest group, assembled in the Green under Thomas MacDonagh, and these men also ended up in Jacob's Biscuit Factory.[9]

Trinity College had been marked for occupation and Paddy Walsh, a member of Moran's D Company, was in charge of the operation. However, it was decided that the taking of Trinity College would mean heavy loss of life, so MacDonagh called it off.[10] At twelve o'clock Thomas MacDonagh set off with his men for Jacob's Biscuit Factory. As they marched through Cuffe Street, women whose husbands had gone to fight with the British army in the war, subjected the men to verbal abuse. The mildest of their remarks were 'Go out and fight with the Germans.'[11]

While in Jacob's Paddy wrote to a friend: 'Whatever happens to us, I know you will be glad that we have made history'.[12] The story of the occupation of Jacob's is told from various sources which give an interesting insight into the situation. Sometime between twelve noon and one o'clock, a group of about 150 men, some armed, broke into the factory and went up the stairs to the top of the building. Still inside the factory were a small number of the workers who were there to carry out maintenance. The workers immediately informed Thomas Orr, the caretaker, and Henry Fitzgerald, the watchman on duty, of the situation. George N. Jacob, the chairman of the company, and Mr Dawson, a manager, were informed by telephone before the wires were cut and they managed to get to the factory. In the meantime a Volunteer officer collected all the workers and placed them under guard at the entrances before allowing them to leave the factory. Thomas Orr told the watchman to get his coat and leave but he himself refused to go. When the watchman arrived back with his coat, the hall door was barricaded and he was detained with Thomas Orr. The remainder of the Orr family was out for the day and their apartment, which was in the factory, was taken over until Sunday 30 April. The rebels had four other prisoners including two Dublin Metropolitan Police detectives.

Volunteers went about securing the building and filling vessels with water in case the water supply was cut off. Thomas Orr made three appeals to the rebels during the week. He asked Commandant MacDonagh to prevent smoking in the factory and MacDonagh issued orders immediately. He asked to be allowed to attend to fourteen horses stabled nearby and even though barricades had to be removed to allow this, MacDonagh gave him permission until he saw danger. Orr also asked for permission to contact Mr Jacob to see if the horses could be removed to safety, but permission was declined. Nevertheless, when the horses were in real danger, he was allowed to see to them. According to Thomas Orr, several rebels were sent out on Tuesday of Easter week to obtain provisions and when they arrived back they had the contents of two bread vans, a large quantity of milk, beef, mutton, bacon and many tins of food. They also had boots and the contents of the tobacco and chandlery stores, McEvoy's of Richmond Hill and Larkin's of Wexford Street. Fitzgerald and Orr refused to peel potatoes but the two Dublin Metropolitan Police detectives were forced to do it. Orr did not see anyone drunk or using bad language during the entire occupation.[13]

Many witness statements give accounts of what happened in Jacob's and they differ in many respects from Thomas Orr's account. According to these, the Volunteers gained entrance to the factory by breaking a window and climbing through it. One young man accidentally let off his gun and Major John MacBride who was inside 'calmly brushed the powder from his moustache and casually warned the boys to be more careful'.[14] Once inside they barricaded the windows and doors using bags of flour and took up the positions allotted to them by the officers. Séamus de Brún describes the incongruous appearance of the garrison at this stage. Some were dressed in full uniform, but it could hardly be seen beneath a mist of flour, others were in civilian garb with a cavalry bandolier or a canvas ammunition pouch. Their arms included double-barrelled shotguns, the Winchester repeater, the Lee Enfield British service magazine rifle, the Howth rifle and small arms from the .22 to the German parabellum.[15] While some men were exploring a cold storage compartment, the door, which was self-locking and could only be opened from outside, almost closed and but for the quick action of one man, who jammed his rifle butt in the door-jamb, the men inside would have frozen to death.[16]

The men in Jacob's and its outposts covered the strategic positions of Dublin Castle, Portobello and Wellington Barracks, Ship Street Barracks and the College of Surgeons. Shortly after five o'clock on Easter Monday a military detachment came down from Portobello. They were fired on by the men at Jacob's and retreated.[17] Some men were sent to Fumbally Lane to occupy an outpost in Barmack's distillery and a Dublin Metropolitan sergeant and two policemen were taken prisoners. A man in plainclothes who refused to move on was shot dead: Michael Walker said the man tried to disarm a Volunteer and was shot and bayoneted.[18] That evening the men from this outpost were ordered back to Jacob's as it was considered too dangerous a post. The people of the area were hostile and were throwing stones at the Volunteers.[19]

On Tuesday, there was regular sniping by a detachment from Portobello Barracks and continuous reply from the roof of Jacob's. Men were sent out to Byrne's and Delahunty's in Camden Street to make contact and assist the men holding Portobello Bridge. On Wednesday, firing started in earnest around the city, but the men inside Jacob's were not engaged in it. However, in the evening sentries were increased and the men in the outposts were not recalled to Jacob's. Flames of fire could be seen lighting up the night sky and at one stage a peculiar yellow smoke was seen over the Four Courts. Major John MacBride exclaimed, 'My God they are firing Lyddite shells.'[20] MacBride knew about Lyddite from his experiences in the Boer and First World Wars. Lyddite shells were the first generation of 'high explosive' shells, and if detonated properly they would fragment and shower shrapnel in all directions with devastating effect. He was probably somewhat relieved to see yellow smoke because it indicated that the shell had simply exploded rather than detonated properly.

The garrison in Jacob's was not attacked directly during Easter week. Some of the men were placed on the roof as snipers to protect other garrisons based in different positions. Others were sent out daily to find out what was happening in other parts of the city. On Thursday, a patrol was sent out under the command of Lieutenant Danny O'Riordan to relieve pressure on the garrison in Boland's Mills under Éamon de Valera and on the way back a Volunteer, John O'Grady, was shot and badly wounded. He died later in the Adelaide Hospital. He was the only casualty among the Jacob's garrison.[21]

On Thursday and Friday night there was a general alarm and everybody rushed to the barricades at the big factory gate in preparation for an attack, but none took place. On Saturday the fierce firing that had been heard all around the area during the previous few days died down and rumours began to reach the garrison that the leaders of the Rising were about to surrender.

On Sunday, Fr Augustine and Fr Aloysius, two Capuchin priests, went to Jacob's to inform the garrison that Pádraic Pearse had surrendered. Elizabeth O'Farrell, who was with the garrison in the GPO, was sent out with Pearse's letter: 'In order to prevent the further slaughter of Dublin citizens, and in the hope of saving our followers, now surrounded and hopelessly outnumbered, the members of the Provisional Government present at Headquarters have agreed to an unconditional surrender, and the commandants of the various districts in the city and country will order their commands to lay down arms.' Thomas MacDonagh, on hearing about the letter, said that as Pearse and Connolly were both under arrest, a letter written by them in custody could have no weight and he could not enter into negotiations with anyone except the general officer commanding the British military.

The priests left to convey that message to General Lowe. He arranged to meet Thomas MacDonagh in St Patrick's Park at 12 o'clock and persuaded MacDonagh to advise his troops to surrender. MacDonagh returned with the priests to consult the men at Jacob's, at the South Dublin Union and at Marrowbone Lane. On his return he summoned a meeting of all his officers in the staff room.[22] Major MacBride sat calmly beside Thomas MacDonagh as he announced that Pearse had surrendered and had issued an order to all units to do likewise. He read the order and pointed out that the men were not bound to obey orders from a prisoner. He solicited the views of those present; each officer spoke up in turn and though some were in favour of fighting it out, the majority counselled obedience to the order. Séamus Hughes wanted to fight and he delivered a fiery speech pointing out that by surrendering the men would in fact be offering their leaders as a sacrifice and that it would be better to die with guns in their hands than to face the firing squad. On the other hand Michael O'Hanrahan in his slow, calm and reasoned tone advised surrender. Éamon Price supported O'Hanrahan. Incendiary shells would destroy the factory and the surrounding thickly populated areas if the fighting continued. MacDonagh listened carefully and then his voice shook as he spoke and finally with tears in his eyes he broke down crying: 'Boys we must give in. We must leave some to carry on the struggle.' It was a poignant moment and one that would remain indelibly imprinted on the memories of those present.[23] Major MacBride tried to cheer up the men by telling them that it was likely they would get another opportunity and he advised that, when they did, they should never again be caught in the cities or within walls; they should take to the open country where they would have a chance to fight.[24]

The commanding officers had to convey the decision to the men and to make the necessary arrangements for evacuation. When the garrison was assembled on the ground floor there was a scene of incredible pandemonium and confusion, as men, seeing their dearest hopes dashed, were weeping openly, breaking their rifles against the walls. Others took things more quietly, but grimly prepared for the inevitable. The young lads and the older married men with dependent children, who were not in uniform, were advised to try to get away. Not all took that course, some stuck manfully to their officers.[25]

MacDonagh then went to the South Dublin Union where he met Éamonn Ceannt. The officers there agreed to surrender. On the way out they had a narrow escape when a soldier fired on them; they ducked and avoided the bullet. The men in Marrowbone Lane were not easily persuaded to surrender but they too finally agreed. Thomas MacDonagh was back in St Patrick's Park at 3 p.m. to meet General Lowe. He removed his belt and handed it with his revolver to the general. When he returned to Jacob's the men were lined up in the basement ready to leave. Suddenly there was a loud noise – looters had broken a window and were inside the building stealing goods. Fr Aloysius spoke to the looters and later said: 'Side by side with the manly and straightforward conduct of those who had borne the brunt of a trying week, I thought their conduct wretched and despicable and I did not mince my words.' The crowd dispersed and many of the looters threw back the stolen goods.[26]

Peter Cushen, an employee of Jacob's, gave an account of what he saw when he went to the factory after he heard of the surrender. He saw about ninety rebels emerging from the factory windows. Looters were climbing up a rope that was hanging from a window and tumbling out sacks of flour. He went in through the caretaker's door into the bake house and found between 90–100 rebels inside. He went to the office to prevent the looters taking the flour and shortly afterwards he was assisted in that by five or six other employees who arrived on the scene. A Volunteer officer, Major MacBride, approached and asked if anyone was able to take charge of the place. He showed Cushen where bombs and hand grenades were stored saying that, if handled wrongly, they would blow up. He left Cushen in charge until someone from the military came who knew what to do with them. Major MacBride had just left when a volley of shots rang out and a bullet pierced a sprinkler over Cushen's head; a bomb that was hurled through the window knocked his hat off but luckily passed through another window and exploded over a refrigerator outside. The soldiers arrived, searched him and demanded that he show them where the rebel flag was hanging. Cushen was more concerned about the bombs he was guarding and having told the soldiers about them he left and lowered the flag.

When the military left, looting started again. Fr Aloysius again spoke to the looters and told them they were a disgrace to the city of Dublin and the looting stopped for a while. The workers secured the premises as best they could before leaving through the Peter's Row gate and down Peter Street.[27]

Éamon Price, on orders from MacDonagh, took command of the garrison. A British officer asked him to arrange for the men to lay down their arms. By a series of parade ground manoeuvres, the arms were laid down and the men formed up in a column. MacDonagh and MacBride, on the order of 'march', took their places at its head. The British supplied an advance guard, a rear guard and lines of side guards. They set off through Dame Street, Lord Edward Street, Thomas Street, past Saint Catherine's church to Richmond Barracks, from where some were to leave for execution, others for prison or exile. 'We still had MacDonagh's parting words ringing in our ears: "We must have some to carry on the fight".[28]

The official police report for April 1916 gives its perspective on the activities associated with Jacob's Biscuit Factory in Easter week. The report says that although the factory did not occupy a strategic position of any importance, it was filled with foodstuffs of various descriptions, and probably in this respect it was deemed necessary to install in it a large garrison, so as to make certain that supplies would be available for the rebels in other places. If this was the idea, it never had the slightest chance of succeeding, as the factory was surrounded early in the week by a military cordon.[29]

The Volunteers in Jacob's did have a ready supply of biscuits. Vinnie Byrne enjoyed eating 'plenty of cocoa chocolate and biscuits galore'.[30] However, biscuits were not considered sustaining enough for fighting men. Séamus Pouch was sent out early in the week to get supplies of bread, potatoes etc. He had a warrant with him, signed by Thomas MacDonagh. He commandeered lard from Garvey's, Wexford Street, and potatoes from Quinlisk's Stores, Cuffe Street, and several trays of loaf bread. He claims that he offered payment to Quinlisk's a few years afterwards but Mr Quinlisk signed a full receipt for the goods in lieu of payment and accepted the warrant as payment. Thus Pouch says, 'I can claim to have paid the first bill due by the Republic.'[31]

Jacob's Factory was, according to Volunteer Seosamh de Brún, the scene of important military activities. The organisation and discipline of the garrison, their ability to conduct raids from the factory and to supply the needs of the troops and the population on the north side of the city made it a strategic site. The part played by Cumann na mBan in its domestic organisation, and by the Fianna Éireann boys in its espionage system proved that MacDonagh, MacBride, Hunter and their staffs achieved a state of efficiency in a short space of time and ensured that the garrison served the needs of the Dublin Brigade as they arose.[32]

CHAPTER 3

INCARCERATION IN BRITAIN

Following their surrender, the prisoners from Jacob's were marched past the Adelaide Hospital to Bride Street and Bull Alley Road where they were lined up with Éamonn Ceannt's men. They were ordered to discard all military equipment and were then marched to Richmond Barracks, Inchicore, Dublin. Those from Boland's Mills did likewise: 'We moved along Northumberland Road with Byrne still in the lead with the white flag of surrender, followed by Commandant de Valera and Captain Hitzen, the officer commanding the British troops'.[1]

Andrew McDonnell describes the conditions in Richmond Barracks:

> Prisoners arriving from all parts of the country were gathered here. We were housed in the barrack buildings, sixty men to every room, cleared out of everything except for a latrine bucket. There was not enough space for all sixty men to lie on the floor: you slept standing up. Food consisted of a bucket of tea and a tin of bully beef once a day – no cups or mugs – you opened your tin of bully beef and dipped the tin in the tea to draw your ration. The hot tea melted the red paint on the tin, and the grease from the tin floated on the tea. There were two large windows to each room but to be seen at a window brought fire from the sentry on the barrack square below.[2]

William Oman, a member of the garrison at City Hall, was in a room at Richmond Barracks with Tom Clarke and Seán MacDermott. Seán MacDermott, when he was taken to the toilet, bribed a sentry for a lump of sweet cake which, on his return, he divided with some of the boys. He said he paid half a sovereign for it.[3]

On Tuesday, the men were taken to the gymnasium and scrutinised by detectives from Dublin Castle. The men thought to be the main leaders were picked out from the rank and file.[4] The leaders were then held in the gymnasium. John MacDonagh expected to be held with them because his brother Tom was one of the leaders. He was not and as he left he turned to see Tom for the last time: 'He waved his hand to me, in the old cheery manner.'[5] The rest of the men were marched under escort to the North Wall where they were put in the hold of a cattle boat.[6]

Paddy Moran was among the 308 prisoners who were deported to Knutsford Prison on 3 May 1916.[7] The boat journey was less than comfortable, there was very little space and all the men were tired. They managed to sleep by sitting back to back in twos, with two others lying across their legs. Men got seasick on one another because there was nowhere to go and no space between them. On the train from Holyhead to London the men spent their time either sleeping or trying, with no suitable equipment, to open the tins of bully beef they had been given. They arrived at Knutsford early in the morning and were allocated individual cells.[8] The prison was used for the detention of soldiers who had been convicted of various crimes, and it was these men who were now guarding the Irish prisoners. The Irish were kept in solitary confinement for twenty-three hours a day for the first few weeks and allowed to walk around the exercise yard in single file for half-an-hour.[9] The routine was strict: the men got up at 6.30 a.m., were taken to a central place to wash in a bucket and then went back and waited in their cells for breakfast at 7.30. The breakfast consisted of a pint of skilly and dry bread, and sometimes a lump of raw meal that was meant to be porridge.[10] They ate at a little triangle of wood inserted in the wall, in the corner of the cell. They were given their half hour's exercise before dinner at noon, a dinner which consisted of two small potatoes, a little meat and watery soup. The potatoes were of poor quality and were usually green in colour.[11] At 5 p.m. they received more skilly and dry bread: 'There was a fierce sense of hunger which was felt very much by the country boys and the cold of the cells particularly at night was very trying.'[12]

The prisoners were not allowed to speak to each other, but some managed to whisper at exercise and to communicate in a kind of Morse code from cell to cell. Bedtime was at 8 p.m. The beds consisted of three planks with spaces between them, no mattress, a raised board for a pillow and two thin blankets to keep out the cold. Frank Robbins brought a carpet rug with him from the College of Surgeons, where he was stationed during the Rising, and it helped to keep him warm.

After two or three weeks the prisoners were given the status of political internees. This meant that they were allowed to speak to each other and to walk around outside for two hours in the morning and two in the afternoon. The cell doors were open during the day and the prisoners had the run of the place.[13] They were also given a mattress and pillows.

Around the same time as their change in status, the prisoners were asked to assemble in the main hall and were told they were being given a form to fill in, which would enable them to make a case for their innocence and would allow them to request release from prison. The words 'Do not sign' were whispered from one to another and the cry eventually rose to such a crescendo that the guards could not control the situation and the prisoners returned to their cells. The forms were distributed later, but not many men signed them.[14]

Following an inspection by a Major General McGregor, the prisoners were allowed a weekly hot bath and were given the opportunity to attend mass. After mass on the first Sunday, as they were leaving the prison chapel, some of the boys started to sing 'Faith of Our Fathers'. All the others joined in and before long they were raising the roof as they continued through all the verses. They also sang 'Hail Glorious Saint Patrick' and they did the same every Sunday afterwards.[15] The people of Knutsford were amazed to hear the sound of hymns sung lustily by 500 prisoners.

Alfie Byrne, MP, a member of the Irish Parliamentary Party, visited and was given a frosty reception by the men there who belonged to the Citizen Army. He told them that the Irish Parliamentary Party was doing its best to secure the release of the prisoners and that they had a definite promise of Home Rule. Frank Robbins took great exception to his words and urged the prisoners to remember what had been brought about by the blood sacrifice of some of the greatest men in Ireland and not to trust what Mr Byrne was saying. The crowd broke up and left Mr Byrne to himself.

The prisoners were allowed visitors and Frank Robbins' relatives walked the eleven-mile journey from Warrington, only to arrive after visiting time, but the prison commandant allowed the visit. The Irish community living in Manchester came and brought sandwiches, cigarettes, fruit, cheese and biscuits, and their visits re-established a connection with the world outside.

The Knutsford prisoners were eventually transferred to Frongoch Internment Camp in North Wales. Each internee was issued with a form to sign:

Notice is hereby given to the above name that an order has been made by the Secretary of State under Regulation 14B of the Defence of the Realm Regulations directing that he shall be interned at the place of internment at Frongoch. The order is made on the grounds that he is of hostile association and a member of an organisation called the Irish Volunteers or an organisation called the Citizens' Army which have promoted armed insurrection against His Majesty and is reasonably suspected of having favoured, promoted or assisted in armed insurrection against His Majesty.[16]

On their arrival at Frongoch, they were met by a colonel who was christened 'Buckshot' because he told them that the guards' guns were loaded with buckshot and that the wires were all electrified and not to try to escape. The sergeant major was christened 'Jack-knives' because he asked every prisoner if he had a jack-knife.[17]

The main building of the camp was a whiskey distillery until 1896 when its owner was killed in a carting accident. The site was deemed suitable for an internment camp and German prisoners of war were kept there initially. It was vacated to accommodate the Irish rebels and received its first internees on 9 June 1916.[18] There were two camps, the north camp and the south camp. The south camp was based in the old distillery building, while the north camp consisted of huts which were constructed to accommodate the large numbers of Irish internees. The rat-infested south camp was uncomfortable and oppressively hot in summer, but the north camp was cold and the ground around it was very wet.

Paddy Moran arrived in Frongoch on 16 July 1916. Each internee was given a bed, an enamel plate and mug, a knife, fork and spoon, a towel and a piece of soap.[19] Thomas Pugh recalled that there was huge overcrowding in the south camp and that in his room the men slept head to tail, with no room between them.[20] The censors allowed the prisoners to have religious articles sent in: some received holy water and one of them, Fuller, decided to ask for poitín to be labelled 'holy water'. He received his poitín and some of those who drank it got so drunk that they fell into a ditch.

The food in Frongoch was little better than it had been in Knutsford. The prisoners were given inferior boiled meat, bad bread, beans and a small potato for dinner. There was a shop run by a Welshman, Johnny Roberts, who was ashamed of how the men were housed and fed.[21] He sold cakes and bread as well as cigarettes, pipes and tobacco at the camp. The men were also allowed to receive food parcels which they shared and which helped them to survive. They were allowed visitors and Paddy Moran's two sisters, Cissie and B, both teachers in Lancashire, visited him in Frongoch.

The regulations were less stringent in the internment camp than in the prisons, but the prisoners were denied prisoner-of-war status; they were, however, treated as special category prisoners. They elected officers from within their own groups to control camp affairs and, once discipline was established the camp ran smoothly. There were, however, tensions caused by the determination of the prisoners to prevent the conscription of their fellow prisoners; some were liable for conscription under the military service acts because they had lived in Britain.[22] In an attempt to confuse the authorities and avoid conscription, the men refused to answer roll call or gave an incorrect name, and this united action ensured that they did not have to compromise their ideals by fighting for Britain.

Frongoch has been called the 'University of Revolution' because among the internees were many who were leaders, including Michael Collins. These men, thrown together in one place, were given an ideal opportunity to meet and plan for the future. Those who were in Frongoch from June 1916 until December 1916 had six months in which to plan a new campaign against the British occupation of Ireland before they were released on Christmas Eve.

While serious plans were undoubtedly made for the continuation of the struggle for freedom, the men also found time for recreational activities. A games committee was established and football matches were organised between the messes in teams of fifteen a-side. Athletic events were proposed for the Wolfe Tone commemoration day and continued throughout the summer. Chess and cards were played; concerts were often held in the evenings.

Route marches were organised two or three times a week and these took the men outside the prison walls and enabled them to admire the surrounding countryside, as well as giving them welcome mental relaxation. They were allowed to sing marching songs and they sang all those they had sung at home before the insurrection.

Some of the men turned to crafts to pass the time: some drawings and carvings have survived and can be seen at the National Museum and at O'Connell school museum in Dublin. A holy water font, now in Kilmainham Gaol, was made there. Reading was another favoured pastime and the men had their own library which included books by Kipling, Chesterton and Shaw. Some newspapers were also supplied.[23] Other activities included drama, choir-singing and step-dancing. Classes in Irish, French, German, Spanish, Irish history, maths, bookkeeping, shorthand and telegraphy were held in the afternoons.[24] Some spent their time writing poetry. The following poem, written in Paddy's handwriting, survives from his time in Frongoch. I am not sure whether he composed it or simply wrote it down:

Four white walls and a stone flagged floor
A window where rays of light
Stray through the bars of an iron door
That's my home tonight
And I sit alone in the prison cell
This den in an English jail
In this latest fight of the Gael
Our foes they sneered at our nation's claim
When the men of our nation prayed
Like beggars in rags in our country's name
Had their sores with whimpering whine displayed
  Yes they mocked us then
  And they scoffed us when
  Our way was the mendicant way
  But our hopes they broke

Then our guns they spoke
And they've ceased to scoff today.

They told us our sins were the cause of our woes
We were liars and savages all
Fit only to grovel and grind for our foes
And snivel and fight at their call
We were great at putting the Turks to rout
Or at giving the Huns cold steel
But at home we could only wrangle and shout
And hurrah for the Iron Heel!
We were good raw stuff for the cannon's mouth
If we fought out in Flanders mud
But to think of home was a joke uncouth
Sure! We hadn't the grit nor the blood
   Yes they bluffed us then
   And they cuffed us when
   Our way was the coward's way
   But MEN have tried
   And MEN have died
   And they've ceased to bluff today.

They smiled at our words with a lofty smile
They hawed and they hemmed and they hummed
When we asked for our rights they gave us a mile
Of promises taped and gummed.
They throttled, and strangled, and burned our race
And they'd mounted a guard oe'r its grave
For our fame they'd uproot, our name efface
'Twas easy, British, 'twas brave
Yes, they'd make our land a brand new land
With Hodge as its uncrowned king
And they'd give us a grave, a brand new grave
Out east where the rifles ring.
   Yes they planned it well

With their schemes from Hell
When our way was the weakling's way.
But in Easter week
They heard MEN speak
And they dread us again today
Thank God
They dread us again today.[25]

However, Paddy was not to have the chance to partake of many of the activities in Frongoch. The Sankey Detention Review committee, so named because Judge Sankey chaired it, had been set up by the British government to investigate each individual prisoner's case.[26] When the majority of the prisoners refused to sign the release form, they were brought down to Wormwood Scrubs Jail, London, in batches of between 50–100, to appear before the committee. Paddy Moran made the arduous journey by train shortly after he had arrived in Frongoch and appeared before the committee in July 1916. He was asked, like all prisoners who appeared before the committee, to confirm his name and address, and was questioned about his involvement in the Rising. He was advised not to take part in political activities on his release.[27] The hearings only took a few minutes and the prisoners were returned to Frongoch after the hearing – they were only told the outcome on the day of their release. On their way to London, some of the men took a chance and left letters for posting on the train seats – most of these were delivered.[28]

It is not clear how the Sankey committee decided who to release and who not to release. Frank Robbins suggests that perhaps it was a case of the committee sticking a pin in a list of names and recommending the release of those names struck. Joe Stanley held a similar view; he suggests that a coin was tossed.[29] Paddy Moran was one of 176 internees released on foot of an order signed by John Sankey on behalf of the advisory committee on 24 July 1916. This was the fifth batch of internees to be released since June.[30] Paddy left Frongoch on 27 July, and arrived back in Crossna on 3 August 1916. His time in Frongoch was short; he was there for less than two weeks.

James Feely of Boyle, County Roscommon, the O/C of the 1st Battalion, North Roscommon Brigade, asked him for an account of where he had been during the Rising and afterwards, when he made his first visit to Boyle after his release from Frongoch. Paddy wrote:

> Patrick Moran, Crossna, Boyle & 160, Phibsboro Rd, Dublin.
> Adj. D Co. Batt. 2, Dublin Brigade
>   Surrendered at Jacob's Factory Sunday eve April 30th '16. Deported to Knutsford Jail (England), May 3rd '16. Transferred to Frongoch Camp July 4th '16. Released from camp after trial in Wormwood Scrubs Jail (London) on July 27th '16. Arrived home at Crossna on August 4th '16. 'With God's help & with God's Blessing a rebel to the end'. P.M. [31]

He also quoted the following poem, although it is unclear whether he composed it:

> 'Tis a fatal thing to love Ireland; she
> spreads her arms her lovers come
> and her kiss is death.
> Ah, for her loveliness and her despair
> She of the shadowed moor the gloomy skies,
> Sorrows are drooping from her hair
> Lost stars are in her eyes.
> She knows the doom that she must bear
> And holds her heart to stay its breathing sighs
> And yet they breathe around her unaware
> They call to all the faithful fond and fair
> They call the knightly dreamer everywhere
> And whoso answers. Dies.
> Patrick Moran

Some of his friends were still interned in Frongoch and Paddy received this letter in August 1916, from Thomas O'Dea:

No. 1094 Thos O'Dea,
Frongoch,
Bala,
North Wales.
Aug. 24th 1916.

Dear Paddy,

Received your card yesterday. Did you have a good day in Galway? What made you send that sort of card, it made every one that saw it curse! Jamie is in hospital, he hurt the cap of his knee, the doctor told him he was to be in bed for a month. Brother J. is suffering all the time from sciatica. W. Neiland is just the same. W. Thornton spent a week in hospital. Why did not you send your address? I do not know where I will send it, I will chance Dublin. Sam has a letter written, he is going to chance Roscommon. Frongoch is the same as when you left it. I suppose there is no chance of us being released at all. All the boys wish to be remembered to you. If you are staying in Dublin, call to see my sister if you can. Dear Paddy I suppose you haven't seen my Mary on your excursion. How is Ciss, also T. Young? No more news, write soon if you get this.

Good Bye from a fond brother,
Thos O'Dea.[32]

Paddy had left his job in Doyle's to take part in the Easter Rising; when he returned to Dublin he obtained a good reference from John Doyle. He described Paddy as of 'irreproachable character, being honest, industrious, sober, and his ability of the highest order in the business'. Paddy worked for a short time in a pub in Leeson Street, then in Lynch and O'Brien, 80–81 Lower George's Street, Dun Laoghaire. Lynch and O'Brien was an impressive shop and in 1911, there were six assistants working there.[33] It sold a variety of goods and its teas were described in an eight-page price list as 'most agreeable and delicious. Flavour, succulency, lightness and quality are their characteristics.' It stocked twenty-two types of cocoa with exotic names like Mazawettee, Kokotee, Malintiko, Rova, Epps and Menier. There was a special section devoted to Heinz preserves – there were thirty different types of sauces. Soups could be bought in tins, glass bottles and packets. In the bar section, an eleven-year-old bottle of whiskey cost four shillings and sixpence; a selection of clarets, sherries, champagnes, burgundies, invalid wines and five different Australian wines were for sale. The shop ceased trading in the 1950s and the name was removed from over the shop in 1958. The premises is now occupied by Shaws.[34] Paddy Moran left Lynch and O'Brien a month or so before his arrest, to become a foreman in Magees', 5 Main Street, Blackrock.

The last of the prisoners held in Frongoch were released on Christmas Eve. It was a very cold night and they were out in snow, sleet and ice. By the time they got on the train for Holyhead they were frozen. They were delighted to be put in a first-class carriage where they were very comfortable. Before they left Frongoch, they were given some of the parcels that they weren't allowed to have as prisoners. Some of these contained gin and whiskey. One large bottle of whiskey was a disappointment; it had been opened and was re-filled with water![35]

In Dublin those who returned home set about re-organising the Volunteers. 'They simply picked up where they had left off and returned to the struggle.'[36] After he returned from internment in 1916, Paddy was living a long way from the area covered by D Company, 2nd Battalion, Dublin Brigade, IRA, but he remained in that company and became its captain.

CHAPTER 4

RENEWAL OF THE FIGHT

Volunteers worked at their ordinary employment during the day and learned to be soldiers by night.[1] They hired halls in the name of various social clubs all over the city. Not much is recorded about Paddy Moran's role in the re-organisation in the period from 1916–1920. However, the late President de Valera, speaking in 1966, said that Paddy 'after his release from prison set about rebuilding the Volunteer organisation'.[2]

Training orders issued for the Dublin 2 Brigade from its headquarters in October 1918, specified that training should be practical and have a definite objective. Half of the training was to be done in open country and Volunteers should learn something new at every parade. A military atmosphere was to permeate every Volunteer function; punctuality, smartness, exactness and thoroughness was to come from the example set by the superior officers. The orders specified that marksmanship was the most important branch of Volunteer training and that a Volunteer must be a good shot. Recruits should first be trained indoors, learning sighting and timing with an unloaded rifle, before being permitted to fire a single shot. They should get plenty of practice with air guns on a rifle range and a register was to be kept of every man's progress in marksmanship. They should learn how to throw hand grenades and how to erect barricades. The Volunteers were urged to practise physical fitness as, being members of a guerrilla force, they would be required to march long distances. They were encouraged to take up walking, running, boxing, wrestling, hurling, football and general gymnastics. Every Volunteer was to become familiar with the district within a ten-mile radius of his battalion area: 'A man who walks with his eyes open will acquire all that is necessary.'[3] Paddy Moran, as captain of his company, had a duty to see that all of the above orders were put into practice and he gained a reputation for dedication, organisational abilities and resoluteness. Paddy had other duties too. His brother, Tom, told Micheál O'Callaghan that Paddy was ideally placed to meet people who travelled between Dun Laoghaire and Holyhead on secret missions for Michael Collins.[4]

Paddy Moran's activities in the period were not confined to his involvement with the Volunteers. He continued to play football and hurling, he was involved in the Gaelic League and he organised dances in the Town Hall, Kingstown (Dun Laoghaire). However, much of his time was also devoted to his trade union activities.

The Grocers' and Vintners' Assistants' Association passed a resolution at a special meeting in 1917: 'that it is the considered opinion of this meeting, that in view of the future outlook of our trade, the time has arrived when it is absolutely necessary that a strong national union of assistants engaged in the grocery and liquor trade throughout Ireland should be formed and become linked up with other labour bodies through affiliation with organised labour in Ireland.'[5] Paddy Moran was one of the founder members of the new union, the Irish National Union of Vintners', Grocers' and Allied Trades' Assistants, in October 1917.[6] The head office of the newly formed union was at 20 Parnell Square, Dublin and Paddy became chairman of the Dun Laoghaire branch and was its representative on the executive of the national union. He was also its delegate to the Bray and District Trade Union Council, a body founded in 1917 to try to combat the effects of the Great

War on the economic and social conditions of the time. Hunger, disease and slum housing were the lot of the poor, and social and economic freedom was considered by the trade union movement to be just as important as political freedom.[7]

Paddy was obviously becoming a key figure in the trade union movement. According to the recorded minutes of the meeting of the Irish National Union of Vintners', Grocers' and Allied Trades' Assistants held on 29 October 1919, he made a very eloquent speech condemning the system of payment of assistants. He decried the system of 'living in' as being nothing but slavery. He proposed that a demand for an all-round wage increase of fifty per cent be made on employers, that the 'living in' system be abolished, and that the amount for living out be revised. Under the 'living in' system, apprentices were required to live on the premises where they were employed. In many cases, they were treated like servants. Strict household rules applied; the apprentice had to be in at night by a certain time or risk being sacked. At mealtimes, food was presented to the boss first and then to the staff in order of seniority; often the apprentice got little or nothing.[8]

At the 14 December 1919 meeting, Paddy elicited a promise from the secretary that he would write to the Great Western Railway to request that a train to the west of Ireland would run on Christmas morning. He and his fellow workers in the grocery and bar trade had no means of getting home for Christmas unless there was public transport on Christmas morning.

There was another period of industrial unrest in Dublin in early 1920 and more than 600 members of Paddy's union ceased work on 1 January 1920. They were looking for a forty-eight-hour week and a fifty per cent pay raise. Two increases in wages had been granted in the previous two years, but the men were working for 35 shillings a week. It was a bitter dispute and many of the strikers were arrested by the military and the police. The publicans had all the force of the British government behind them; some of them boasted that with one word they could have all the pickets transported to Wormwood Scrubs. The men on strike supported themselves for the first two weeks and were then given strike pay by the union. The employers expected that when the strike pay was exhausted the men would crawl back to work, but the strike lasted for ten weeks.[9] The dispute was finally settled at a conference presided over by the Lord Mayor, Alderman L. O'Neill. The terms of the settlement were favourable to the men and they were congratulated on the fine spirit displayed during the whole period of the dispute.[10] The agreed terms were a forty per cent increase in wages for men at the two senior grades and a thirty-three and one-third per cent increase for those at the two lower grades of apprentice. The men also secured a fifty-six hour working week, a half day each week, one Sunday in four off and a day off on Christmas day and St Stephen's day. An assistant who changed from living in to living out was granted an increase of 30 shillings a week.[11]

Paddy was one of those arrested during the strike. He was charged, along with James Glynn, with intimidation, assault and threatening behaviour. Thomas Brady told the court that a crowd of 200–300 persons assembled outside his premises in Upper George's Street, Dun Laoghaire, when a consignment of porter arrived. The two defendants put their hands on him when he tried to unload the dray. Sergeant Dowling, Dublin Metropolitan Police, said that the two accused prevented Mr Brady from unloading the dray by seizing his arms. On the charges of assault and threatening behaviour, fines of 10 shillings were imposed or seven days imprisonment in respect of each of the summonses. The prisoners declined to pay the fines and were imprisoned. Mr Woods, defending, said that the attitude of his clients was that they had done no moral wrong and therefore preferred to go to prison.[12] Paddy went to Mountjoy Jail on 19 January 1920 and was released on 1 February 1920. His address at that time was recorded in the prison register as 43 Mulgrave Street, Kingstown, and according to the register he had brown hair, blue eyes and a fresh complexion, weighed 140 lbs and he was five feet six inches in height.[13]

In September 1920, Paddy was elected president of the Grocers', Vintners' and Allied Trades Union and often received letters from men seeking work in Dublin.[14] Peter O'Hara wrote to him from Adela Street, Belfast, asking him to help get a job for a companion:

Dear Patck [*sic*],

Just a note, as you will have heard of my becoming one of the common enemy, and also my repulse back to the proletarian ranks. A couple of months ago, a friend of mine, Jimmie Boyle, and I started on our own in joint partnership and in the riots we were burned out. I have succeeded in getting a job but Boyle is still out. Things are so bad here owing to so many houses being destroyed that it is impossible to get started so I thought you might be able to fix Boyle up in Dublin. Your Jimmie [Paddy's brother] knows him well as they worked together in the Strand. I was going to write to Hughes but I thought he might be out of town. I trust I am not taking any liberties upon you personally or upon the Union as I presume Dublin members have first preference to jobs.

I was glad to hear through E. Cooney that you had aspired to the Presidency of the Union; the Bungs (?) may look for trouble now.[15]

You might let me know before the weekend if there would be any chance of a job up there as he intends going to Glasgow next week if nothing turns up.

Thanking you in anticipation,

Yours fraternally, Peter[16]

Ross Connolly writing in the *Irish Press* in March 1971 said Paddy 'was an attractive personality and his activities on behalf of his union soon earned him election as president of the union, as well as being chairman of the Dun Laoghaire branch.'[17] It may be that Paddy's personality and active participation was the reason for his election as president, but there is some evidence that the trade union movement was subject to infiltration by members of the IRB. John Anthony Caffrey, an IRB member, gave an account of a meeting that he and three others were instructed by the IRB to attend. They were given the names of three men and told to vote for them when their names were proposed at the meeting. The three men were duly proposed for the offices of chairman, treasurer and secretary. Caffrey was not sure what the purpose of the meeting was, but says that it occurred to him later that it might have been a union meeting.[18]

Caffrey's daughter, Teresa O'Carroll, told me a story her father had told her about Paddy Moran and three others, Bernard Ryan (also executed on 14 March 1921), John Anthony and another man whose name Teresa could not recall. All four went to get a photograph taken in the Volunteer uniform; however, they had only one uniform between them so each had to dress in it in turn for the photograph. As will be evident later, it might have been better for Paddy Moran to have avoided being photographed in uniform.

After his release from Frongoch, Paddy found himself engaging further in nationalist politics. On his visits home to Crossna, he helped to revitalise the Sinn Féin organisation there and a new club, called the Thomas Clarke club, was formed in May 1917. One hundred people attended the first meeting.[19] The police were aware that the returned prisoners were reorganising their branches and that they were holding secret meetings. An intelligence report from 1917 mentioned Roscommon as an area where this was happening.[20]

On Easter Sunday 1918 Paddy attended a meeting in Glynn's of Cootehall, County Roscommon, convened to organise another Sinn Féin club. Larry O'Hara recalled that Terence Glynn, Drumshinney, Cootehall, was one of those in attendance at that meeting.[21] Terence worked with Paddy in Lynch and O'Brien in Dun Laoghaire, before taking up a position as manager in the grocery and spirit shop of Thomas Hogan, Dame Street, Dublin, in 1917.

Following the 1916 Rising, no progress had been made on the implementation of Home Rule. In 1917, Lloyd George, the British prime minister, offered two alternative proposals for the governance of Ireland. The first was that Home Rule should be applied immediately in twenty-six counties and six counties would be excluded. A Council of Ireland would be set up with the same number of representatives for the twenty-six counties as for the excluded six counties. This first proposal was rejected by John Redmond and the Irish Parliamentary Party. The second proposal was that the terms of an alternative to the limited Home Rule suggestion should be discussed at a Convention of Irishmen and proposals submitted to the cabinet for the future government of Ireland. Sinn Féin declined to participate in any convention unless the terms of reference were favourable: it wanted the convention to be free to pronounce the complete independence of Ireland and it wanted the British government to publicly pledge to the United States and the powers of Europe to ratify the decision of the majority of the convention. It also wanted only people elected by adult suffrage in Ireland to take part in the convention and the Irish prisoners at Lewes and Aylesbury Jails to be given prisoner-of-war status. When the composition of the convention was announced, Sinn Féin was offered five seats, but because their conditions were not met, the party declined to participate.[22] The convention went ahead, but achieved little except the release of prisoners from English jails.

In February 1917 Sinn Féin had its first electoral success when Count George Noble Plunkett was elected at a by-election in North Roscommon. Séamus O'Doherty, a native of Derry and a commercial traveller for M.H. Gill & Sons, a publishing firm in Dublin, became Director of Elections for the Count. He was ably assisted by Fr Michael O'Flanagan, still curate in Crossna. Fr O'Flanagan was the main driving force in the election campaign for the candidate. *The Irish Times*, commenting on the result, said, 'For twelve days and nights he [Fr O'Flanagan] was up and down the constituency like a whirlwind and talking to the people at every village and street corner and crossroads where he could get people to listen to him.'[23] Paddy's two brothers, Tom and Batty, were among the many who joined him to help with the campaign. Many of the leaders of the Republican movement, including Michael Collins, came to canvas for Plunkett.

Paddy Moran knew Séamus O'Doherty well. He was at that time a regular visitor to the O'Doherty household in 32 Connaught Street, Phibsboro. He endeared himself to the family and was held in high esteem by them. The family moved to Philadelphia in 1920 and a letter from Mrs Kitty O'Doherty from Philadelphia testifies that he was a favourite with the family: 'I have as many callers as I had in 32 but I shall never find friends as true and constant, and I never yet found one that walked into all our hearts like yourself, Paddy'.[24] Dan Breen met him in O'Doherty's; he said of him that he was 'an upright and a faithful soldier'.[25]

Paddy managed to send a note to Séamus, when the latter was a prisoner in Mountjoy in 1919, by pinning it inside an overcoat. When Mrs Kitty O'Doherty doubted that it would get through Paddy said, 'We have a friendly warder named Berry who will see to it.' In 1920 Paddy carried Feichín O'Doherty, aged 3, on his shoulders to the boat at the North Wall, Dublin, and saw the family off to join their father in Philadelphia.[26]

As the First World War progressed, Lloyd George needed more manpower to fight for Britain. He decided it was time to force the Irish to join the British army and introduced the Conscription Bill in April 1918. He proposed to enforce conscription first and then to introduce a measure of Home Rule for Ireland. The Conscription Bill was passed without the consent of the Irish Parliamentary

Party; they wanted to see Home Rule granted first. A conference of representative men from Sinn Féin, the Irish Parliamentary Party, Labour and an independent representative, T.M. Healy, was convened by the Lord Mayor of Dublin in the Mansion House in Dublin at which it was decided to resist conscription 'by the most effective means at our disposal'.[27] On 23 April 1918, a general strike of twenty-four hours was called. The British cabinet received reports of Ireland's grim resolve and sent Lord French to Ireland as viceroy. His intentions were clear:

> Home Rule will be offered and declined, then conscription will be enforced. If they leave me alone I can do what is necessary. I shall notify a date before which recruits must offer themselves in the various districts. If they do not come we will fetch them.[28]

In May 1918, in an effort to frighten the men of Ireland into submission, a number of prominent Sinn Féin members were arrested, including Arthur Griffith, Éamon de Valera, Count Plunkett, William T. Cosgrave, Countess Markievicz, Maud Gonne MacBride and Mrs Tom Clarke. They were imprisoned in England without charge but the explanation given in the papers for the arrests was that they had entered into treasonable communication with the German enemy.[29] On 21 June 1918, a by-election took place in east Cavan and Arthur Griffith, although in prison in Gloucester Jail, England, was elected for Sinn Féin. The people of Cavan demonstrated that they were not about to be coerced into joining the British army. Conscription was never enforced and the armistice was announced on 11 November 1918.

Fr Michael O'Flanagan became acting president of Sinn Féin when de Valera was imprisoned in May 1918. He took a very active part in the Cavan by-election. He was suspended by his bishop for addressing three public meetings in three parishes during the election campaign without the permission of their respective parish priests. The people of Crossna sent a very strongly worded remonstrance to the Bishop of Elphin.

A Remonstrance

ADDRESSED TO THE MOST REV. DR COYNE, BISHOP OF ELPHIN AND SIGNED BY ALMOST EVERY MAN, WOMAN AND CHILD IN THE PARISH OF CROSSNA.

To the Most Rev. Dr Coyne, Lord Bishop of Elphin.

It is with feelings of pain that we, the people of Crossna, have to appeal again to your Lordship to remove the ban imposed on our beloved priest, Fr O'Flanagan, a ban imposed, we feel constrained to say, for no crime except that his honesty, his sincerity, and passionate love of country is to lie construed into crime.

It has been rumoured that the cause of his suspension is the neglect of his spiritual duties, and on this matter we should know something, and we have no hesitation in declaring that from a spiritual point of view no better priest ever set foot in our midst.

We should, indeed, be very slow in saying anything that might be tortured into an offence, or seem disrespectful to your Lordship, or to impute to you anything in the nature of partiality on a matter so serious and fraught with so many unpleasant consequences.

We know your Lordship well and long, and your elevation to the See of Elphin sent a thrill of joy and pride through our hearts, still, it is very hard to believe but your Lordship's latest act is unconsciously playing into the hands of the bigots who now trample on everything which your Lordship should foster and hold dear. And surely it is not too much to ask your Lordship to desist from a course which, if persevered in, will only rise a turmoil the like of which never before in Ireland occurred between a bishop and his flock.

We earnestly entreat of your Lordship allow Fr O'Flanagan his full liberties.

It is heart-rending to look upon the treatment he is receiving and impossible to keep silent. We hear the howls of orange bigots, such as Lord Carson and Sir Edward Carson [*sic*], for the return of the penal days. We see the youth of our country feebly plodding under a cloud of slavery, the dreadful menace of conscription, which hangs over their heads. And to all this what answer has your Lordship given? A sinister one undoubtedly. You have stilled the one potent voice that was left to cheer and guide them. You have done in 1918 what Dr Troy did in 1798, when at the feasting table of Mountjoy and Carew the excommunication of Fr Murphy was decreed, and for all this what will your Lordship gain? – the applause of the arch-enemy of your religion, the Freemason clique of England. The *London Times* may praise you and throw its bloody garment round you. The rag which sneered at Daniel O'Connell and which blackguarded John MacHale and which has no better name for the priests of Ireland than 'Surpliced ruffians'. This rag may take you to its bosom. And what will you lose? Certainly the wishes and prayers of a now devoted people. Fr O'Flanagan was suspended because he was, and is, an Irish patriot priest, and an Irish priest is no innovation in Irish public life. Religion and patriotism in Ireland are inseparable.

Ever since, and even before, the blessed Oliver Plunkett was compelled to cast his dying eyes on his burning bowels, the twin sisters – religion and patriotism – have been transmitted from father to son, and today they shine brighter than ever. They have been wound into the warp and woof of Irish life and cannot be divorced. And your lordship cannot stop the onward march or stem the rushing tide. Others have tried it and have miserably failed.

The insults that are now poured on Fr O'Flanagan will do him no harm. A grateful and warm-hearted people will only cling more tightly to him in the hour of his affliction. And whether your Lordship took dictation from non-Catholics such as Lord Middleton, or from influential Catholics, such as the Anglicised Sir Thomas Stafford, it matters little. When these calumniators are dead and gone, and when their names shall only be recalled with horror and disgust, the name of the patriot priest of Crossna will shine as bright and clear on the pages of Irish history as the morning star that circles the heavens, pointing out to future generations of Irish men and women the road to glory, to honour and to virtue.

And as a protest against your Lordship's action, we have closed Crossna church, and it will remain closed till Fr O'Flanagan is restored to the mission. Your Lordship may look on our actions as extreme, but pray remember the awful malediction conveyed in those dreadful words: 'Woe to the man whom history shall accuse and whom posterity shall judge.'

To this tribunal we leave your Lordship's action and our own.[30]

Fr O'Flanagan could not now say mass or perform any other duties associated with his priesthood so he devoted much of his time and energy to Sinn Féin. He was invited to say the opening prayer at the first meeting of Dáil Éireann on Tuesday, 21 January 1919. He said that prayer in Irish:

Tar, a Spioraid Naomh, ath-líon croidthe t'fhíréin, agus adhain ionnta tine do ghrádha. Cuir chughainn do Spioraid agus cruthóchfar iad agus athnuadhfaidh Tú aghaidh na talún.

Guídhimís

A Dhia, do theagaise croidthe na bhfíréin le lonnradh an Spioraid Naoimh, tabhair dúinn, san Spioraid chéadna, go glacaimíd an ceart agus go mbéidh síorgháirdeachas orainn de bharr a sholais sin. Tré Iosa Críost ár dTighearna. Amen[31]

The translation:

Come, Holy Spirit replenish the hearts of the faithful and kindle in them the fire of Thy love. Send forth Thy spirit O Lord and they shall be created and Thou shalt renew the face of the earth.

Let us pray:

O God, who by the light of the Holy Spirit didst instruct the hearts of the faithful, grant us the same spirit to relish what is right and ever to rejoice in His consolation through Jesus Christ our Lord. Amen.[32]

Paddy Moran must have been disappointed at the circumstances of Fr O'Flanagan's dismissal from his priestly duties but was, no doubt, proud of his elevation to higher office in Sinn Féin and his continued devotion to the cause of freedom and social justice.

CHAPTER 5

BLOODY SUNDAY, 21 NOVEMBER 1920

After the death on hunger strike of Thomas Ashe, in September 1917, the Volunteers began to drill and march openly in defiance of police. In March 1918, a general headquarters staff was established with Richard Mulcahy as chief-of-staff, Michael Collins as the director of organisation, Rory O'Connor as director of engineering, Seán McMahon as quartermaster general and Dick McKee as director of training.[1]

Politically, Sinn Féin was gaining support at the expense of the Irish Parliamentary Party and won seats at by-elections in North Roscommon, South Longford, Cavan, East Clare and Kilkenny. When the general election was held on 14 December 1918, Sinn Féin won 73 of the 105 seats; twenty-six unionists and only six Irish Parliamentary Party candidates were returned. Nationalist Ireland had moved from support for the Irish Parliamentary Party, who advocated Home Rule, to Sinn Féin who wanted an independent sovereign Ireland. The newly elected Sinn Féin representatives did not take their seats in the Westminster parliament but decided instead to establish their own parliament, Dáil Éireann, and on 21 January 1919, the First Dáil convened.

In August of that year a motion was passed in the Dáil requiring all elected members to take an oath of allegiance: 'I do solemnly swear (or affirm) that I do not, and shall not, yield a voluntary support to any pretended Government, Authority or Power inside Ireland hostile or inimical thereto; and I do further swear (or affirm) that to the best of my knowledge and ability I shall support and defend the Irish Republic, which is Dáil Éireann, against all enemies foreign and domestic and that I will bear true faith and allegiance to the same and that I take this obligation freely without any mental reservation or purpose of evasion. So help me God.'[2]

The same oath was administered to all Volunteers in their own companies in the presence of a representative of the brigade headquarters.[3] The Volunteers were now members of the Irish Republican Army (IRA), Óglaigh na hÉireann.

On 21 January 1919, the day that Dáil Éireann was convened, two members of the Royal Irish Constabulary were shot dead at Soloheadbeg, County Tipperary, and this signalled the beginning of the War of Independence. During the previous three years, the Volunteers had confined themselves to raiding barracks for arms but few resorted to violence causing death. However, from January 1919 to the end of December 1920, 193 police were killed,[4] 174 were wounded, sixteen soldiers were killed, sixty-one were wounded, 484 barracks were burned and 2,861 raids for arms were carried out by IRA.[5]

When he took over as director of intelligence in January 1919, Michael Collins set up two groups within the IRA; an intelligence staff and a group of men, trained to shoot to kill, known as 'the Squad'. The intelligence staff gathered information about the enemy from contacts sympathetic to the republican cause in places such as government departments, Dublin Castle, the sorting office at the General Post Office, the telephone exchange, hotels, restaurants, railway stations, mail boats, within the ranks of the police and among the warders in the jails. Each company of Volunteers had an intelligence officer who reported to the brigade intelligence officer and thence to intelligence headquarters.

The Squad comprised twelve or so men who were full time and were paid £4 10s per week.[6] There was no room in it for anyone having scruples about the use of violence. Members of the Squad shot Detective Smith on 31 July 1919, Detective Daniel Hoey on 12 September 1919, Detective Barton in November 1919 and Detective Redmond on 21 January 1920.

In 1920, Sir Nevil Macready was appointed commander-in-chief of the British forces and was instructed by the British cabinet 'to suppress the rebellion by whatever means may be requisite'.[7] Faced with the deterioration of law and order in Ireland, the British government recruited a division of ex-officers of the Great War to assist the police in Ireland. When they arrived on 25 March 1920, they were dressed in khaki coats with black trousers and caps and were promptly named the 'Black and Tans'.[8] They were paid 10 shillings a day. A second force was recruited in May 1920 and at first they were known as cadets, then special constables and finally auxiliaries to the police. These were paid one pound a day. Their commander was General F.P. Crozier, a unionist whose ancestors came from County Leitrim.[9]

Brigadier Cecil Prescott Decie, Divisional Commissioner of the RIC for Munster, wrote a letter to John Taylor, Assistant Under-Secretary, Dublin Castle, in which he said, 'I have been told of the new policy and plan and I am satisfied, though I doubt its ultimate success in the main particular – the stamping out of terrorism by secret murder.'[10] Lieutenant Colonel Smyth, a fellow divisional commissioner of Decie's, delivered a speech in Listowel, County Kerry, in the presence of General Tudor, government advisor on policing matters. He urged his constables to shoot anyone whom they considered suspicious: 'You may make mistakes and innocent persons may be shot but that cannot be helped and you are bound to get the right parties sometime. The more you shoot the better I will like you, and I assure you no policeman will get into trouble for shooting any man.'[11] Smyth was shot dead by IRA gunmen on 17 July 1920. The Restoration of Order Act of August 1920 ensured that the maintenance of order passed into the hands of the military. It substituted courts-martial for the civil judiciary; military courts of inquiry replaced the coroner's court. Police no longer feared exposure at the coroner's court which up to then had 'kept a check on their activities'.[12]

The Black and Tans were deployed immediately on arrival in Ireland to assist the police, without any training for their new position.[13] They were accused of many atrocities in the weeks and months that followed their arrival. John O'Hanlon of Turloughmore, County Galway, was shot in front of his parents, his wife and two small children; Fr James O'Callaghan was shot dead in Cork, as was James Coleman when he opened his door in response to a knock. They went from his house to Stephen Coleman's home and not only shot him, but also a young man named Hanley who pleaded with them not to shoot him as he was his mother's sole support. Fr Griffin disappeared in Galway in November 1920, and his body was found a week later in a bog hole with a bullet wound in his head. Five men with revolvers entered the public house owned by Michael Walsh, a Sinn Féin member of Galway county council, cleared out the customers and helped themselves to the money in the till and to free drinks, telling Michael's terrified daughter: 'We are English secret service men and we know what we are doing.' When they left they took Michael with them, and a week later his body was found in a river with a bullet through his head.[14]

The British government often attributed theses atrocities to the IRA. General F.P. Crozier, the commander of the Auxiliaries, resigned after less than a year in command and claimed that 'the crown forces under his command were guilty of a systematic policy of murder, theft and torturing of prisoners, and that this policy is not only officially condoned, but that the very highest officers in the service have conspired both to suppress and invent evidence relating to these crimes.' General Crozier maintained that cadets, who were dismissed from the force for serious misconduct, could always be reinstated by threatening to tell what they knew regarding the involvement of high-ranking police officers in murders.[15]

Crozier was convinced that if these forces were under the control of the army, rather than the police, they couldn't have behaved as they did. 'We murdered the Irish, very often the innocent Irish, and then we said that the Irish murdered each other.[16] He blamed British government policy for this:

Let it be said that the British army in Ireland behaved well in the most trying circumstances; they worthily upheld tradition in 1920–1921. But the British government, knowing how the army would behave, raised a division of ex-officers of the Great War and allocated to them, as policemen, the task of organised murder, which disciplined soldiery would not, and never could, contemplate … I resigned not so much because I objected to giving the Irish assassins the tit-for-tat, but because we were murdering and shooting up innocent people, burning their homes and making new and deadly enemies every day.[17]

In the House of Commons, Lloyd George claimed that after three years of restraint in the face of murder, the patience of the police and army had given way and there had been some severe hitting back. He was accused of giving an incomplete account of the forms that reprisals were taking. There was apparently overwhelming evidence that property was burned and destroyed, rifles were fired and bombs were thrown at random, killing and wounding civilians. Women and children were driven in terror into the fields and mountains. In Balbriggan, County Dublin, twenty-five houses, shops and a hosiery factory were set on fire and two young men were bayoneted to death in reprisal for the killing of District Inspector Burke and the wounding of his brother. In County Clare three people were killed, and the towns of Lahinch, Miltown Malbay and Ennistymon were burned following an ambush in which five members of the crown forces were killed. Judge Bodkin, opening the Ennis Quarter Sessions, condemned the outrages on both sides saying that the actions of the IRA shamed their common humanity, while the reprisals by the crown forces should be known by their legal names ... arson and murder.[18]

The Dublin Castle authorities recognised that information was being passed on to the IRA. A professional soldier, Sir Ormonde Winter, who had experience of intelligence work in India, was appointed director of intelligence at Dublin Castle and organised 'an intelligence system by recruiting ex-officers, and this organisation was of great value in collecting intelligence in Dublin'.[19] By October 1920, a number of these intelligence officers had come to Dublin and were living in lodgings in different parts of the city; they were often referred to as the 'Cairo Gang'. There are a few different explanations given for the name 'Cairo Gang': one, that the campaign was planned in Cairo by a number of army intelligence officers who met there at the instigation of Sir Henry Wilson, Chief of Imperial Staff;[20] two, that the officers frequented a Dublin café called the Café Cairo; or three, that the officers who were recruited had served in Cairo. Their sole aim was 'to track down and destroy Collins and his intelligence lieutenants'.[21]

These officers did not work during the day, but slipped out in civilian clothes after curfew to join raiding parties and pick up their targets. On 22 September 1920, John Lynch, a Limerick man, was killed in The Exchange Hotel, Parliament Street, Dublin; one of those responsible was Captain Bagally, a court-martial officer. Vaughan's Hotel was raided but Liam Tobin, who was staying there, managed to spin such a good story that he got away. He recognised two of the 'Cairo Gang', Lieutenant Peter Ames and Captain George Bennett, among the raiders.[22] On 19 November 1920, it was stated in the House of Commons that a plot to murder soldiers and to infect army horses with glanders[23] had been uncovered in papers taken when Professor Michael Hayes' house at 49 Longwood Avenue, South Circular Road, was raided a week earlier.[24]

The IRA leadership realised that British intelligence was becoming very effective and that the net was closing in around it. Collins made it clear that it was time to act or the 'Cairo Gang' would succeed in annihilating himself and his men. Collins' men spent several busy weeks gathering information about these special officers. Joe Dolan, one of Collins' intelligence officers, was sent round to all the hotels and boarding houses where they were living to collect information from waiters, footmen and others.[25] A list of targets was drawn up by the staff of IRA GHQ and 'every effort was made to see that the evidence against the men on the list was irrefutable'.[26] Michael Collins wrote to Dick McKee, commander of the Dublin Brigade of the IRA, on 17 November 1920. He was brief and to the point: 'Have established the addresses of the particular ones. Arrangements should now be made about the matter. Lt G is aware of things. He suggests the 21st. A most suitable date and day I think.' Lt G was a civil servant whom Collins had persuaded to work for him.[27]

The day of action was fixed for Sunday, 21 November 1920. Many of those who took part in the shootings said, in their statements to the Bureau of Military History, that the operation was sanctioned by the Dáil and that they were acting on orders. Frank Thornton, HQ intelligence staff, was in charge of compiling all the information and he and Brigadier Dick McKee, Dublin Brigade, presented a full report to a joint meeting of the Dáil cabinet and the army council. He was asked to prove that every man on the list was a secret service agent.[28] Cathal Brugha, Minister for Defence, worked through the files of information and he was not satisfied with some of the evidence. He was 'very conscientious and adamant in his judgement. If, to his mind, there was the slightest loophole for uncertainty about an agent or a spy, then that individual could not be dealt with. About fifteen names were rejected at that interview.'[29] Richard Mulcahy, chief-of-staff of the IRA, who was on the run at the time, said that he spent the night before Bloody Sunday with Cathal Brugha, after they had met with Collins and Dick McKee to discuss the shooting of the detectives.[30] 'Those chosen to carry out the raids were a mixture of Squad and Dublin Brigade men; most often the Squad members led the parties.'[31] Michael Collins, Dick McKee, Peadar Clancy, Paddy Daly and Seán Russell met on Saturday night, 20 November, to finalise operations.[32] The raiding parties were given detailed information about the houses to be visited, the situation of rooms, descriptions of agents and routes of approach and retreat.[33] Denis Begley, a member of E Company, 2nd Battalion, Dublin Brigade, recalls being summoned to Carpenters' Hall, Killarney Street, Dublin, to be briefed by Seán Russell. He organised a party of ten men to go to 22 Lower Mount Street.[34] Harry Colley said that eight men were selected for each operation by the officer in charge of them, and that the instructions and a list of addresses were given to that officer a week before Bloody Sunday. During the week, each company officer had to make himself familiar with the location of the operation under his command. The final arrangements were made on the night before, at 9.30 p.m. in Tara Hall, Gloucester Street (now Seán MacDermott Street), Dublin. 100 Seville Place was the original venue for the groups of eight and their officer to present themselves at quarter-hourly intervals to be briefed, but it was raided just before the appointed time and a change of location was quickly made. Colley recalled:

> Seán Russell, the officer commanding the Dublin Brigade, explained that the men to be shot were members of a new secret service which the enemy had brought into the country; that many of them had great reputations as secret service men working for England during

the war; and that it was vitally necessary for the success of the fight that they be removed. No country had scruples about shooting enemy spies in wartime but if any man had moral scruples, he was at liberty to withdraw from the operation and no one would think worse of him; he wanted every man to be satisfied in his conscience that he could properly take part in this operation.

Harry Colley also said that on that Saturday night, Dick McKee ordered the mobilisation of two squads for two additional operations.[35]

Groups of Volunteers were briefed for different houses in the Baggot Street, Leeson Street and Mount Street areas. According to Harry Colley all eight operations planned were carried out. However, some statements detail operations that were sanctioned for the northside of the city but were unsuccessful, either because the officers listed for assassination were not there or the Volunteers detailed to carry out the operation did not turn up. In their books James Gleeson and C.S. (Todd) Andrews give details of other operations on the southside that were also unsuccessful.

The execution of the British secret service agents in the Gresham Hotel was entrusted to D Company although the location of the hotel was not within the company area.[36] Paddy Moran, the only non-Squad member to take charge of an operation, was given thirteen men from D Company, Second Battalion, Dublin Brigade. Paddy Kennedy, intelligence officer with D Company, related what happened at the briefing:

On the Sat before Bloody Sunday I was instructed to report to 100 Seville Place that night where, I was told, I would receive specific instructions regarding an operation to be carried out the following morning. When I arrived at Seville Place that night I discovered that a number of specially selected men from my company were present and that Paddy Moran, my company O/C, was in charge of them.

Seán Russell took charge for that night, and he gave our instructions for the following morning. He explained that a big swoop was to be made simultaneously on all British agents residing in private houses throughout the city and that the operation was to be carried out at 9 o'clock sharp. He detailed Paddy Moran to take his party to the Gresham Hotel and eliminate three British intelligence officers who were stopping there. Lieutenant Colonel Wilde and Captain McCormack were two of the British agents; I cannot remember the name of the third man.

I arranged with Paddy Moran to meet him next morning in North Earl Street. I met him as arranged and we proceeded to the Gresham Hotel. As we entered the hotel the other members of our party, who were in the vicinity, came in after us. Our first job was to disconnect the telephone. As we knew the rooms in which the intelligence agents were located, our party split up, as pre-arranged, and proceeded to the rooms allotted to them by Paddy Moran. I remained with Paddy Moran while the shootings were taking place. There were people in the dining room and we took up position at the door and held them there.

Two British agents were eliminated that morning, the third man escaped. He was a Catholic, I believe, and had gone out to early mass. The whole operation lasted less than ten minutes.[37]

James Foley became company captain following Paddy Moran's arrest. He said:

The execution of the two British secret service agents in the Gresham Hotel, Dublin, was entrusted to D Company although the location of the hotel was not within the company area. The members who were present were as follows: Capt. Patrick Moran, Adj. Michael Kilkelly, Section Commanders Arthur Beasley, James Foley, Volunteers Michael Noone, Nicholas Leonard, Joseph Glynn, John Cullinane, William Hogan, Richard McGrath, Morgan Durnin, Joseph Doyle, Patrick Kennedy and George McCann.[38]

Paddy Daly confirms that Paddy Moran was in charge at the Gresham:

> Seán Russell picked the men for the various operations. Paddy Moran was not a member of the Squad but volunteered for the job. He was Captain of D Company, 2nd Battalion, and on that account Seán Russell did not put a member of the Squad in charge of the Gresham Hotel operation, knowing that he could not improve on Paddy Moran. Paddy Moran was not in Mount Street on Bloody Sunday.[39]

The hall porter from the Gresham said, at the military court of inquiry into the deaths, that the raiding party asked to see the hotel register and then asked to be conducted to rooms 14, 15 and 24. The porter told them there was nobody in No. 15. He brought them to No. 14 where Lieutenant Colonel Wilde was shot and to No. 24 where Captain McCormack was shot.[40]

The following extract is from the Dublin Metropolitan Police report sent to London following the events of Bloody Sunday morning:

GRESHAM HOTEL

About 8.55 E.L. Wilde, aged 30, and a Patrick McCormack were shot dead in their bedrooms at the Gresham Hotel by a number of men, 12 or 14, who went to the hotel, held up the staff and some guests, and at the point of a revolver compelled Hugh Callaghan, the porter, to conduct them to No. 14 and No. 24, rooms occupied by the deceased. They were all armed and unmasked and one carried a heavy hammer. They first knocked at Mr Wilde's door No. 14; he opened the door and was immediately shot dead, two or three shots being fired. He was in pyjamas and was found lying on the floor face downwards. Then they went to No. 24 and on the door being opened they entered and Mr McCormack was shot dead while lying in bed. There were five wounds on the head and body. Callaghan does not know any of the raiders. Dr Flanagan of Sligo who was staying in the hotel examined the bodies immediately after the occurrence.

Ex-Captain Mr McCormack has been staying in the hotel from time to time during the last six months.

Mr Wilde about whom no information has been obtained has been staying three weeks. He does not seem to be engaged in any occupation.[41]

Eleven British officers, one civilian and two cadets were killed on Bloody Sunday morning, while four officers and one civilian were wounded. Colonel Montgomery, who was wounded, died of his wounds on 9 December. In the Shelbourne Hotel, three men rushed up the stairs and one of them saw a man with a revolver approaching so he fired. The man with the revolver was himself; he did not realise that he was looking in a mirror! The targeted officer heard the shots, left his room and went hastily to another floor higher up and escaped. Captain Newberry's pregnant wife was in the room with him when he was shot in Baggot Street and she delivered a stillborn baby a week later.[42]

On the IRA side, Frank Teeling was captured when he was injured in the leg as he tried to scale a wall at the back of 22 Lower Mount Street, where Lieutenant Angliss was shot. Teeling was about to be shot when General Crozier, the commander of the Auxiliaries, arrived and he ordered his men to bring him to hospital for treatment and to keep him in custody. Billy McClean, a member of the IRA, was wounded in the hand when he reached out to shoot at Auxiliaries approaching the front door of 22 Mount Street, but he escaped.

The shooting of Captain McCormack in the Gresham caused controversy immediately, because it was claimed he was not working for British intelligence. He was a veterinary surgeon, a native of Castlebar, County Mayo, and was married to a daughter of James O'Connor of The Abbey Hotel, Roscommon. He had served in the Royal Army Veterinary Corps in France and in the Near East, was retired, and had recently returned from Cairo.[43] Mr McCormack's mother wrote to Richard Mulcahy, Minister for Defence, on 23 March 1922 asking for an explanation for her son's death:

Mrs Kate McCormack
3 Adelaide Street,
Dun Laoghaire.

I am the mother of Mr P.J. McCormack Ex-Captain in the British army who was shot in the Gresham Hotel on the morning of Sunday 21st November 1920. <u>I wish to ask if you will let me know the circumstances of my son's death or what the charges were against him.</u> I am 75 years of age and naturally I felt deeply the loss of my only support in life, but I feel more deeply still that charges of dishonourable conduct against his country should be preferred against him by people who have always known him to be a supporter of the national aspirations of the Irish people. It is only recently that an old friend let me know what was being said with reference to my son, and as I have a number of important facts which may possibly clear his name, I would feel grateful for an enquiry into the matter.

Principally I rely on the point that another Captain McCormack who lost his hand in a Clara ambush and who is reported to have sat on a court-martial at the trial of Kevin Barry is at present in England and it is possible my son may have been mistaken for him. Secondly it is stated that my son died worth £5161.00. This was a printer's error. The facts are that Probate of his Will was granted showing that he died worth £516.00, which was lying to his credit in Holts Bank in London but this £516 was part of a cheque for £1,200 which was cabled to him by a Mr Montessian of Cairo for the purchase of a horse from Mr J.J. Parkinson. My son appears to have spent £684 (the remainder of the £1,200) on hotel bills, etc. and on the necessary outfits for his wife and child whom he intended taking back with him to Alexandria. When his death took place it was necessary to put £500 for which his life was insured to the £516 in order that Mr Montessian should have his horse, his father-in-law supplying the deficiency. You will therefore see that he died without any assets and that I am at present living on the charity of my daughter-in-law's father.

The Recorder of Dublin early last year awarded me £750 which I never got, and it was stated in evidence and by the Recorder that my son was in no way connected with the Irish Troubles.

Mr J.H. Callan, who is my solicitor, is a man whom I know to be very friendly disposed towards the republican movement, and he examined all the effects, private documents etc. of my son, and I am sure if he is questioned he will be able to assure you that nothing of an incriminating nature against the republican movement was found.

My son had been appointed official starter to the Alexandria Turf Club at a salary of about £600 a year, his practice, commission on horses etc. being close to £2,000 in perspective, and as he intended going into the horse trade in a big way it was his intention to return to Cairo on 16 October but the difficulties of arranging berthage for himself and family and horses took so long that the final arrangements were not made until a few days before his death, and he was to have sailed on 2nd December 1920. Mr Callan can testify to shipping correspondence.

Might I mention that I am a cousin of the late Michael Davitt, and a sister-in-law of the late Dr McCormack, Bishop of Galway; that in younger days I took a leading part in the 'plan of campaign' and the Land League and that my son was thoroughly Irish in his education and upbringing. I therefore find it impossible to believe that he should have been mixed up with anything discreditable, and I will feel relieved beyond measure to know that you have investigated the matter and satisfied yourself that a grave mistake has been made.

May I mention that my son would never have been in the army at all were it not that he was compelled by reason of his occupation (Veterinary Surgeon at the Curragh) to join up or lose his means of livelihood.

I am Sir,

Yours faithfully,

Kate McCormack (widow)

The underlined sections were marked A and B and Mr Mulcahy wrote asking Michael Collins how they should answer these. This was his reply:

To Minister for Defence

With reference to this case you will remember that I stated on a former occasion that we had no evidence that he was a secret service agent. You will also remember that several of the 21st November cases were just regular officers. Some of the names were put on by the Dublin Brigade. So far as I remember McCormack's name was one of these.

In my opinion it would be as well to tell Mrs McCormack that there was no particular charge against her son, but that he was an enemy soldier.

M.O.C. 7–04–1922

Mr Mulcahy replied to Mrs McCormack:

11–04–1922
Mrs Kate McCormack

Dear Madam,

With reference to your letter of 23–03–1922, I have to say that inquiry into the matter of your son's death on 21st November 1920, disclosed the fact that there was no particular charge against him except that he was an enemy soldier.

I wish to take this occasion of expressing my very sincere sympathy with you.

Beir Beannacht
Aire Cosanta

Mrs McCormack replied:

23 Mellifont Avenue,
Dun Laoghaire

20th June 1922
R.J. Mulcahy Esq.,

Dear Sir,
Protracted illness prevented my acknowledgement of your letter of April 11th earlier.

I have to thank you for your kind expression of sympathy contained therein.

My mind is relieved that my son's character is above reproach, and that he has done no act unworthy of his name, or given any cause for his cruel death. I would like however to point out that there appears to be some misconception with regard to Mr McCormack's position. He could not have been an enemy soldier as he had been demobilised nine or twelve months previous to his death, and from the time of his demobilisation until his death he was engaged on his business as Veterinary Surgeon in Egypt, in Cairo and Alexandria, and only returned to Ireland in connection with the purchase of horses for Alexandria.

If you can help me with more definite reasons for the sad tragedy which has left me childless and heartbroken, I shall be very deeply obliged.

I am dear Sir,
Yours faithfully,
Kate McCormack

Mulcahy replied:

Dear Mrs McCormack,
I regret very much that I am not in a position to give any more definite reasons than were given in my letter of 11–04–1922.
Mulcahy[44]

The manager of the Gresham, James Doyle, in his statement to the Bureau of Military History, said that McCormack was in the hotel from September, that he had purchased racehorses and that he was booked to return to Egypt in December. 'Although he had been a Veterinary Surgeon in the British army there would appear to have been grave doubt as to his being associated with British intelligence.' He said that Mr Wilde had been there for a considerable time before Bloody Sunday. 'When Archbishop Clune visited the hotel again, I mentioned the shooting to him and he told me that Wilde had been put out of Spain; that he was well-known there as a British agent.'[45]

On 18 November 1920, a few days before he was killed in the Gresham, Mr Wilde wrote a letter to Mr Arthur Henderson of the Labour Party in England, possibly to cover his real activities in Ireland:

For some time now I have been an interested witness of the Labour Party's magnificent fight for real democracy and my object in addressing this letter to you is to beg you to be so kind as to put me in touch with those who can advise me as to the best method of consecrating my life to this cause. I am at present interested in the Irish Question and as an eyewitness to the 'George and Greenwood' administration, I must say first it is not British rule and second Ireland will not be coerced. Ireland is essentially a tradition-loving people and her traditions must be respected by those who govern her. My knowledge of her history might prove useful to the Labour Party and I should be happy to assist in propaganda work in England and I trust that my little quota to the settlement of Ireland may help to make the world realise that Ireland is a pillar of the Empire and Ireland is proud of her work in building and maintaining the greatest democratic Empire that the world has ever known. Kindly let me know to whom I may communicate on the subject of this letter. Believe me,
Yours faithfully,
Leonard Aidan Wilde[46]

The debate still goes on as to whether P.J. McCormack was a

secret service agent. Tom Bowden, University of Manchester, outlined what he considered was a career pattern indicating secret intelligence service for Captain McCormack. McCormack had just returned from Egypt, which was at the time the focal point of intelligence operations. As a veterinary surgeon and an Irishman he had an excellent natural 'cover' for intelligence work in a rural community. McCormack may have been in Ireland to assess the threatened use of germ warfare (the plan to infect army horses with glanders) by the IRA.[47] An entry by Sir Mark Sturgis, senior Dublin Castle administrator, in his diary for Sunday 21 November says: 'two secret service men were assassinated in the Gresham Hotel'.[48]

Charles Townshend casts doubts on Bowden's assertions and quotes the correspondence with Mrs McCormack from the Collins Papers to support his claim that McCormack was not a secret service agent.[49] James Gleeson called Captain McCormack's killing 'a tragic mistake'.[50]

It seems strange that McCormack was staying in the Gresham Hotel for several weeks when his mother was living in Dun Laoghaire, and his wife and child were also in Ireland. The manager of the Gresham said that McCormack slept late and did not go out until the afternoon. The maids who worked in the houses where the intelligence officers lodged and who gave information to the IRA said that was the pattern of activity those officers followed.[51]

When Michael Collins and Richard Mulcahy replied to Mrs McCormack, were they hiding behind the Dublin Brigade men who were not there to answer for themselves? Brigadier Dick McKee, the officer commanding the Dublin Brigade, Vice-Brigadier Peadar Clancy and Paddy Moran were, by this point, dead. If there was not a body of convincing evidence against McCormack, would Cathal Brugha not have removed him from the list?

In a memo sent to London from the chief secretary's office at 10.00 p.m. on Bloody Sunday, 21 November 1920, the assassinations were described:

Fourteen assassinations in cold blood and five cases of wounding were perpetrated about 9 a.m. this Sunday morning upon members of the crown forces and others resident in different parts of the city of Dublin. These murders were carried out on a concerted plan by separate murder groups armed with revolvers and ranging between 4 and 20 men in number. In all seven houses in different parts of the city and one hotel were visited, and one murder or more was done at each place. In almost each case the method of procedure was the same. One or two of the raiders knocked at the door and at its opening the whole party entered the house and having sought out their victim or victims shot them dead. Some were shot in bed, some were taken to another room and shot, some were shot out of hand on the stairs or wherever they happened to be; most of the men murdered were officers connected in some way with the administration of justice, either as court-martial officers or as officers concerned in the various stages of the preparation of cases for trial by court-martial. From this fact, coupled with facts concerning recent activities of the forces of the crown in suppressing crime, lies something of the motive and reason of this calculated and savage act. It would seem as though the gang which has made the murder of crown servants its business for some time past had become more and more concerned of late at the pace of the pressure with which the machinery of justice has been exercised against them. They had become actively conscious that the crown has gained of late, knowledge not only of their methods and plans but also of their names and whereabouts and of their criminal history individually. Murder plans were being frustrated, arrests of members of the murder gang and their associates were being made in greater numbers and with fuller prospects than ever before of securing that our end of justice should be attained and the criminals brought to book. It was in these conditions chiefly that the criminals concerned saw fit apparently to launch an attack of assassination against that part of the army specially concerned with bringing them to justice and in this desperate last effort there lay the twofold motive not only of scotching the machinery of justice but also of terrorizing the officers and our government with it.[52]

The shooting of the British officers in the morning only accounts for part of the events on 'Bloody Sunday'. The central council of the GAA had taken up a challenge from the Tipperary football team to prove their superiority over the Dublin team and a challenge match was arranged for Croke Park on Sunday 21 November. Challenge matches were organised regularly for the Republican Dependants' Fund and the Dublin senior board asked all the members 'to be at Croke Park ... not later than 2.00 p.m. to act as stewards in the Dublin/Tipperary contest which will start at 2.45 p.m'.[53] Earlier in the day, Dunleary (Dun Laoghaire) Commercials, a team founded by Paddy Moran, defeated Erin's Hopes, the St Patrick's College, Drumcondra, team in an Intermediate Championship game also held in Croke Park.[54] The Tipperary vs Dublin game was in progress when shooting broke out. Thirteen people lost their lives, some instantly, others died later as a result of their injuries. The Hogan stand in Croke Park is named after Michael Hogan, a Tipperary footballer who died from his injuries. Jane Boyle was watching the match with her fiancé when she was shot dead. They were to be married on Wednesday, 24 November 1920 (see Appendix 5).[55]

Major E.L. Mills, Auxiliary Division, Beggar's Bush Barracks, Dublin, made a statement on 22 November 1920, which, it is alleged, was not laid before the military court of inquiry into the shootings at Croke Park. He said that at 1.30 p.m. on 21 November 1920 he was detailed to take charge of a mixed force of RIC and Auxiliaries to hold up and search people as they filed out of Croke Park. He was ordered to leave the barracks at 3.20 p.m. As he approached the Railway Bridge he heard a considerable amount of rifle fire but no shots were coming from the football field. Firing was going on within the football ground when he reached it; he says he put a stop to it. The crowd was in a state of panic and people were being carried out dead or injured. He says that no arms were found and that he did not see any need for firing at all.[56]

In response to a parliamentary question asking why Mr Mills' evidence was not laid before the court of inquiry, Colonel Browne, the Dublin district commander, stated that Mills was called as a witness and gave evidence orally to the court. He also said that Mills 'is no longer an Auxiliary and was not under military command at Croke Park on 21/11/20'. A second police witness told the court that Mills was in Croke Park.[57] Mills resigned after Bloody Sunday.[58]

Sir Hamar Greenwood, chief secretary for Ireland, said in the House of Commons:

The round-up and search was carried out according to a preconcerted plan with the object of securing Sinn Féin gunmen who had taken part in the assassinations that morning of fourteen British officers, who in some cases were believed to have come into Dublin under cover of attending the match in the afternoon. Events in the football ground go to show that this belief was well founded and that a considerable number among the football crowd were carrying arms on their persons. That was proved beyond doubt by their efforts to escape, which had fatal consequences to a number of innocent people. It had been arranged that the military should surround the field and that the officer should announce to the crowd by megaphone that a search was to be made by the police and that no anxiety need be felt. The police force approached the neighbourhood of the field while the military were encircling it. Before the military cordon was complete the police were observed by civilians evidently posted to watch the approaches to the field. The police were fired upon from two corners of the field. Simultaneously men fired – from their places on the grand stand, with revolvers, into the air. Of this there is considerable evidence. It seems clear that these shots were a pre-arranged signal as a warning to a certain section of the crowd. A stampede was caused, not alone by the firing, but also by the rush of men seeking to make their escape from the field. Through the fall of a corrugated iron railing a number of people were crushed. Meanwhile a number of armed pickets outside joined, no doubt, by gunmen making their escape from inside, were maintaining a fire in the direction of the police, who returned it. The firing lasted no more than three minutes. About thirty revolvers thrown away by men who formed part of the spectators were picked off the ground.

Twelve persons lost their lives, eleven were injured seriously enough to warrant their detention in hospital, and about fifty persons sustained slight injuries.[59]

Lieutenant Commander Kenworthy asked Sir Hamar if he was aware that 'many eye witnesses are prepared to swear that no shots were fired at the police and that the so-called pickets were men selling tickets outside the field, and does he justify firing into a struggling mass of people including women and children in an attempt to pick out a small number of armed men out of 15,000 people?'[60]

Mr Kelly asked Sir Hamar could he explain when 'it became necessary to turn a machine gun on the people and how it happened that a little boy, ten years of age was bayoneted to death. Was that done by gunmen?'[61]

Sir Hamar replied that he was 'not aware that any machine gun was used and I do not believe that a boy of ten years was bayoneted'.[62]

A few boys from Wicklow who were in the grandstand for the match gave an account of their 'terrifying experience':

They were grouped together in the grandstand when the military appeared and began to fire. Some sought shelter under the stand while one made for the gate. A shop assistant from Mr L. Byrnes, Wicklow, obeyed the command of the civilians to drop to the ground. He remained in this position for some time and succeeded in reaching the gate by creeping, where he joined a huge crowd who were being held up. He was ordered to put up his hands and was obliged to keep them above his head for at least one hour before he was searched and allowed to go. While the officer was searching the crowds at the gate, Auxiliary police discharged shots over the people's heads and warned them not to rush. They ceased firing when ordered by the military officer. The other Wicklow boys, one of whom had the startling experience of seeing a man shot dead at his side, succeeded in getting free from Croke Park after being searched on three different occasions. Public transport ceased and the Wicklow boys had difficulty getting to their homes, two got home on Sunday night, another on Monday morning and the remainder on Tuesday night.[63]

Another young man who was at the match said it had been in progress about ten minutes when forces of the crown broke in at all the gateways, having completely surrounded the ground: 'They rushed in as though they were attacking the Germans and began firing straight away.' Several witnesses said that 'an aeroplane appeared over the grounds shortly after the match started and flew over at a low altitude above the throng'.[64]

The RIC men who gave evidence to the court of inquiry said that police did not fire first and that the firing came from the football grounds. All the evidence from civilians on the other hand said that men in uniform came in the main gate firing and that the first firing came from the bridge on the road leading past the main entrance. This seems to corroborate what Major Mills said. The court, however, found that firing was started by civilians, that the RIC's firing was carried out without orders and was in excess of what was necessitated by the situation.[65]

Brigadier Dick McKee and Vice-Brigadier Peadar Clancy, two of the organisers of the IRA's Bloody Sunday operation met with Michael Collins on Saturday night in their regular haunt, Vaughan's Hotel, Parnell Square, when they had finished their briefing of some of the participants for the operation next morning. There they met Conor Clune, a young man from County Clare. The three men left the hotel and went to Fitzpatrick's house, off Gloucester

Street where they were staying.[66] The house was raided following a tip-off from James Ryan, a military police sergeant engaged in intelligence work in Dublin Castle. All three were arrested and taken to Dublin Castle where they were interrogated. McKee and Clancy were tortured before they and Conor Clune were killed on Monday 22 November at the Castle. In retaliation Ryan was tracked down and shot by the IRA on 5 February 1921.[67]

Dick McKee's sister Moira gave oral testimony to Ernie O'Malley and said that Dick had bayonet wounds in both hands and along his arms and a big wound, about eleven inches, in his side. He had a gunshot wound in his neck. Peadar Clancy was very white and he had a great wound in his head. Conor Clune had one wound, but he hadn't been tortured.[68] Volunteers Pat McCrea and Tommy Gay went to St Brickin's Hospital to see the remains of the three men. Peadar Clancy had a large hole in the temple between the eye and the ear which was plugged with cotton wool, he had been badly wounded about the throat and it was covered with cotton wool. Dick McKee's face and head were badly marked.[69]

The Dublin Castle authorities said that the three men were wounded while trying to escape. One Volunteer, who was brought to Dublin Castle after Bloody Sunday and was in the room where Dick McKee, Peadar Clancy and Conor Clune were killed, said 'a mouse or a midge could not have escaped from that room'.[70] Dr McLysaght, whose father owned the seed and nursery plant in Clare where Conor Clune worked, described giving Clune a lift to Dublin, where he hoped to meet Piaras Béaslaí to discuss the Gaelic League. Clune arranged to meet Dr McLysaght near the entrance to Croke Park the following day. He did not turn up and McLysaght read in the evening paper on Monday that he was one of three men killed 'while trying to escape' from the Castle. Michael Collins sent Dr McLysaght to London to refute the propaganda surrounding the death of Conor Clune. On his return he was arrested and was taken to the same room in the Castle where the three men were killed and an Auxiliary officer pointed to the bullet holes in the woodwork and said, 'That's where we shot the other bastards, we'll probably do the same to you.'[71]

Sir Ormonde Winter gave what seems to be a totally preposterous account of what happened in the guardroom where McKee, Clancy and Clune were held. He said that the three prisoners attacked the one sentry left in charge while the other sentries were having breakfast. The sentry on duty fired a shot to warn the guard and then had his rifle taken from him. When the other guards came to his aid, an Auxiliary was attacked by a prisoner with a spade, while another prisoner fired a shot from the sentry's rifle, narrowly missing the commander of the guard.[72]

According to Michael Hopkinson, 'The events of Bloody Sunday were the most dramatic of the War of Independence, they represented a microcosm of the whole conflict in respect of the role of intelligence, the appalling violence, the thirst for revenge and the inextricable link with propaganda.'[73] Were the killings of British officers justified as claimed by the IRA, or were they callous murders as claimed by the British press? Were the shootings in Croke Park a reprisal, or were they caused by chaos and confusion? Arthur Griffith, when he came to his office on the morning after Bloody Sunday, was badly shaken. He thought the killings in Croke Park were dreadful, but that was a British crime. The other killings were not: 'How can we justify the killing of men on a Sunday morning in their homes in the presence of their wives?'[74] Robert Brennan, his director of publicity, pointed out that these men were 'not merely British officers. They were a special squad, recruited for the purposes of spying and murdering. They had themselves individually and collectively carried out a number of murders of our men. They had been recruited at the instance of Sir Henry Wilson, who, though an Irishman himself, was bitterly anti-Irish. He made no secret of his belief that the way to meet and beat Sinn Féin was by naked terrorism.'[75]

Cardinal Logue, the Archbishop of Armagh and Primate of all Ireland, condemned the Bloody Sunday atrocities when he wrote a pastoral letter in November:

> Assassinations of individuals is a detestable crime and a terrible outrage against God's Law but it is a greater shock to humanity and a graver outrage against the divine ordinance by which human life is protected, to turn lethal weapons against a defenceless, unarmed closely packed multitude, reckless of the number of innocent people who may fall victims.[76]

Collins had no doubt that he had done the right thing by ordering the Bloody Sunday operation:

> My one intention was the destruction of the undesirables who had continued to make miserable the lives of ordinary decent citizens. I have proof enough to assure myself of the atrocities which this gang of spies and informers have committed. Perjury and torture are words too easily known to them. If I had a second motive it was no more than a feeling such as I would have for a dangerous reptile. By their destruction the very air is made sweeter. That should be the future judgement on this particular event. For myself my conscience is clear. There is no crime in detecting and destroying, in wartime, the spy and the informer. They have destroyed without trial. I have paid them back in their own coin.[77]

Richard Mulcahy, Chief-of-Staff of the IRA, was quite clear about the responsibility of those against whom the IRA directed their operation on Bloody Sunday, when he spoke to Ulick O'Connor in later life. He said 'they [the British officers] were members of a spy organisation, that was a murder organisation. Their murderous intent was directed against the effective members of the government as well as against GHQ and staff of the Dublin Brigade.'[78]

Very few people knew that Paddy Moran was involved in the

Gresham Hotel on Bloody Sunday. Within the Moran family it is clear that two of his brothers, Jim and Tom, knew, but kept it a secret throughout their lives from his five sisters and probably from his other three brothers, John, Joe and Batty. In conversation with my brother Seán, a nephew of Paddy's, it emerged that he was told by my father about Paddy's part in the operation, but he understood from the circumstances in which the disclosure was made that it was intended to be in confidence while any of Paddy's immediate family was still alive. Faced with the evidence provided in the witness statements and in the O'Malley notebooks, Seán disclosed what had been related to him. Paddy Moran told his brother Jim, when he visited him on the night before his execution, of his involvement. The one thing that laid heavily on his conscience as he went to the gallows, was that P.J. McCormack might have been unjustly killed.[79]

It is unclear whether many of his fellow Volunteers knew of his involvement, or simply chose not to divulge the information. Dan Breen, Ernie O'Malley and many commentators over the years declared him completely innocent of any involvement in the events of Bloody Sunday. Those who were directly involved in the Bloody Sunday operations kept very quiet afterwards and John Horgan was told by Seán Lemass that 'firing squads do not have reunions' when he tried to question him about his involvement.[80] Paddy Kennedy's wife did not want Ernie O'Malley, when he took statements from participants in the 1950s, to say that her husband was involved. There was a veil of secrecy surrounding the activities of many of those involved in the whole War of Independence. Most of their families did not talk about it in later life. Within the IRA organisation itself there was a secrecy and a reticence to share experiences with units other than one's own. Perhaps that was because many of the men were members of the IRB and a very strict cell system existed in that organisation. I discovered that if I wanted to get any information about Paddy Moran in the witness statements taken from surviving participants of the War of Independence in the late 1940s and early 1950s, I had to look for statements from people who were in his own company, D Company, 2nd Battalion, Dublin 2 Brigade.

After the action in the Gresham, Paddy probably went back to report to Seán Russell at Byrne's, 17 Richmond Street, Dublin. He may have gone to the executive meeting of the Grocers', Vintners' and Allied Trades' Union being held in Parnell Square, which was part of his alibi. Almost certainly he went to Croke Park to see his team, Dunleary Commercials, defeat Erin's Hopes, the St Patrick's College team, in a replay of the Intermediate Football Final. But we do not know if he remained in Croke Park for the challenge match and witnessed the mayhem there in the afternoon. Sunday was his last time in the city of Dublin as a free man; he was at work in Magees' of Blackrock on Monday and worked as usual until he was arrested the following Friday, 26 November 1920.

CHAPTER 6

KILMAINHAM GAOL

Paddy Moran was arrested on Friday 26 November 1920, five days after Bloody Sunday. Three or four officers came into Magees' shop in Blackrock and asked for Captain Moran. When he said, 'My name is Moran', they told him to get upstairs. They searched his room but found nothing. One officer said, 'Did you not know we were raiding around here this morning, why did you not clear out?'

'Why should I clear out?' was his reply.[1]

A list of IRA members was found in a raid on Richard Mulcahy's house around this time. Between Bloody Sunday, 21 November 1920, and 21 February 1921, 1,745 people were arrested in the Dublin area.[2]

Paddy Moran was taken to Dun Laoghaire and later that day transferred to the Bridewell, Dublin. He was detained there for a fortnight during which time he was involved in two identification parades. He was taken to Arbour Hill prison, Dublin, on Saturday 11 December 1920, and there he was involved in a third identification parade. On Friday 17 December, there was yet another identification parade and this time Paddy Moran noticed an officer and two privates standing in a group in the yard to view the men going down to stand at the window through which prisoners were viewed during identification parades. The officer was Major Carew;

he lived at No. 28 Upper Mount Street, Dublin; the privates were Lawrence, Major Carew's batman, and Snelling. Snelling was a motorcyclist who was held up on Bloody Sunday morning, had his bicycle taken from him and was held up again in Upper Mount Street and taken to No. 38. These three soldiers were the witnesses for the prosecution at Paddy Moran's trial. Private Lawrence had met Paddy Moran and another unidentified man in Mount Street on the eve of Bloody Sunday when Paddy and his friend tried to help a lady who was in some kind of distress. Lawrence questioned the two men because it was past curfew and they should not have been out. Paddy spoke in a cockney accent and managed to convince Lawrence that they were *bona fide*. The fact that Lawrence had seen Paddy in Mount Street was critical in the building up of the case against Paddy. The motorcyclist, Snelling, claimed that Paddy was the man on the steps of No. 38 Upper Mount Street, who covered him with a revolver and made him cross over to that house.

Paddy Moran wrote an account of the identification parades for his solicitor, Michael Noyk. He did not know the names of his accusers and refers to them as 'Private Black Eyes', 'Private Grey Eyes' and 'the Officer'. He believed this identification was set up specifically to select him. He was not identified at the window and went with his fellow prisoners to the gymnasium, but the last ten men were called out again, including Paddy. One of the three military men he had seen standing in the yard, 'Private Black Eyes' (Snelling), then picked him out and asked him to stand beside another prisoner, Kevin Halpin. Both men were asked to go and shave and Paddy was brought out and placed with seven others in the yard. He was then the only clean-shaven man among them. 'Private Black Eyes', 'Private Grey Eyes' (Lawrence), and 'the Officer' (Carew) all now consulted and Private Snelling then came over to Paddy and said to him: 'Yes, you are the man who held me up with a revolver on Sunday 21 November 1920 in

Upper Mount Street.' When Paddy said that he was not, Snelling asked him to walk a few paces and said, 'Yes, you are the man, did I not identify you before?'

On hearing that he had not identified Paddy previously, he asked for Paddy's name and then turned to Major Carew and said, 'There's something wrong here, that's not the name.' Paddy asked a police officer, Sergeant Nixon, to take down all that was said and to give him the names of those present, but Nixon refused to do either. Private Snelling walked away and Private Lawrence came over and said, 'Yes, you are the man who held up my chum.'

'Would it surprise you to know that I was at my breakfast at the time?' Paddy replied.

Paddy was placed in a cell on his own and that night he was moved to Kilmainham Gaol. Before he left Arbour Hill the staff sergeant told Paddy that there was a doubt in his case and that he was not going for trial but to be put beside another man for yet another identification parade.[3]

Shortly after his arrival at Kilmainham, Paddy sent out his laundry with a message hidden inside the detachable collar of his shirt:

> This place is the limit. I would not be here at all but one young soldier thought he had identified me before which he hadn't. When he heard the name he said there's some mistake that's not the name but the second soldier said 'twas me so I'm here on suspicion. I was not in Mount Street for years so I hope the scales come off their eyes. Of course I can prove I was miles away but let them see their folly out, I'll make no statements.[4]

He described his new abode in a letter to Mary Farrell, a friend from Dun Laoghaire, as a 'gloomy old pile'. The Farrell family had a dairy near Lynch and O'Brien in Dun Laoghaire, where Paddy had worked up to a month before his arrest. His girlfriend was one of the Farrell girls, Bea (B). He asked Mary to get his razor, brush, strap and soap and a mirror 'to see myself as others see me'. He understood that he was there for another identification parade and felt confident enough to say that if the authorities hurried up he might still be free for Christmas.[5]

He wrote to Mary again on 3 January 1921:

My dear Mary,

I have just noticed this is the first time I wrote 1921 and wish you a Happy New Year which you can distribute to all my friends. I am getting accustomed to the routine of this place and it isn't as bad as it looks outside, and I shall be expecting to see the outside appearance soon again. The 'grub' here is plentiful and good, and what with all the parcels you and my other friends send I'll have to start entertaining if I am to get rid of it all. I gave B my washing this morning though I'm not in any need as Clare brought me enough some days ago to tide me through unless I'm going to be kept here indefinitely. I'm sorry I delayed answering your letter so long but I would have written today in any case. And B forgot to put the two medals in the parcels or envelopes. I did not get them with the others. Perhaps they may be mislaid in the office here and will turn up later. I suppose you have the same dismal weather outside that we have here, but one satisfaction, it isn't cold and we can't complain all the same. Just when I got this far Annie and Clare have arrived with more parcels and a flask of tea, this was just at dinnertime. So I had a good dinner and a bowl of tea after, it takes some beating anywhere. I got the chocolates all right, convey my thanks to the donor but they are sweetness wasted on me as I rarely eat sweets so somebody else will get the majority of them. There is no news in this place to send that would interest you. I suppose I have to sit quiet and be patient and I suppose all my many friends will have to do likewise, then some fine day I'll bump into all of you. With every good wish for the new year to yourself and all my Dunlaoghaire friends.

Yours sincerely,

Paddy Moran

The expected identification parade took place early in January and this time he was placed between two men, O'Reilly and Adams. He was taken to Dublin Castle on Friday, 7 January 1921 and charged with the murder of Ames and Bennett at 38 Upper Mount Street on 21 November 1920. Private Lawrence, the batman to Major Carew, was there. When Paddy Moran complained that the officer present was not taking down the evidence, the officer jumped up in a rage, went to his coat and took out a revolver, opened it up to see if it was loaded and said, 'You keep your mouth shut, you see that, you know what it is, you are very fond of them.' When another officer entered the room the first officer asked him if he had a gun. When he replied that he had, he was told to keep it handy and not to mind if it went off in a hurry.[6]

Others have described interrogations at the Castle that were more severe. Ernie O'Malley was arrested in the Inistioge area of Kilkenny in December 1920 and was interrogated in Dublin Castle. He described how Captain Hardy, a famous and greatly feared interrogator, tried to extract information from him by pointing a red-hot poker at his eyes. Major King, who was with Hardy, beat O'Malley with his fists so hard that his face was cut, his eyes swollen and he felt the salty taste of blood run down his throat.[7]

Paddy returned to Kilmainham with a charge of murder hanging over him and later wrote to his youngest sister, Maggie, who was living at home with his parents, and to his sisters Ciss (Mary) and B (Bridget), who were both teaching in England at the time, to reassure them:

Kilmainham Gaol, Thursday

My Dear Maggie,

I was very glad to get your letter to know yourself and all at home were quite well. I really never felt so fit in all my life myself, and the conditions here are not so bad as they were at first. I had a letter from Ciss on Friday, & B and herself are very well. Annie [sister] told me she was writing to let you know that I will be getting tried soon. Let this news cause you no alarm. I suppose they are not putting the charge for fun because it is serious enough, but I can't look at it in that light. I haven't been in the street where the shooting took place for a couple of years. It was just my ill luck to be like someone or perhaps not at all like someone who was there that morning. Such a charge can't stand a test and with God's help if there is a trial its outcome will be to my advantage. I do not expect to be tried next week, possibly the week after. The sensation is of course a new one. But it doesn't worry me and I do not want it to worry anyone at home – as with God's help & the best legal advice, I'll come through all right. Neither I nor you are the only individuals and friends who have the same trouble (?) these times. No action of mine was responsible for the charge so I feel no personal responsibility for any annoyance it may cost my friends or myself. Now I think that's enough about the serious side of the question.

Oh but Heavens!

I had many a good laugh at Cissie's letter with all the local humour it contained, I could see Charlie after the feed of herrings, telling Johnny he'd give his two eyes for another piece of a herring – he would! and then his troubled look as he contemplated what he would suffer that night. Sorry to hear of Miss Lane's death, she was about as sweet with the rod as Larry was with the knife. I too dream many a time of you all. I thought Dada was in a row, fancy & got fined £4 thro false evidence, and that Jim had some trouble with Pat Mac. I was dreaming of Charlie also but beyond the fact that he had a great lorry of spuds in the garden I do not remember any more. Mamma and all of you have cropped up sometime. So I suppose it's telepathy.

I had a long letter from Ciss and Annie has just been outside with a parcel. Clare [cousin] will be here this evening so with other people's kindness I'm having a high time. Do not forget to write soon and send all the news.

With best love to Dada, Mamma and you all, remember me to all the friends etc.

Your loving Bro,
Patk

Kilmainham Gaol, Dublin, Monday

My dear Ciss & B,

I was very glad to get your letter and to know you are both so very well. I was sorry to see you were troubled as really, though things may appear serious, I know that such a charge can't stand the test of truth. I was thankful for the prayers and picture, I had a lot of devotions before but am adding on those which I think powerful. I had a letter from Mag, they are all well. I never wrote to Miss McKenna since she wrote [to] me. As a matter of fact I dropped all my correspondents & am sorry now because letters are better than anything here. Annie has just been here with a parcel. I get too much food and often thought of suggesting that she shouldn't be going to the expense and then she has such a rush – while she could write as often as she liked. The conditions here have improved a good deal and everybody is feeling very well. I do not think I was ever much better myself, I should be sorry if anyone was worrying too much but as no action of mine was responsible for the charge being brought I do not feel any personal responsibility. The trial was to be on next Saty [sic] but the solicitor said that he could not proceed on that day so I do not know for certain when it comes off. In any case I'm quite at ease on the matter. Write soon, with very best love to you both.

Your fond Bro,
Patk

Frank Teeling, the only man captured in action on Bloody Sunday, was lodged in Kilmainham around the same time as Paddy Moran. Frank had been shot in the hip when he tried to scale a wall at the back of 22 Lower Mount Street on Bloody Sunday morning; he fell back into the garden and was captured.[8] Ernie O'Malley was imprisoned under the name Bernard Stewart, the authorities unaware that they had in custody a much-wanted man. Thomas Whelan from Clifden in Galway, Michael J. Tobin, Edward Potter, William Conway, Jimmy McNamara, Patrick Rochford and Jimmy Boyce were also awaiting trial for their alleged part in Bloody Sunday. Fr Dominic O'Connor from the Franciscan Capuchin Friary in Church Street, was arrested along with Fr Albert Bibby on 17 December 1920, in a raid on the friary. Fr Dominic was charged with making seditious statements, sentenced to five years penal servitude and taken to Kilmainham Gaol. While he was there, Paddy was his mass server and they became good friends.[9]

The prison was under the command of the 2nd Welch Regiment. There was a strict routine for the prisoners: reveille was sounded at 6.30 a.m. by the sharp ringing of bells; before breakfast at 7.30 a.m. all blankets were returned to the store, latrine buckets emptied, cells scrubbed out and generally cleaned, and prisoners themselves washed and properly dressed; after breakfast, plates and cooking utensils had to be thoroughly washed. The officer commanding the prison conducted an inspection daily at 9.30 a.m. and prisoners were expected to be standing outside their cells. There was a period of exercise morning and afternoon, dinner was at 12.30 p.m., tea at 4.30 p.m., blankets were issued at 8.00 p.m. and prisoners were in bed by 8.30 p.m.[10] At first relations between the prisoners and their captors were tense, but gradually the regime became more relaxed and the prisoners were able to mingle at exercise, to talk to each other at cell doors and even to visit each other's cells.

Family and friends delivered food parcels at the gate and Paddy's sister Annie, a student nurse at the Mater Hospital, and his cousin Clare Moran, who lived in South Circular Road, Dublin, brought him anything he required. His girlfriend delivered a flask of tea and often an apple cake for him. He had a photograph of her in his pocket and Ernie O'Malley recalled him showing it to him. Paddy said, 'That's a great girl', and shook his head with a remembering smile.[11] Like all the prisoners, Paddy carried his home place in his mind and could talk to O'Malley of Crossna and the people he liked. He recalled 'the lonely shores of Lough Allen, the bare recession of hills towards Leitrim and the smells of the ferny undergrowth of woods near the lakes of Skean and Meelagh'. In order to while away the time and to take Paddy out of himself, O'Malley asked him 'to walk down the right bank of the Shannon from Lough Allen to Carrick-on-Shannon and come back on the opposite side'. When Paddy walked behind O'Malley at exercise they would recall the 'colour of the curlews (near Boyle) after rain and the reeds near the shore in the early morning'. They thought about how it would feel 'to stand on the Rock of Courage in Lough Key and look across at the Rock of Doon'.[12]

Paddy had a visit from Colonel F.D. Martin, a court-martial officer, on 19 January 1921. He brought with him a letter which asked Paddy to give him notice if he wished to be legally represented at his trial which was expected to take place on or about 29 January. It said that every facility would be given to him to employ a solicitor or counsel and to interview any witnesses he might wish to call. If he was not in a position to employ civil legal advice, a qualified legal officer would be assigned to him to assist him in his defence. The summary of the evidence against Paddy and a Notice of Prosecution by counsel were attached. The notice read:

Whereas you are alleged to be guilty of crimes under the Restoration of Order in Ireland Regulations in respect of which you will be tried by court-martial. Take notice that by virtue of rule 88 and 89 of the Rules of Procedure 1907 the prosecution will be conducted by Counsel at your trial in respect of said crimes. Given under my hand at Headquarters, Dublin District, this 18th day of January 1921.[13]

The summary of evidence contained the evidence of five unnamed witnesses (I have inserted the names in each case) and it was supposed to be the evidence sworn in Paddy's presence at the Castle. Paddy studied it and wrote notes in the margin where he pointed out the differences with what was in fact sworn:

First witness [Private Lawrence]

I am batman to [Officer Carew] who is employed at Dublin Castle. At about 11.30 p.m. on 20 November 1920, I was just about to enter No. 28 Upper Mount Street where I lived with my officer. I was stopped by two men who, after telling me a long story, made a certain request [*Paddy wrote that at the Castle, the batman had sworn that the request was to come with them to stop a woman being ill-treated*] and asked for certain information. I did not give them any.

I eventually left the men and entered No. 28. It would then be nearly midnight. As I was opening the door one of them shouted after me a question. [*He had sworn at the Castle that they asked, 'Did he live there?'*] When I got in I made a report to my officer as to what happened.

The next morning, Sunday 21 November, between 8.45 and 9.00 a.m., I happened to look out the sitting-room window, which is on the top floor, when I saw a man walking up and down outside No. 38 Upper Mount Street, which is practically opposite. I saw him suddenly quicken his step, pull a revolver out of his pocket and point it at the Private who had just come up. I later found the Private's name to be Private [Snelling] and now know him well. I ran and told my officer what was happening. He was in bed.

The officer ran into the sitting room with his automatic. I followed him. He opened the window and shouted something. I saw the Private was then standing on the steps of No. 38 and the man I had seen before was pointing the revolver at him. My officer fired and I stepped back from the window.

I went away to fetch my service revolver and when I returned both the Private and the man had disappeared.

The accused I see here before me now who answers to the name Patrick Moran is the man who held up the Private. I identified him at Arbour Hill about the middle of December last and picked him out from about 15 men (*Paddy put ?? in margin here and wrote in '7 men'*). I asked for him to be shaved to make absolutely certain he was the right man.

Second witness: the officer [Major Carew]

On 20 November 1920 my servant Private [Lawrence] was very late returning home. I looked out of my sitting-room window which is on the top floor and looks on to Upper Mount Street and saw him talking to two civilians near the front door. Directly I looked out they left him and he came upstairs and made a report to me.

Next morning between 9.00 and 9.30 I was in bed when my servant ran in and told me something as a result of which I got out of bed and took my automatic with me, which I had under my pillow and went into the sitting-room and opened the window.

At the house opposite I saw a civilian holding up a soldier. In his hand he had a Webley pistol. [*Paddy Moran inserted a ? and wondered how he could know that it was a Webley from the top floor of a tall building.*] I cannot swear to him positively.

Shortly after the soldier and the civilian disappeared into the house, I heard several shots. Fifteen or twenty [men] ran out of the house. I fired at them and some fired at my window. I think I hit two as I saw them squirm but they ran on. [*Paddy wrote 'I was not searched for bullet wounds'.*]

Third witness: the motorcyclist [Private Snelling]

At about 8.40 a.m. I left the Castle on a Triumph Combination to go to Rathmines to fetch my officer. I went via Dame Street and Grafton Street. Just as I turned out of Grafton Street, I heard shots which sounded as if they came from the other side of the Green but I could not say exactly where they came from.

I went on and entered Lower Baggot Street. When I was about fifty yards from the house where _____ lived which was on the right-hand side coming from the Green and which I now know is No. 119, I heard shots and saw about twenty men running from the direction of 119. They were straggling across the road. I noticed one in particular had bright red hair and a curious bow-legged run and he turned his toes in.

A little higher up Baggot Street, I saw a man lying half-way out of a window covered with something like a sheet. He was bleeding badly.

I went on and turned down Herbert Place. When I was about fifty yards from the corner of Herbert Place and Upper Mount Street, I saw a crowd of men come running out of Upper Mount Street. I judged them to be the same men I had seen in Baggot Street. I noticed the red-head among them. Some of them spread across the road and pointed revolvers at me. They were all armed with service revolvers. I got off and put my hands up. I left the bicycle and started running towards Kingstown Road. After I had gone a few yards one fired after me and called on me to stop. I did so and came back.

One man said, 'Go down this way' and pointed down Upper Mount Street. I walked on and he walked behind me. I saw a man standing outside a house in Upper Mount Street [No. 38]. He pointed a revolver at me and beckoned me to come over, I did so.

He kept me covered as I was walking towards him and I naturally kept my eyes fixed on him. He pressed the revolver in my ribs [*Paddy noted here that at the Castle he said 'Guts' but the officer said that doesn't read nice*] and told me to give four knocks on the door. The door did not open so the man called 'Open the door boys.' [*Paddy noted here that when he gave this evidence in the case against Thomas Whelan he said it was someone inside who said, 'Open the door boys.'*] I picked him out from ten men. [*Paddy inserted a ?*] In the house a man fired one shot, I then heard two shots. [*Paddy noted that the medical officer said there were ten wounds on Bennett and seven on Ames.*]

Fourth witness: The medical officer at King George V Hospital, Dublin

On the 22 and 23 November I examined the bodies.

In the case of Lieutenant Bennett there was a small puncture wound on the top of the head with a larger wound at the back of the head, two wounds close together at right forehead, one wound in front of chest, three wounds in back and two wounds in the right forearm.

In the case of Lieutenant Ames there were two wounds in the right armpit, one in right upper arm, one in front of chest, one in right chest, one in right flank and one in right side of back. I extracted a bullet from under the skin which I now identify. [*Paddy noted that he did not have any bullet but that one was brought in for him at that point.*]

The cause of death in both cases was shock and haemorrhage.

Fifth witness: Arresting officer

On 7 January 1921 I arrested and charged the accused. Paddy Moran said, 'I was not in Mount Street that morning.'

The accused persons Patrick Moran and Joseph Rochford having been duly warned, declined to make a statement.

I certify that the evidence contained in this summary of evidence has been taken down by me in the presence and hearing of the accused persons, Paddy Moran and Joseph Rochford, at Headquarters, Dublin district on 7th, 8th and 9th days of January 1921 in accordance with the provisions of the Army Act and the Rules of Procedure framed thereunder and that the requirements of the Rule of Procedure 4(c), (d) and (e) have been complied with.

The two accused men were asked if they wished to examine any of the prosecution witnesses, but they declined.

The charge sheets were not included but were sent later:

Charge Sheet 1:

The accused Patrick Moran, 5 Main Street, Blackrock, and Joseph

Rochford, 11 Elmpark Avenue, Ranelagh, civilians charged with:
(a) committing a crime within the meaning of Regulation 67 of the
Restoration of Order in Ireland Regulations, that is to say MURDER
in that they in Dublin, Ireland, on 21 November 1920, feloniously,
wilfully and of their own malice aforethought did kill and murder
Lieutenant A. Ames.

(b) Committing a crime within the meaning of Regulation 67
of the Restoration of Order in Ireland Regulations, that is to say
MANSLAUGHTER in that they etc.

Charge Sheet 2:
Same wording but referred to murder of Captain Bennett.

Charge Sheet 3:
The accused Patrick Moran of 5 Main Street, Blackrock, a civilian,
is charged with contravening the provision of an order made by the
Competent Military Authority under regulation 9A of the Defence
of the Realm Regulations and in force in Ireland as if it had been
made under the Restoration of Order in Ireland Regulations, that is
to say carrying firearms not under effective military control in that he
in Dublin, Ireland, on 21 November 1920, did, contrary to an order
of competent Military Authority dated 28 September 1918, carry
firearms, namely a revolver, not under effective military control.[14]

Paddy spent some time pointing out inaccuracies in the summary
of evidence and writing out his own statement for his solicitor,
Michael Noyk.

There were other things on his mind too. In well-established
IRA tradition, plans began to be made for escape, in particular
for the escape of Frank Teeling who was tried by court-martial on
25 January 1921 and sentenced to death. Several prisoners were
snatched from jails in Ireland and in England during the War
of Independence and by 1 January 1919 over thirty Republican
prisoners had escaped from Irish prisons.[15] Robert Barton left a

cheeky note for the governor when he escaped from Mountjoy in March 1919, saying that owing to the discomfort of his cell he felt obliged to leave and asked the governor to retain his baggage safely until he sent for it.[16] There was, however, no record of any prisoner ever having escaped from Kilmainham Gaol up to this point.

Two soldiers, Private Holland and Private Roper, came to know and like Frank Teeling and offered in hushed tones to help him escape. Herbert Conroy was released from Kilmainham Gaol in December 1920 and told Oscar Traynor, the officer in charge of the Dublin Brigade, about the two friendly soldiers.

Paddy Moran was a friend of Séamus Kirwan, a fellow Volunteer in D Company, 2nd Battalion, who owned a public house at 49 Parnell Street, Dublin. One of the soldiers called there early in January 1921 and brought with him a note from Paddy asking for outside help. For several days meetings were held between the soldiers, Oscar Traynor and his men. Notes were sent to and from Kilmainham through Kirwan's in Parnell Street and Sean Farrelly's public house at 141 St Stephen's Green. The plans were narrowed down to two alternatives: a rope ladder for the wall or a bolt-cutter for a rusty padlock on an unused gate.

Mick Smith procured the bolt-cutter from Breen's garage in Donnybrook, Dublin, where he worked.[17] In 1936 Smith wrote a letter to the editor of the *Evening Herald*, in response to an article by Denis Begley, in which Begley claimed to have sourced the cutter. Mick Smith described how Herbert Conroy conveyed a message to him from Tom Ennis at GHQ requesting him to go to general headquarters, Printer's Hall, Gardiner Street, Dublin. Mick Smith was then asked to get a bolt cutter about one foot long, which could be carried into the jail unnoticed. He explained that such a cutter would be of little use, as it would only cut a small bolt. He went to the garage and explained to the owner what was needed. They both agreed that the cutter would need to be four or five feet long. They decided to cut the handles from a cutter and were intending to adjust it so that it could be reassembled again easily with bolts and steel tubing. Mick Smith then thought of making the handles from the steel tubing so that they would slide on and off easily. They cut the handles from a three foot cutter with a hacksaw, fired the forge to heat the steel tubing, placed the cutting portion of the cutter on the anvil, hammered on the steel handles and the result was a bolt-cutter with removable handles. It took them about six hours to do the job. Mick Smith brought the cutter to Tom Ennis and then to Oscar Traynor at 21 Clonmore Road, Dublin. In Traynor's sitting-room they tested the cutter and soon had several bolts cut. The steel tubing used was heavy gauge; it was the carting shaft from an old Lagonda motor car. Smith finished his letter saying: 'I still have in my possession the wire-cutter that was left in my house three days later by Denis Begley'.[18]

Opinions are divided as to whether the ladder or the bolt-cutter was tried first. Ernie O'Malley, who was inside the jail, describes the failure of the bolt-cutter on the first attempt;[19] Christy Byrne and Mick Smith, who were on the outside also think that the cutter was tried first.[20] In contrast Oscar Traynor maintained that it was the rope ladder that was tried first and that this plan failed on two occasions before the bolt-cutter was used. He repeated that assertion in his statement to the Bureau of Military History.[21]

There are also different accounts of the dates of the escape attempts. Séamus Kirwan recalled that a few attempts were made but without success, causing Michael Collins to doubt the sincerity of the two soldiers. Paddy Moran informed Kirwan that the soldiers were absolutely genuine and that they were even prepared to risk their lives to see the matter through. 'But you can trust them,' Paddy wrote, 'you can depend your lives on them.'[22]

Some accounts say that the first attempt was made on Sunday 6 February. Three soldiers who were found with their girlfriends near the jail were taken captive and kept for a week in a house in Inchicore until after the escape. The girls' parents were informed of their capture, given assurances that they were perfectly safe and warned to keep quiet. Others recall that the first attempt was made on Sunday 13 February, and that the bolt-cutter and the rope were both tried. When the bolt-cutter failed, a rope was thrown over the wall which landed with a thud on a galvanised roof: it had a heavy weight on the end to stabilise it. It was drawn back and when the prisoners tried to pull it over the wall on the second attempt, it caught in a crevice and broke. These accounts say this was the night that the soldiers and their girlfriends were taken prisoner.[23] Private H. Townshend, one of those British soldiers, gave evidence at the court-martial of Holland and Roper, on 7 March 1921. While he did not mention girls being there, he said that while he was sitting on a wall outside the jail on 13 February, he was approached and asked to put his hands up. He was blindfolded and taken to a place he did not know. He was kept there until the evening of 15 February 1921, when he was released at the tram terminus in Inchicore, Dublin.[24]

The two soldiers, Holland and Roper, were just as disappointed at the failures of the escape plans as the men inside and one of them arrived in Kirwan's on Monday 14 February. He met Oscar Traynor and told him, 'I'll cut the so-and-so padlock myself.'[25] The padlock that was cut with the bolt-cutter was given to the National Museum in 1935 and is held in Collins Barracks Museum.[26]

Whether the rope ladder or bolt cutter was used first, in the end it was the bolt cutter that was used in the successful escape. On the evening of Monday 14 February, three prisoners, Frank Teeling, Ernie O'Malley and Simon Donnelly walked out through a disused side gate. Simon Donnelly had only been in Kilmainham from Friday 10 February, just two days before the escape, but he was well known to the authorities and was on a list of persons suspected of complicity in the murder of police and civilians as early as November 1919.[27] As a result he was likely to be quickly convicted, so it was considered important to get him out of Kilmainham as soon as possible. The escapees boarded a tram: Simon Donnelly got off in Camden Street and Teeling and O'Malley got off in Heytesbury Street, Dublin. The latter two went to Malone's, a safe house, and later that night, Áine Malone, fearful that the house might be raided, linked arms with these two men and brought them to another house near Mount Street Bridge.[28]

Desmond Fitzgerald, arrested on 11 February, and Seán Kavanagh had given the escaping men money for their tram fare.[29] Fitzgerald is reported to have said that he would not go along with the men when they told him that the gate was open, as a crowd might hinder the escape.[30]

The jail was in the area covered by the men of F Company, 4th Battalion, Dublin Brigade, and they were given the task of watching the jail to assist the escapees to get safely away. Seán Dowling and Christy Byrne took charge and Jimmy Donnelly picked the men and women he needed to help: Bill Kelly was an employee of the cleansing department of Dublin Corporation; he and Mick Heffernan were given hard yard brushes and told to sweep around the jail gates every morning. 'They did so much cleaning that they had the old gutters nearly swept away.'[31] The men of F Company had to be careful because the city was under curfew. About twenty of them went along the canal every evening to get outside the city boundary and stayed in a hay-loft. During the night they travelled back along the canal to the jail to keep watch. They did this for a week.[32] Paddy O'Connor and Barney Keogh made the rope ladder. O'Connor said that they were at the jail every morning at 5.00 a.m. and every evening at 7.00 p.m. for about a week. O'Connor and Paddy Rigney were to act as an escort for Teeling and O'Malley and they had their own guns as well as two with ammunition for the escapees.[33] On Sunday, 13 February, Jimmy Donnelly was called to Kirwan's pub and told that the soldiers had arranged for the escape to take place at 8.00 p.m.; it was now 7.00 p.m. He managed to have sufficient men ready to cover the escape and he brought the rope ladder to the prison.[34] On the night of the successful escape, Paddy O'Connor saw three men walk past him, heard an alarm sound and only afterwards realised that the three men were the escapees, who did not need help from the men stationed outside.[35]

Ernie O'Malley later wrote extensively about the escape.[36] He got the bolt-cutter from one of the friendly soldiers who had hidden it inside the leg of his trousers to get it into the jail and that soldier also brought him a revolver. O'Malley implies that he walked around with the cutter inside his trousers and the revolver in his pocket inside the jail![37] Most other accounts say that the contact was made by Herbie Conroy, Ginger McNamara and Paddy Moran, and that the bolt-cutter was brought to Frank Teeling because he was the one most likely to be able to use it as he had worked in an iron works in Inchicore, Dublin. The cutter and the revolver were hidden under rubble in a disused cell inside the jail. There is no mention of Ernie O'Malley as the organiser of the escape in the accounts that I have read from those who gave statements to the Bureau of Military History or from the accounts that Ernie O'Malley himself took from participants and that can be read in the O'Malley notebooks.[38] Ernie O'Malley and Simon Donnelly both said that they tried to persuade Paddy Moran to escape with them, but he refused.[39]

In so far as the witness statements are accurate, there is evidence that there was an order, imposed from GHQ, for the men escaping. Frank Teeling, already tried and convicted, was a Dublin Brigade man and the brigade insisted that he should be first on the list. Richard Mulcahy tried to put Ernie O'Malley first, but the men of the Dublin Brigade were adamant that Teeling would be the first to go; second place went to O'Malley; third to Paddy and fourth to Simon Donnelly according to Harry Colley.[40] However, Donnelly was there for such a short time that it seems doubtful that he was on the list. O'Malley said that Chief-of-Staff Richard Mulcahy had told him in a note that any plan for escape should include Teeling and himself.[41] Paddy O'Connor recalled that when the plan was first drawn up it provided for the escape of only two prisoners, Teeling and O'Malley.[42] Anna Kelly, in her articles on prison escapes, argued that there was a lapse of a week between escape attempts. If that is so, then Simon Donnelly was not in the prison on the first attempt (6 February 1921) and that might explain why Paddy Moran had given his place to Simon for the subsequent attempts.[43]

So why did Paddy Moran not try to escape with the others? The main reason for the escape was to free Frank Teeling. The whole operation was regarded as full of potential hazards and Paddy Moran felt that, for it to be a success, only two men should try it as the escape had to be accomplished within five minutes, between the warders' patrols.[44] Paddy also said that if he escaped he would have to go on the run and be useless to the Volunteers; besides he expected to be acquitted at his trial.[45] Anna Kelly mentions that he sent a note to the O/C (Oscar Traynor) saying that he would stand trial and not let down his witnesses.[46] Denis Begley, E Company, 2nd Battalion, recorded that Paddy Moran said he would not come out because he had a perfect alibi.[47] Michael Noyk, his solicitor, said he was convinced that he had a perfect defence and would not stand in the way of another prisoner escaping. Diarmuid O'Sullivan, another prisoner in Kilmainham at the time, corroborated that evidence.[48] In a letter to his sister after his trial, Paddy admits that he could have escaped, 'I need not have been there to stand my trial if I did not think I would be all right.'[49]

When Oscar Traynor broadcast an account of the escape in the late 1930s, Paddy's brother, Jim, who had been with him the night before his execution, wrote to the editor of the *Irish Press*:

Sir,
In his recent broadcast on prison escapes, Oscar Traynor referred to my brother, Patrick Moran, as a man who paid the penalty because of

his belief in 'British Justice'. Mr Traynor must have known that my brother was in the Volunteer movement from the start, that he was out in 1916, and that he was Captain, D Company, 2nd Battalion, Dublin Brigade at the time of his arrest. He was a man who knew what the movement meant as well as any, and better than most, and he was not in it by accident.

There was an article written some time ago by Simon Donnelly in the *Evening Telegraph* when that paper was in existence. It gave his story of the escape, but was, to my mind, hardly fair to the dead. I refrained from writing then, but now that the same story is broadcast, I feel it my duty to tell what my brother himself told me.

I was speaking to him in his cell on the eve of his execution, and, among other things, we discussed the Kilmainham escape. He told me then that he considered that Ernie O'Malley 'a much-wanted man who was there [as] a prisoner under an assumed name', should be one of the limited number who could safely escape. From the location of their cell, if he himself tried to get away it might spoil O'Malley's chance.

He had no regrets for the decision he made, saying that if he were not glad to die for Ireland it would be a direct contradiction to the sentiments of a lifetime.

Yours truly,
Jas Moran[50]

Ernie O'Malley had been moved into the cell next to Paddy, just before the escape.[51]

Undoubtedly and with hindsight Paddy Moran could have taken his chance and escaped with the other three men. However, there was no certainty that the escape would succeed and if Paddy had gone and it had been a failure he would surely have been perceived as guilty. Paddy made his choice in the firm belief that he would be acquitted. It was not unreasonable for him to think that because there were others already acquitted. James Boyce, Michael J. Tobin and Jimmy McNamara were tried with Tommy Whelan and found not guilty, so surely he had as good a chance as they had. In the Tobin and McNamara case the evidence of Snelling, the cyclist, was not accepted, yet it was accepted in Paddy's case.[52]

Paddy thought he had a cast-iron alibi and he had an array of witnesses who were prepared to testify to that alibi. He would only find out in the following days at his court-martial in City Hall that the police had in their possession statements from two of his fellow workers that supported a completely different alibi. He knew he wasn't in Mount Street on Bloody Sunday and that Private Lawrence, the batman to Major Carew had placed him there because he had met him in Mount Street on the eve of Bloody Sunday. He thought he had supplied his legal team with enough information to prove beyond doubt that he was falsely identified.

Paddy also was aware that O'Malley would be hanged if the authorities realised who 'Bernard Stewart' actually was, so it was important that nothing would hinder his escape. There were others in Kilmainham who had already been convicted for the Bloody Sunday murders and who were not involved in the escape. Edward Potter and William Conway were convicted at the end of January along with Frank Teeling for the murder of Lieutenant Angliss at 22 Lower Mount Street. Their sentences were later commuted to life imprisonment, but only after Teeling's escape.[53]

Tommy Whelan was convicted on 1 February for the murder of Captain Bagally at 119 Baggot Street.[54] GHQ staff were the only ones who knew exactly who was involved in Bloody Sunday. They knew that Tommy Whelan was not involved and yet no effort was made to assist him to escape.

There were other prisoners in Kilmainham whose fate hung in the balance, their cases not having been tried. Frank Flood, Patrick Doyle, Thomas Bryan, Bernard Ryan and Diarmuid O'Sullivan were there, charged with high treason for their involvement in an ambush in Drumcondra on 21 January 1921. They were removed to Arbour Hill on the night the escape was discovered and were tried on 22–24 February 1921, found guilty and sentenced to death. Diarmuid O'Sullivan's sentence was commuted to life because of his youth; he was just fifteen.

The Dublin Castle authorities were severely shaken by the escape. General Macready wrote to Joint Under-Secretary to the Lord Lieutenant, Sir John Anderson:

My dear Anderson,

We have had a real disaster. The man Teeling and two other unimportant men escaped last night from Kilmainham Prison and got clean away. It is about the worst blow I have had for a very long time, and I am naturally furious. I will not make any remarks about it until I get the Inquiry, which is being held, but it is perfectly obvious that the escape would not have happened without the collusion of the Welch Regiment who was on duty there. I will certainly take the most drastic action I can against those responsible. Personally, I had not the faintest idea that important prisoners were interned in that old ramshackle place next door to the new prison which is used as quarters for troops.[55]

He wrote again the following day:

The inquiry into the escape of Teeling will if humanly possible be finished today and again if humanly possible, shall go over tonight. What appears in the *Daily Mail* today about a lorryload of people dressed up as soldiers making fools of the guard has not one word of truth in it. So far as I can at present make out, the men were let out of prison through the courtyard door, which has not been opened for centuries, the big padlock being filed through, which must have been the work of several days. It looks as if certain men of the Welch Regiment were all paid for their assistance, and if it should turn out to be so, I hope they will spend many years in Portland before they are able to enjoy themselves with Michael's [Michael Collins] money. It was very cleverly done, and I rather admire Michael, and it just shows how careful people have to be. Mulcahy was known to be in that direction, which is out of his usual beat, the evening of the escape.[56]

Following the escape all army personnel employed in the jail were relieved of their duties pending an internal inquiry. A court of inquiry was set up in Kilmainham courthouse on 15 February 1921 to ascertain the circumstances surrounding the escape. Lieutenant R.W. May, 2nd Battalion Welch Regiment, Commandant of Kilmainham Gaol said that Private Roper had keys to Simon Donnelly's cell (No. 2) and Bernard Stewart's (No. 10) (Ernie O'Malley's) on the middle landing and that he had a skeleton key to Teeling's cell (No. 18) on the top landing. Private Roper testified that he put chamber pots into the cells at 8.50 p.m. and that the prisoners were there. However, Sergeant Austin said that he passed three cells on the ground floor at 8.40 p.m. but he did not see any warder there.[57]

Lieutenant May said that bloodhounds were brought to the prison and they tracked the escape route from the middle landing, down the stairs to the ground floor, out by the first door on the west side of the building, across the courtyard to the west gate, through the gate out of the prison precincts, then a sharp turn to the left, over a low wall, into an empty shed and by a tortuous track beside a small stream in a westerly direction for about 200 yards, then turning north to Kilmainham Road. On the road, they lost the scent.

Major General G.F. Boyd went to Kilmainham to investigate the escape on 27 February. He interviewed fifteen soldiers who were under arrest and concluded that Privates Roper, Holland, Williams, Caveney, and Sergeant Austin and Lance Corporal Lewis should be detained. Sergeant Austin and Lance Corporal Lewis were, he said, guilty of negligence but the four privates were responsible for the escape.

General Macready wrote to Sir John Anderson advising him that the soldiers involved in Teeling's escape were to be tried by court-martial. When it was finished he proposed 'to move the regiment to the most God forsaken part of the country I can find. Only I should like you to keep this to yourself as if it gets out before it is done, the Welsh spirit in our Lloyd [Lloyd George] may rise up and make difficulties.'[58]

Privates Williams and Caveney were released, but Private James Holland and Private Ernest Edgar Roper were charged with wilfully allowing civilian prisoners committed to their charge to escape. They were sentenced to eight years' penal servitude each.[59] Captain Herbert Nixon wrote a letter from The Old Town Hall, Belfast, to General Macready in August 1921 asking for a lesser sentence for James Holland. Alderman William H. Roper, 16 Brynsfi Terrace, Swansea, wrote to Sir Alfred Mond, MP for Swansea, asking him to consider the position of his son, now that there was talk of a settlement of the Irish Question. Both requests were refused.

General Macready wrote from the War Office in England on 25 September 1922, asking for further information about the part played by Holland and Roper in the escape, so that he could brief the secretary of state who was meeting a deputation on their behalf. Mr Wroughton, Dublin Castle, replied that he and his chief intended to recommend to the army council that the remainder of the sentences be remitted as soon as the British army was out of the country.[60]

Paddy Moran was brought to City Hall for his trial the day after the escape, 15 February 1921. His trial should have taken place on 4 February; it was postponed because one of the prosecution witnesses, Major Carew, was injured and unable to attend, so the president of the court cancelled the proceedings. He said he had received a message from the convening officer that a witness for the prosecution was not able to give evidence, owing to wounds inflicted on him by an assassin.[61] Michael Noyk, referring to the claim that Major Carew was shot by the IRA on 3 February, the day before the court-martial was due to begin, while having tea in a tea-shop on Dame Street, Dublin, said it was apparent to him from his inquiries that the shooting was not carried out by the IRA.[62] Major Carew had initially identified Paddy, but had changed his mind and would now not positively swear to his identity in court.

After his resignation, General Crozier wrote an article for the *Daily News* in which he alleged that the very highest officers in the service in Ireland had conspired to suppress and to invent evidence, and that he himself had helped in some cases to pervert the course of justice.[63] In Paddy's case, the fact that he knew he was being framed for the Mount Street assassinations made him feel confident that the evidence against him would not stand up in court. If he had known his fate, perhaps he would have been the fourth man out of Kilmainham Gaol on that fateful night, 14 February 1921.

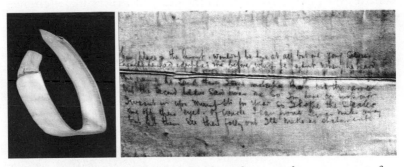

Photographs of the collar which Paddy used to smuggle a message out of Kilmainham

CHAPTER 7

THE COURT-MARTIAL

Patrick Moran, 5 Main Street, Blackrock, County Dublin, and Joseph Rochford, 11, Elm Park Avenue, Ranelagh, Dublin, appeared before a field general court-martial which started in City Hall, Dublin, on 15 February 1921.[1] It was held in the council chamber, which was stripped of all its appointments and furniture; entrance was gained by passing through the Lower Castle yard, Upper Castle yard, through a narrow passage and out into Castle Street. The whole area was patrolled by the military; sentries were posted with machine guns and rifles to watch over Dublin Castle and City Hall.[2] Michael Noyk had difficulty getting counsel to defend his cases and was disappointed with some of those who refused. Finally he got Mr Williamson, KC, a good Unionist, who threw himself wholeheartedly into the case. Noyk described the trial as the highlight of the court-martial trials because, while not as spectacular as that of General Seán MacEoin, it was the only trial where they could put up a watertight defence.[3]

The members of the court-martial were Kenneth Marshall, Judge Advocate, Major F.S. Montague Bates, president, Major E. Morton, Lt Col E.H. Chapman, Major L.C. Dorman, Captain E.W. Avenell and Captain D.G. Romanis.[4] They sat at a long table, each with a revolver in front of him. The room was full of secret service men; one could hardly raise one's eyes without being aware of someone's scrutiny.[5]

The prosecuting counsels for the crown were Travers Humphreys and Roland Oliver. For the defence James Williamson, KC, and Charles Power, instructed by Michael Noyk, appeared for Paddy Moran. Mr McElligott, KC, and Gerald Farrell, instructed by Mr O'Farrell, appeared for Joseph Rochford.[6] Both men were charged with the murder or alternatively the manslaughter of Lieutenant Ames at No. 38 Upper Mount Street. Opening the case, the prosecuting counsel said there was no suggestion that either Moran or Rochford actually committed the murder in the sense of physically committing it by shooting but, it was alleged, that they were partners in a conspiracy by which Lieutenant Ames and another officer were murdered. Once again Private Snelling identified Moran as the man who held him up with a revolver at No. 38 Upper Mount Street. The batman (Private Lawrence) testified that he saw Snelling being held up from a window on the fourth floor of No. 28 and he too identified Paddy Moran as the assailant. Major Carew testified that he saw a man holding up a soldier in the street, that he opened a window and pointed a revolver at him, but did not fire. He then saw fourteen or fifteen men come out of No. 38 and he fired at them.[7] Private Lawrence identified Joseph Rochford as one of the men he saw running away from the scene.

For the defence Rochford's parents, his brothers, his sister and a lodger in his home gave evidence that he was in bed that Sunday morning until 11.00 a.m., that he left the house to go to 12.00 mass and returned around 2.00 p.m. The Judge Advocate, Kenneth Marshall, when summing up later, said that there was only one witness who could profess to identify Rochford: Private Lawrence, the batman. Marshall said it would be unsafe to act on the evidence of only one identifying witness and so the court acquitted Rochford.[8]

James Williamson, KC, opening the case for Paddy Moran, drew attention to the discrepancies between Carew and Lawrence's evidence. The officer said that the hold-up on Bloody Sunday had taken place at 9.15 a.m., he knew this because the batman had brought him his tea. Yet the batman swore that he hadn't brought the officer any tea at all. If the court could not rely on the evidence of the batman in the Rochford case how could they, he asked, rely on it in Patrick Moran's case? Snelling had that morning, according to his own statement, seen over sixty people. When he arrived in Baggot Street, he saw an officer hanging dead out of a window, he was arrested by two men, his motor cycle was taken from him and he was driven away by two men, one armed with a revolver and another with a gun. He was fearful and trembling and he naturally made a mistake in the identification that many a man before him had made. On the crown evidence alone, Williamson continued, Moran was entitled to an acquittal.

Paddy Moran, in his own statement to the court gave his well-rehearsed alibi evidence:

> I had nothing to do with the murders committed on 21 November. My movements that morning were public and quite innocent. I am at business in Blackrock, and on that morning went to 8 o'clock mass, which was over about 8.30. I walked back to the place where I work with a young lady friend, whom I met at mass. I went inside and had my breakfast about 9 o'clock. After breakfast I took the first tram for town, leaving Blackrock about 9.30. I did not know there was any commotion in Dublin until I reached Lower Mount Street, where the tram was held up. I got out at Nelson's Pillar [O'Connell Street], and went to Banba Hall, where I had to preside at an important meeting of my trade union, of which I am the president. The meeting began at 11 o'clock and lasted until about 1 o'clock. That is all I have to say.[9]

Several witnesses testified in support of his alibi. Margaret O'Flanagan of the Technical School, Blackrock, lived on the school premises with her mother. She was a member of Cumann na mBan and organised the witnesses to support the alibi for Paddy. She said she went to 8 o'clock mass in Blackrock, she saw Moran and he asked her to come in through the sanctuary door. She sat next to him all the time, walked with him as far as a shop called Wilson's. He told her he was going to Banba Hall, Parnell Square, Dublin. She knew him well as they used to meet at jazz dances.

Joseph Cannon, 23 Temple Road, Blackrock, was a collector at the sanctuary door at 8 o'clock mass on Sunday 21 November. He remembered seeing Miss O'Flanagan coming in with a man and bade her good morning. He did not know the man's name, but remembered that Miss O'Flanagan had said 'I am going off now', as a joke. He met her later in the day and asked her what he should call her now and she said 'Moran'. He told her about the trouble in the city and she said, 'I wonder if Mr Moran went to Banba?' He remembered this because of the trouble that Sunday and of the conversation with Miss O'Flanagan. He said he did not belong to any political party.

Mary Francis Aylward, 4 Montpellier Terrace, Monkstown, was a shorthand typist at Hughes and Co., 71 Dame Street, and she testified that she met Moran at mass and greeted him. She knew him well and was a customer in the shop where he worked.

Mrs Finn, Brosna Cottages, Blackrock, lost her husband in the First World War. She was at 8 o'clock mass and saw Miss O'Flanagan and Paddy Moran in front of her. She knew him by sight from the shop; she saw him later at Wilson's shop and saw him go in Magees' door. On the Friday when she learned that someone had been arrested she asked which assistant it was, that is how she remembered the incident.

Henry Costello, Deansgrange, said that he saw Moran going in the sanctuary door to mass. He knew him from Lynch and O'Brien, where he sold groceries and alcohol. He heard of his arrest on the following Sunday at mass, but knew he could not have had anything to do with it as he was at 8 o'clock mass the previous Sunday.

William Duffy, 4 Stradbrook, Blackrock, testified that he saw Moran and a lady coming through the sanctuary door. They crossed the church and knelt on the left-hand side of the sanctuary. He saw him again getting his paper and tobacco in Wilson's. He had no speaking acquaintance with Moran but knew him from the shop in Dun Laoghaire. He was wearing a fawn coat and a slightly darker fawn hat. 'I remember the Friday following 21 November, because I had heard that Moran had been arrested that day and this fixed the Sunday in my memory. In discussion with friends on the subject they suggested that I contact Mr Noyk which I did.' Duffy said he had no interest in Moran and he was not a member of any political party. He usually went to 11 o'clock mass but went that day at 8 o'clock because he was going to Dalkey to visit his in-laws.

Mr Pims was an old soldier who served in India, Gallipoli and France. He said he was at mass and saw Moran there and at Hughes' confectionery shop that morning. He said he did not hold with this Sinn Féin business and had nothing to do with it.

Patrick Nolan, 12 Cullen's Cottages, Deansgrange, said he went with H. Costello to mass. He said he was surprised to see Moran in Blackrock that morning; he was not aware he had left Lynch and O'Brien, Kingstown (Dun Laoghaire).

J.P. McCabe, Vice-Chairman of Blackrock Urban Council, said that he also saw Moran at 8 o'clock mass and again five minutes after mass standing in the street opposite the Technical School talking to Miss O'Flanagan. He remembered him since the time of the Grocers' Assistants' strike. He used to be down picketing at his establishment.[10]

Mary Tracey, 19 George's Avenue, Blackrock, owned a tobacconist business in Dun Laoghaire but lived in Blackrock. She described seeing Paddy (she was a customer of Lynch and

O'Brien) coming out of Magees' and he walked in front of her to Bath Place, the tram stop.

Mr Doheny, a Labour Exchange employee, Phoenix Terrace, Blackrock, said he was standing outside Magees' about 9.30 a.m. on 21 November and saw Moran coming out of Magees' and getting on the tram.

James Swan, 32 Victoria Buildings, Blackrock, the tram conductor, said he knew Moran because he used go to football matches. He knew him well and spoke to him and to Mr Mirrelson that morning when the tram was stopped in Mount Street. Moran said 'things are very hot here'.

Joseph Mirrelson, General Dealer, 74 York Road, Kingstown, swore that Paddy Moran was on the first tram that left Blackrock at 9.30 a.m.

Kate McGough was a housekeeper at Magees' and said that Moran came into the kitchen and asked if breakfast was ready. She asked if he was in a hurry and he said he was going to town. He asked was it near nine, and she said it was about five to nine. Another man, O'Connor, and Moran were in the breakfast room at about five to nine. She did not see them again that day. Moran was in the kitchen about ten minutes before breakfast was brought in.

M.S. O'Connor, Phoenix Terrace, Blackrock, an employee of the government in the Labour Exchange, said that he was going to 10 o'clock mass in Monkstown and saw Moran standing outside Magees' house. He used to chat to Mr Moran when he was in Lynch and O'Brien and he knew him well. He was passing through Blackrock on Friday 26 November, and saw a military car outside Magees' and a man being taken away in it. Someone in the street told him it was Moran; then he remembered seeing him the previous Sunday.

As well as all the eye-witnesses who were there to establish Paddy's alibi, the defence also had witnesses to throw doubt on the stories of the prosecution's witnesses. One of the prosecution witnesses, Private Lawrence, had said that he knew the time of the hold-up in Mount Street by the chiming of the church clock. However, Francis Harvey Stewart, rector of Church of Ireland, St Stephen's Green, testified that the church clock did not chime. James Traynor, sexton at St Stephen's Green church, also provided evidence and proved his unbiased credentials by explaining that he was an Englishman and an old soldier. He was discharged in 1907, became attached to St Stephen's Green church in 1908, joined the army again in 1915, fought through the First World War and was discharged on 1 March 1919. He then went back to his duty as sexton at St Stephen's Green church. He explained that while there was a clock on the church, it never struck or chimed, and had not done so for eight years because the strikes had been taken off. The bell rang for service on Sunday mornings at 8 o'clock, the next service was at ten and the next at eleven, and he said that the bell always rang 5–10 minutes before the service.

A Nurse Daly gave evidence regarding the time Private Snelling had sworn the events he witnessed had happened. She lived in Lower Baggot Street and swore that she heard the shots in Baggot Street. She went out, and on going to cross the street, she stood aside to let a soldier pass on a motor cycle and saw him go across Baggot Street Bridge. She said she thought this happened at a quarter past nine. However, her evidence was discounted because she said that she started doing a few jobs in her house that took about thirteen minutes at 8.45 a.m. and when she went out she said it was about 9.15 a.m. The times did not quite add up.

P. Hughes, secretary of the Irish National Union of Grocers' Assistants, said that Moran was president of the union and presided at a meeting on 21 November at 11 o'clock. He signed the minutes of the previous meeting and these were produced in court.

Three men from Paddy's workplace, Magees', made statements to Michael Noyk. Two of these, William Doyle and Eugene McCourt, were not called to give evidence because Noyk discovered that they had made statements to the police that differed from those made to him. In his statement to Michael Noyk, Eugene McCourt, who worked as an assistant in Magees', said he worked in the shop all day on Saturday with Paddy Moran. They had supper and went to bed at 10 o'clock. Moran, O'Connor, Doyle and himself had breakfast together the following morning at 9.15 a.m. After breakfast McCourt went to mass in Blackrock, returning at 11.30 a.m. None of the staff were there then. He did not see Moran after that until late that night. 'I made a statement to the detectives when they called. I do not go in for politics.' (Written on his statement to the police is IRA, E Company, 4th Battalion.)[11]

William Doyle testified that he worked with Paddy all day on Saturday and they both went to bed that night at 10.00 p.m. They had breakfast about 9.45 a.m., but it might have been a quarter or twenty minutes earlier. They had no clock upstairs. He asked Moran if he was going to town and he said he himself was going to Dun Laoghaire. He asked him if he was going to Banba Hall and Paddy said he was. 'I made a statement to the police but before I signed it I told him there might be a slight mistake about the time as I could not be accountable after such a lapse of time.'

However, in statements to the police made on 23 December 1920, William Doyle said he got up on (Bloody) Sunday morning at 10.00 a.m., he had breakfast with Paddy Moran, he left at about 11.00 a.m. to go to mass in Marlborough Street, Dublin, and Paddy was in the house when he left. He returned home at 10.30 p.m. and Paddy Moran was in his own room at that time. Eugene McCourt said that he and Paddy Moran had supper on Saturday night at about 10.15 p.m. and breakfast on Sunday morning around 9.30 a.m. He saw Moran in the house at 11.00 a.m. when he was leaving to go to mass.[12]

Doyle, McCourt and Mr O'Connor, the owner of Magees', had been arrested without charge and were interned in Ballykinlar camp in December 1920. Although O'Connor had made a statement, unlike Doyle and McCourt, he was not summoned to appear in court.[13]

The prosecution acknowledged that several witnesses testified that Paddy Moran was at 8.00 a.m. mass and that he was on the first tram to town at 9.30. It was suggested that that evidence could be true but the period between 8.30 and 9.30 a.m. had not been accounted for except by Miss McGough, the housekeeper. She said that he had breakfast at 9.00 a.m. with three others. Two of those, however, had given statements to the police that were inconsistent with her evidence. The prosecution suggested that the accused could have been in Mount Street if he had a motor cycle, a bicycle or even a horse conveyance, but Daniel McCarthy, Dublin Metropolitan Police, said that he was on duty in Main Street, Blackrock, from 6.00 to 9.00 a.m. and that no motor car or bicycle came out from the city to Blackrock on that Sunday.

In his statement to the Bureau of Military History, Michael Noyk described the evidence of Doyle and McCourt to the police as an obstacle that was difficult to overcome. He decided to keep them in his office and told them not to go near City Hall during the trial unless he telephoned for them. Sir Travers Humphreys was apparently white with rage when the defence closed without calling them.[14] He asked the court to recall Miss O'Flanagan and produced a photograph of Moran with a revolver and asked her if it was Moran.[15] She said she did not know Moran had a pistol and was doubtful whether the photo produced was of the accused. This was probably the photograph that was taken with three of his comrades, when they had to take turns to be photographed in the one uniform they possessed. Michael Noyk claimed that the photograph was captured in a raid on Phil Shanahan's public house, but the police said it was found in Paddy's lodgings in Magees' of Blackrock.[16] The photograph was produced, but not admitted as evidence when the defence objected.

Humphreys then asked the court to call the detectives who had taken the statements from Doyle and McCourt in December, but again the defence objected and after an adjournment the objection was sustained. Noyk observed, 'It was obvious the court could be gracious enough to sustain the objections; they had seen all they wanted to see when they saw the photograph.'[17]

Mr Charles Power made a magnificent closing speech for the Defence. Although Judge Advocate Kenneth Marshall, when summing up, paid tribute to Power's summation, the rest of his own speech was very pro the prosecution.[18] He reiterated all the evidence given by the prosecution witnesses and found excuses for the differences in the evidence with regard to whether the officer had been given his tea, whether a clock chimed, how the identification was made, or why an identifying witness asked to have Moran shaved. Marshall did not refer to the fact that the batman was looking out a top floor window, four storeys up and that it could hardly be possible to see a face at that distance, nor to the fact that the officer, Major Carew, was not willing to swear to Moran's identity in court.

The prosecution then referred to the defence witnesses and said that Miss O'Flanagan was identified as largely responsible for the evidence of some of them. She clearly was a great friend of Moran and it was only natural for her to want to help him if she believed his innocence. He was not suggesting that she was guilty of perjury, but she might have quite innocently persuaded herself that she was at mass with him on 21 November when in fact it could have been a different Sunday. He referred to the evidence of the housekeeper, Miss McGough, and the fact that Doyle and McCourt were not called to corroborate her evidence. Mr Power then pointed out to the judge advocate that he had not mentioned the fact that a defence witness had told the court that the clock did not chime at all, even though the batman testified that he knew the time from the chiming of the said church clock.[19]

The court retired to consider the evidence and after about an hour and ten minutes returned to give the verdict. Joseph Rochford was found not guilty on both counts. Patrick Moran was found not guilty on the charge of manslaughter, but guilty on the charge of murder. He was asked if he had anything to say and replied in a firm voice: 'I have nothing to say, but I repeat, I was not in Upper Mount Street that morning and I never saw any of the people before in my life that swore about me until I saw them at Arbour Hill.'[20]

Michael Noyk was not surprised that Joseph Rochford was acquitted. He believed that in all cases tried by court-martial one or two people were tried against whom there was very little evidence. This was done to show how fair 'British justice' was – Rochford was a 'foil' for Moran.[21]

Paddy Moran was not the man who held up the soldier motorcyclist (Snelling); it was in fact Mick Lawless who held him up. He was on patrol outside No. 38 Mount Street and hearing the footsteps of a man running and glancing over his shoulder, he saw that the man was in khaki uniform. He walked past No. 38, wheeled around quickly and held up the soldier with his revolver. Snelling cried out, 'Don't shoot, don't shoot!' Lawless ordered him to go up the steps and knock on the door. Lawless heard a shout from the house opposite (No. 28), looked up and saw a man (Major Carew) with a revolver. He used Snelling for cover and, pointing the revolver at the man, shouted to him to get in from the window. The door of No. 38 was opened and Private Snelling was placed in a room on the ground floor.[22]

Vinnie Byrne described the action inside No. 38 Mount Street. As he was marching the officer, Captain George Bennett, down to the back room where Lieutenant Peter Ashmun Ames was, he heard the doorbell ring. Snelling walked in, Byrne ordered him to raise his hands and placed him under guard in the hall. He went to the back room where he shot both Ames and Bennett. Byrne then returned to the hall and wondered whether to shoot Snelling. He thought, 'well, he is only a soldier' and did not shoot him, but told him not to stir for fifteen minutes. When Snelling swore at the court-martial that Paddy Moran was the man who held him up outside No. 38 Mount Street on Bloody Sunday, Byrne was sorry that he had let him go free.[23]

The authorities were aware that Paddy was not in Upper Mount Street on Bloody Sunday, but they probably knew that he was active somewhere that morning. They had a photograph of him in uniform, they had two statements from his fellow workers that differed from the alibi evidence of the other witnesses and there was a lapse in time that was not accounted for. According to the alibi evidence Paddy arrived in O'Connell Street at 10 o'clock but did not arrive at Banba Hall, a few paces away, until 10.45.[24]

A note written in pencil by Paddy Moran on the witness Mary Tracey's statement for the solicitor asks, 'Did she know of Dunleary match?', the first clue that there was another match in Croke Park on Bloody Sunday. Written in ink underneath is the reply 'knew of football match'.[25] I did not understand the significance of the reference to the match until I read in the Dublin GAA history that there was another match in Croke Park on Bloody Sunday. It was a replay of the Intermediate Football Final between Erin's Hopes and Dunleary Commercials and was played in the early part of the day, probably at 11.45 a.m. Dunleary Commercials were the winners; the score was 3-2 to 0-2. As Paddy was the founder of the Dunleary Commercials, it is likely that he was in Croke Park to see his team play. He probably went first to Byrne's in North Richmond Street to report to Seán Russell and he also probably got rid of his gun there.[26]

The note on this witness' statement to the solicitor seems to confirm that it was to the match in Croke Park he went following the action in the Gresham rather than to the Union meeting in Parnell Square on the morning of 21 November.

The minutes of that Union meeting were presented in court:

Executive Meeting. Sunday, 21 November 1920.
The committee met this day, Mr P. Moran presiding, and the following members were present. Messrs J. Garry, J. Cullen, J. Canavan, P.

O'Keeffe, D. Dowling, P.F. Flynn, Lee O'Neill, W. Cummins and J. Nolan with P. Hughes, general secretary.[27]

Working hours, wages and duties of the staff were the only items on the agenda for the special executive meeting on 21 November. These and arrangements for the payment of contributions were discussed. The meeting was then adjourned.

However, the minutes of the meeting held on the previous Sunday set the day for this special executive meeting for Friday 19 November at 10 o'clock.[28] Did it happen on Friday as arranged and was the date changed to Sunday 21 November? Was this part of the alibi that was constructed for Paddy?

Margaret O'Flanagan had tried to give him a watertight alibi. There was a gap between the time he said he arrived in the city centre and the time he said he arrived in Banba Hall, Parnell Square, Dublin, a short distance away, which was noted by the prosecution.[29] The prosecution also exploited the fact that Margaret O'Flanagan said that she asked several witnesses about the sequence of events on that Sunday, 21 November 1920, sometime in the second half of January 1921. They argued that it was unlikely that anyone would remember exactly what happened on a particular day so far back without prompting.

It is sometimes suggested that Margaret O'Flanagan was Paddy's girlfriend and the prosecution implied this, but she was not; he referred to her formally as Miss O'Flanagan in a letter to his sister Annie from Mountjoy.[30] He had a girlfriend, Bea Farrell, and he carried a photograph of her in his pocket. They were about to be engaged when he was arrested and they exchanged a gold locket and a cross just before his execution. Immediately after the trial he sent out a note to Bea:

My Dear B,
I hope you're not worrying over the result of the case. I can't conceive

Paddy Moran's brothers and sisters at the opening of Moran Park, Dun Laoghaire. Front row, L to R: Lena Fitzpatrick, Bridget Moran, Annie Moran. Back row, L to R: Jim Moran, Tom Moran, Joe Moran and Batty Moran. Seán Moran, Paddy's nephew, can be seen slightly to the right of his father, Tom. The man wearing a hat in the background on Tom's left is Tommie McDermott (RIP), a neighbour from Crossna.

Above left: *Memoriam card for Patrick Moran.*
Above right: *The cross that was given to Paddy by his girlfriend Bea Farrell at the time of his execution. Photo taken by John Keaney.*

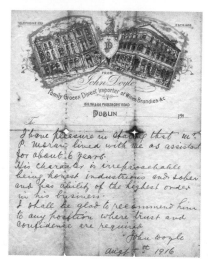

Reference given to Paddy from John Doyle of Doyle's Pub at Doyle's Corner, Dublin.

Father Michael O'Flanagan.

Left: *Execution at Kilmainham Gaol.*

Below left: *Grocers' Assistants' Gaelic Football Team. College Green Division Winners 1913.*
Front row, L to R: *P. Moran, J. Foy, W. Coates, S. Murphy, G. Healy.* Middle row, L to R: *L. Emo, J. McConnell, M. Furlong, J. McNamara, P. Dobson.* Back row, L to R: *A. Cooke, J. Connelly, P. Smith, J. McConnor, P. Sheridan, H. Gilligan (hon. sec.), J. Farrelly (president).*

The account of where Paddy was during the Easter Rising and afterwards, written on his first visit to Boyle after his return from internment in England in 1916 and returned to the Moran family by James Feely, Boyle.

Left: *Paddy's father and mother, Bartholomew and Brigid Moran (née Sheeran).*
Top right: *The house in Crossna that was Paddy Moran's birth place.*
Bottom right: *The graves of the nine men who were reburied in Glasnevin cemetery on 14 October 2001, as they are today. Photo courtesy of Claire Moran, grandniece of Paddy Moran.*

Paddy Moran with a gun. A copy of the photograph that was produced at his trial.

A memoriam card for Paddy Moran.

Michael Noyk, the solicitor who organised Paddy's defence. Courtesy of Anthony (Tony) Behan.

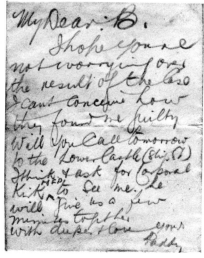

The note that Paddy Moran sent to his girlfriend Bea after he was found guilty.

The surrender 1916. Rebels are marched to Richmond Barracks.

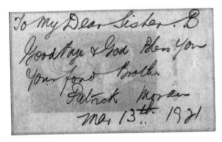

Final message to Paddy's sister Bridget.

Paddy and his girlfriend Bea Farrell.

Paddy's nephews lifting his coffin in Mountjoy. Far side: Barty Moran (RIP, partially obscured), Mickie Duignan, Seán Moran, Paddy Moran, Joe Duignan and Padraic Fitzpatrick. Courtesy of Jim Mitchell, Irish Prison Service.

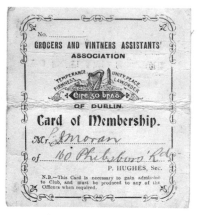

Paddy Moran's Card of Membership for the Grocers' and Vintners' Union.

Paddy Moran and Thomas Whelan. Photo taken just before their execution. Courtesy of Allen Library, North Richmond Street, Dublin.

Right: *Mountjoy Jail in earlier days showing the burial plot inside the cordon.*

Presentation of portrait of Paddy Moran to the Moran family, October 2001. Front row, L to R: *Mary Keegan (née Moran), Mary Larkin, President Mandate Trade Union, Anna Sheerin (née Moran), May Moran, Barty Moran (RIP) and Sandra Browne, Mandate.* Back row, L to R: *John Douglas, General Secretary of Mandate, Mary Lock (née Duignan), Bridie Plummer (née Moran), Rita Moran, Mickie Duignan, Paddy Moran and Seamus Nolan, Mandate. Courtesy of Danny Donnelly.*

Christmas card from Joe Moran to his sister Bridget sent from Athlone Detention Centre. Joe escaped from Athlone and arrived home on Christmas Eve.

Paddy Moran and Tommy Whelan with warder Lester Collins.

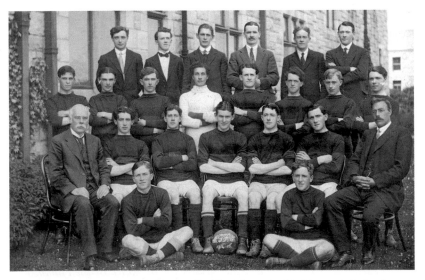

Marlborough Rangers football team. Paddy Moran is third from right in the middle row.

The unveiling of the memorial in Mountjoy in 1961.

Richmond Barracks, Inchicore. Troops with rifles slung over their backs are put through their paces. Courtesy of the National Library of Ireland.

Paddy Moran's cell in Kilmainham Gaol.
Courtesy of Niall Bergin, Kilmainham Gaol Museum.

how they found me guilty. Will you call tomorrow to the Lower Castle (Ship Street) I think & ask for Corporal Kirk to see me. He will give us a few minutes together.

With deepest love,

Your Paddy.

Two policemen from the Kingstown area were asked by the authorities about Paddy Moran's character on 8 February 1921.[31] Sergeant James O'Sullivan had known him for about three years and had arrested him and James McGlynn and charged them both with intimidation and assault on James Brady, publican, 17 Upper George's Street, Kingstown, on 14 January 1921 (when they restrained a man unloading a dray during the Grocers' Assistants' strike). 'Moran was remanded on bail and after the remand he was convicted and fined 10 shillings and put under a rule of bail of £20 for two years by Mr Cooper, divisional magistrate, on the assault charge, and was sent for trial to the county commission on the charge of intimidation.'[32] Sergeant O'Sullivan said he took an active part in the strike and he knew him to be an advanced Sinn Féiner, and saw him frequently in the company of (Ginger) McNamara and (William) Keogh, both assistants in Lynch and O'Brien. (Both had been arrested following Bloody Sunday and were members of the same company as Paddy, D Company, Dublin 2 Brigade, and both worked in Lynch and O'Brien, Lower George's Street, Dun Laoghaire. They were later released.)

Twenty-four political prisoners including Messrs Conway, Potter, Whelan, Flood, Ryan, Doyle, Bryan and O'Sullivan were removed under a strong police escort from Kilmainham Gaol to Mountjoy Jail during curfew on Wednesday, 16 February.[33] Paddy Moran (Prisoner No. 439) joined them on Friday night, 18 February, after his trial. He had spent fourteen days there in early 1920, but this time his situation was much more serious.

CHAPTER 8

MOUNTJOY JAIL

Paddy adapted to his new surroundings in 'C' wing of Mountjoy Jail and began writing to his parents, brothers and sisters to tell them how he felt after the trial. He wrote to his sister Annie, a student nurse at the Mater Hospital, Eccles Street, on Saturday 19 February:

My dear Annie,

I am writing this to you as my first letter since I saw you last at the Castle. I came here last night and was not sorry to part company with that place. I think I had a rather unfair trial but the dice was well loaded against me and I have a gripe against those who defended me in a couple of things that, though they got me to write out the identification scene in Arbour Hill, they did not at all cross-examine the cyclist on the vital points nor did they call a witness who could prove the scene.[1] I am wondering now if this is really to be the last shift. It might and it might not. I need not have been there to stand my trial if I did not think I would be all right and I believe after all the prayers that prompting must have been for the best. I'd like to know how you are feeling about the present stage now and how all at home look at it. I never gave it a thought until I saw how worried people looked as I came out of court. I expect to get this out today, send a copy home and one to Ciss. I will write to B tomorrow or perhaps today – we are allowed one official letter each day. I suppose there may be no limit to how many we get in. We can also get parcels etc. but I do not want you to send too much. I want some hard plug [tobacco] and matches and some butterscotch. I suppose if there is any worry on either side you are all fretting for me and I'm thinking of those outside and am A1 myself so do not worry. Give my love to all and particularly to B [his girlfriend] and Clare [his cousin] and all at SCR [South Circular Road, where his cousins and his uncle lived]. I send all my love to all at home and to Ciss and B [sisters]. Remember the blackest cloud has a silver lining and I am not a bit downhearted. Get a permit at the Castle. I gave your name, B and Clare first and also Peg Aylward and Miss O'Flanagan, but there are so many I'd like to see, I hate to make exceptions. With my best love and hoping to see you when the clouds roll by.

    Your fond brother,

    Patrick

On his second day in Mountjoy, Paddy took on the task of writing to his parents:

My dear Parents,

I suppose, indeed I'm sure, you have all been anxiously looking forward to my trial and I know you are disappointed at the result. I was always so certain I would be set free that I was taken aback myself. In fact I never thought the case would come off on the nature of the evidence I had heard against me, but my witnesses, though I had a host, seemed to carry no weight and it went against me. I've got so accustomed to consoling myself lately that misfortune and myself seem fast friends and we get along very well together. So for myself, I've no worries and I hope you will all rise to the occasion and do not grumble at the present outlook which might be worse. I'm not guilty; that's one consolation you have, and I expect things will right themselves yet. I saw Annie at the Castle when the trial was on. She is looking fine and is a brave soul though I'm sure she is worried now. I wrote to her yesterday and had parcels from herself and Clare. At the rate stuff is coming in I will not have room in my cell shortly and there's no danger I'll be hungry, and I've kept my appetite all right.

Now you must realise this is a hard sort of letter to write with so much uncertainty in the future, one can't settle down to discuss random topics. You can keep hoping and praying for the best, and you will not be disappointed, I'm sure. I hope Tom, B & Jim, Maggie and Joe are quite well and with best love to your dear selves.

Your fond son,

Patrick Moran

All his letters were censored (the originals are all marked by the censor), so it is not surprising that he professed his innocence so vehemently in many of them. Writing to his sisters in England, he said that he was so full up of the idea of getting out of it that he hadn't given the result much thought. But he also said 'I have an easy mind on the matter and that's more than can be said for those who swore against me.'[2]

In Mountjoy, he was with many of the men who had been in Kilmainham with him for the past few months: 'I have a few more here in the same boat as myself, so I am not too alone.'[3] Thomas Whelan (Prisoner No. 422) from Clifden, County Galway, was there and they became close friends in the last weeks of their lives. They also made friends with the warders guarding them, in particular Warder Daly, Warder Lester Collins and Warder Wheeler.

Paddy continued to receive letters from friends – he asked his sister Annie to acknowledge them as he was restricted to one letter a day and could not manage to reply to all of them himself. His girlfriend Bea and her family continued to send him 'the most luxurious parcels'.[4] He told Annie that he was eagerly looking forward to a visit and enquired whether her permit was issued. He was feeling very contented and was hopeful because, as he said, his 'case was getting a bit of attention now and I expect to be vindicated all right'.[5] Mountjoy, he observed, was much cleaner and more regular than Kilmainham and his meals were everything to be desired.

Apart from writing letters to his family, Paddy put his thoughts on paper in the form of poetry, to while away the hours. He called this poem 'Our Day':

I sit alone in Mountjoy Jail;
So far away from hill and dale
I sit alone and heave a sigh;
As I think of happy days gone by.
The prison bell it rings out clear;
And makes my lonely cell more drear
But as it rings, it seems to say:
Old Ireland yet shall have her day.

My prison bed lies on the floor;
The warder locks the iron door
I kneel and say my evening prayer;
And then lie down in cell so bare,
And soon I dream of my country's woes;
My country gripped by foreign foes
But in my dreams I hear God say:
Old Ireland yet shall have her day.

And in my dreams I once more see;
Old Ireland Free, Old Ireland Free,
Her mountains blue, her scene so grand;
Old Ireland blest by God's own hand
The prisons open wide their doors;
And Irish boys are free once more
See in the streets the people pray
Thank God Old Ireland's won her day.

But as I dream in my lonely cell;
I hear once more Old Mountjoy's bell
The warder knocks on my cell door;
I rise and dress, my sleep is oe'r,

> I make the bed, I clean the cell;
> What this day holds but one can tell
> And now once more I kneel and pray;
> That Ireland fights and wins her day.[6]

Paddy continued to write his daily letter:

My dear Parents,

I was delighted to get your letter Mamma & to hear you are all bearing this mutual trouble so well and that you have confidence in my ability to clear myself of this charge. Not one word sworn against me applied to me I assure you and I do not feel the least bit worried. I had a long letter from Ciss yesterday and Cecilia had a word in it to say she was writing today. I do not suppose I was ever in better health. I have my pipe, plenty of reading, an easy conscience and a great trust in prayer, and feel every whit as solid as the wall that surrounds me and I'm a Dutchman if I do not again show fair play between you both in your combat for the spectacles. Annie, Clare and my other friends are having a very busy time keeping me supplied with all my necessities and have proved themselves real bricks. I accept your word in full that none of you are worrying. I give you mine that I'm not. We can but trust that God will take a hand in the dispensing of justice and then all shall be well.

With my best love and good wishes to you all.

Your fond son,

Patrick Moran

On 23 February, he wrote again to his sister Annie, who still hadn't received her visiting permit. He asked her to try to bring his girlfriend, Bea Farrell, and his cousin Clare with her when she got it. Referring to Bea he said, 'I am very glad to know you've grown to like somebody so much, the seal of your disapproval would be an awful barrier, you're such a keen judge and I know your loving interest in me.'[7] He acknowledged the prayers of his many friends, 'for me I never prided myself, at least not since my early days, at being much good that way, but I do devote a fair share of time just to help and to show I'm not altogether indifferent.'[8]

Outside Mountjoy, Paddy's case was, as he said, getting attention. Louise Bennett, the honorary secretary of the Irish section of the Womens' International League, sent a telegram to Viscount French, Vice Regal Lodge, Dublin, on 26 February 1921, calling for a reprieve for Potter, Conway, Moran and Whelan, and stating that the members of the League were convinced, 'as were the majority of the Irish People', that their guilt was unproven.[9]

A report from the police headquarters to Assistant Under Secretary, Sir Andy Cope, on 27 February 1921, in response to the doubts cast on Paddy's conviction stated that 'a certain amount of weight may fairly be given to the fact that the police had in their possession a photograph of Moran in IRA uniform with a revolver in his hand and that on the day before the initial trial date, an attempt was made to murder Major Carew.'[10] The report concluded that the court was justified in coming to the decision to which it came, and that there were no grounds upon which any interference with the sentence could be recommended.[11]

Paddy's meals were no longer everything he desired and he was now making arrangements to have meals brought in each day. He wrote to Gogan's of Phibsboro himself, as he did not want his friends to bear the expense. He asked Annie to call on Mr Deakin, a chemist in Phibsboro to get another bottle for his stomach like the ones he sent to Kilmainham; the food there had reawakened his stomach trouble.[12]

By 9 March, he was receiving his meals regularly and now wanted a fresh boiled egg for his breakfast. His boots were worn and leaking and he asked his sister Annie to get another pair from his trunk, but asked her not to buy new ones. The next day, 10 March, his boots or the boiled eggs became the least of his worries: he was told that he would be executed the following Monday. It was an unwelcome gift on his birthday. *The Irish Times* carried the announcement made by general headquarters on the evening of 9 March: 'In the case of Patrick Moran, the general officer commanding the forces in Ireland confirmed the sentence of death.'[13] Five other men's sentences were confirmed at the same time.

The six men, Frank Flood, Thomas Bryan, Patrick Doyle, Bernard Ryan, Thomas Whelan and Paddy, were transferred from 'C' wing to 'D' wing when their sentences were confirmed. 'D' wing held the condemned cells and the execution chamber.[14] Whether Paddy was still able to get his meals from Gogan's is not clear, but when Thomas Bryan's sister called at the prison on Saturday with his breakfast, it was not accepted because his sentence had been confirmed.[15]

Paddy wrote his last letter to his parents:

My Dear Parents,

I suppose ere this reaches you, you will have heard all the news there is to hear about me and I pray [to] God to give you the grace to view my fight with death and my triumph over it with equanimity. I was told today, by way of a birthday gift I suppose, that myself and another prisoner named Thomas Whelan are to go the same road as Kevin Barry went not long ago next Monday morning. I know it will be very hard for you all to bear and I hope you will see it in the light that I do and bear it just as bravely as I do and as I will. Perhaps it is the will of God. I'm sure it is, that I should get such notice of 'when, where and how' my earthly course finishes and that I never again might get the same chance for a thorough preparation. I expect to die in the grace of God as I am now, I hope. I crave His mercy and expect to meet you all in a brighter and better world and I want you all to look forward and to strive for that Eternal reward. I had a visit from Annie and Sister today. She will tell you how I feel about it; the question of whether anyone else should travel to see me was a sore one with me. No child ever had better parents; I did my best as a dutiful son and brother. I hope my efforts pleased God almighty and you. I feel strong in myself now for what I do not look on as an awful ordeal, and a meeting with those I love so well might not do either of us any good so unless you wish otherwise I shouldn't advise anyone to travel to see me. I pray God almighty to bless you all. Do not worry for me, pray for me instead and shed no tears and always hold your heads high because I die a martyr not a criminal, as they would paint me. Am rushed now, will write again to Mag. and the lads and yourselves,

    With best love,

    Your fond son, Patk

He wrote the following day to his sisters in England and to his brothers and sisters at home in Crossna:

Mountjoy Prison, 11 March 1921:

My dear sisters Cissie and B,

After all the hopes, delays, etc., connected with my charge I have to state at this period that on yesterday (my birthday) I was informed that a fellow prisoner named Thos Whelan and myself are to be executed on Monday morning 14th inst. You I know are quite satisfied with my innocence, so are the public and I of course know I am. In this case I die a martyr and so does the other man. I am quite resigned to my fate and have trust in God's mercy and his divine will that this is perhaps his way of giving me what we all hope for and for what I have prayed for, a Happy Death. I pray that God may give you all the grace to bear this bravely, as you can rest assured I will. I hope to meet you all whom I loved so well (and who were so worthy of a great love) in Heaven. I saw Annie and we agreed that it might be better for the composure of all of us that no one should travel to bid me goodbye. May God bless you all – shed no tears for me, pray for me and I hope to aid you all in your passage towards me by my prayers. I can't express my love for you,

    Your fond brother, Patrick

P.S.

I meant to write [to] each of you but I found the task hard just because I know what your feelings will be, not for my own, I'm feeling as well as you ever knew me.

Mountjoy Prison, 11/03/1921

My dear Brothers and Sisters,

I write this on Friday night and I suppose you are not new to the news about my impending execution. I hope my loved parents and you will bear the news bravely as you know I will and am. I should write to each one of you individually but those letters to loving parents, brothers, sisters, are the hardest of this trial. I am thoroughly resigned to die if it is God's will and might not again have as good a chance of making my eternal salvation secure. My brother prisoner Whelan and myself are very happy and give each other great help in our spiritual preparation. When we look on all the sudden and unprovided deaths which take place these times we might perhaps be thankful to escape such an end. It is arranged that it takes place at 6 a.m. on Monday morning. Do not shed any tears for me but give me your prayers and I will aid you all in your fight to become united in the next world where a just and merciful judge will dispense justice and mercy. I name you all in my mind and bid you a loving goodbye. To Moran and family, Ned Doyle and family, C. Bruen and family, I do the same & to all the neighbours and friends, Mattimoes, Sheerins, etc., and give them my love and remembrance. I should have to write [to] the whole countryside if I mentioned all the names I call to mind. Goodbye and God bless you all, with my love and prayers,

Your fond Brother,
Patrick Moran[16]

His older brother John was a policeman in Lancashire, England, at this time and he wrote to him:

My dear Brother John,

I hope you will bear with fortitude the news I send you today that I am to be executed on Monday morning 14th. You can rest assured that I die innocent and with a perfect assignation to God's Mercy, I expect to be the first of us in Heaven and my prayers will be always for you all so that we may all meet there, the same happy family that we were on this Earth. This must be God's will that I was to have such notice of when, where and how I was to die and to make secure my eternal salvation. Do not worry for me, I will go through my part all right, comfort Dada, Mama and the rest at home. I have no worry for myself but I can't help taking on myself a little share of what this will mean to you all. Goodbye and God Bless you.

> Your loving Bro,
> Patrick[17]

The verdict on Paddy caused consternation amongst legal people and prompted Archbishop Walsh of Dublin to get his secretary to ring Michael Noyk and tell him that he was sending him a letter giving his views and giving him permission to publish the letter in the press:

Dear Sir,

I see that your name is signed as solicitor to a very impressive memorial which was brought to me with a request for my signature. The prayer of the memorial is for a commutation of the death sentence in the case of Patrick Moran now lying in a Dublin prison, convicted by a court-martial of the murder of a military officer.

The memorial, in my judgment, shows conclusively that the evidence adduced in support of the charge altogether fails to sustain it.

I have always understood from that great jurist the late Chief Baron Pallas, as the result of several serious conversations with him, that when the evidence on which a charge is based fails to sustain it – not merely in case of a capital charge, but in case of any charge, great or small – the only result consistent with justice is withdrawal of the charge, and acquittal.

I apply this without hesitation to the case of your client.

Believe me,

Dear Sir,

Faithfully yours,

+ William J. Walsh

Archbishop of Dublin[18]

This memorial was sent to the secretary to Lord French, the Lord Lieutenant for Ireland, at the Viceregal Lodge, for the attention of Lord French. Sir Andy Cope replied from the chief secretary's office, Dublin Castle on 11 March, saying that the Lord Lieutenant had directed him to acknowledge receipt of Michael Noyk's letter and the enclosed memorials on behalf of Patrick Moran and Messrs Flood, Doyle, O'Sullivan, Bryan and Ryan, and to say that they would receive his most careful consideration.[19] A similar memorial for a reprieve for Thomas Whelan had already been sent.

The memorial was also sent to Cardinal Logue, Archbishop of Armagh, and a telegram was received in reply stating that he, Cardinal Logue, did not know the case and could not allow his name to be used. The memorial was sent with a copy of the Archbishop Walsh's letter to the Archbishop of Canterbury. Fr Bell, his chaplain, replied that the Archbishop could not take any personal steps as there was nothing he could do except transmit documents which were already in the hands of those to whom they were addressed. Lord Hugh Cecil, MP, received the memorial but replied that he did not think it desirable that MPs should use their influence in respect of the prerogative of mercy. Lieutenant Commander John Kenworthy, RN, MP, received a letter from Michael Noyk on 7 March 1921 and replied that he had taken the matter up with Sir Hamar Greenwood, MP, and would let Noyk know the result as soon as possible. However, when the memorial arrived on 11 March, Kenworthy was out of town. He replied on 14 March, saying that he had received it but could not do anything and now 'poor Moran was executed'.[20]

The *Daily News* on Friday, 11 March 1921 raised its voice in support of Paddy Moran and also Thomas Whelan:

It is officially announced that sentence was promulgated in Dublin yesterday on Patrick Moran, convicted for the murder of Lieutenant Ames on Sunday, 21 November. The general officer commanding the forces in Ireland has confirmed the sentence of death. Confirmation was announced on Sunday of the sentence of death passed on Thomas Whelan for the murder of Captain Bagally. The *Daily News* learns that very grave doubts exist as to the evidence on which these men were convicted. Evidence of identification regarding Whelan was given by an officer who swore with equal confidence to the identity of a man named Boyce. The same court-martial acquitted Boyce. Whelan was also identified by a soldier who swore to the identity of two men named Tobin and MacNamara.[21] Both the latter were acquitted by the court-martial. Witnesses for the defence swore that at the time of the murder Whelan was at mass some miles away. Their evidence was in no way broken down by cross-examination.

Patrick Moran was convicted of the murder of Lieutenant Ames at a similar court-martial on 17 February. The evidence against him was principally that of a soldier-cyclist who had already identified two other men [Michael J. Tobin and Jimmy McNamara] as being concerned with the murders but who were acquitted.

For the Defence, nineteen independent witnesses, none of them in any way related to the accused, testified at the trial that the accused was in Blackrock (five miles from the scene of the murder) in or about the time of its commission.

In Moran's case no suggestion was made by the prosecution that any of the alibi witnesses were in any way connected with Sinn Féin, and in point of fact, the majority of them were either ex-soldiers or ladies and girls who had lost their brothers and husbands in the late war.[22]

Five other witnesses came forward to try to prevent Paddy's execution: Matthew Fennell, Frank Blades, Martin Doheny and Thomas Crimmins made statements on 13 March that corroborated alibi evidence given at the trial. J.P. McCabe, Blackrock, who was one of the witnesses for the defence at the trial, drove these men into Dublin to give their evidence. He was in communication with a government official at 10 p.m. on Sunday 13 March, who informed him that due consideration would be given to the fresh evidence.[23] However, a report written for Sir John Anderson concluded that there was no new evidence in these four statements.[24]

The fifth witness made a completely new statement and it caused some consternation in the Castle. Madge McLaverty contacted Michael Noyk and made a statement which he forwarded to the lord lieutenant. It cast doubt on the ability of the chief witness for the prosecution, Private Snelling, to remember the events of Bloody Sunday:

I am the wife of Robert A. McLaverty, FRCPI, Master of the Coombe lying-in hospital and reside with my husband at 55 Merrion Square. On the morning of 21–11–1920 between 9.00 a.m. and 9.30 a.m. I was in my bedroom which is at the back of the house. One of my servants came to me and asked me did I hear the shooting. I went to the room in the front and I looked out the window and saw a young soldier coming from Upper Mount Street and entering the house. I went downstairs to the study and there saw the young soldier, he was in a Private's uniform and I would know him again. He was very agitated, had his tunic open and his face was the colour of death. His cap was on the back of his head and he was on the point of collapse. He told me that the 'Shinners' raided him and took his dispatches from him, and that he was put with his face to the wall and nine shots fired all round him. I asked him, as his story was confused, who had attacked him and taken his dispatches from him and he replied 'I do not remember anybody or anything more'. He was unable to use the telephone and one of the maids rang up Dublin Castle for him, while

I rushed away to get restoratives. I am prepared to give this evidence on oath, and to produce witnesses to verify it. Neither my husband nor myself have any connection with politics nor has either of us any knowledge of the accused.

Signed Madge McLaverty

Witness James D. Kelly, MD B Ch BAO

Coombe Lying-in Hospital.

10–03–1921[25]

A secret memo from general headquarters, Parkgate Street, Dublin, dated 12 March 1921, was marked 'urgent' and sent to the under secretary, Dublin Castle. It referred to the statement from Mrs McLaverty and said that the soldier (Private Snelling) was wired for and was expected to arrive at the Dublin district headquarters the following morning.[26]

Mrs McLaverty wrote to General McMahon and asked for his assistance in getting her a hearing in the right quarters to give her evidence. Her own words were, 'I am profoundly convinced that the soldier in question could not possibly have had such a clear recollection of facts as stated in his evidence.'[27] McMahon forwarded her letter to General Macready with a memo attached: 'I know Mrs McLaverty to be a lady of the highest honour and reliability who has no political leanings and who acted as a noble person on 21 November, in sheltering the young soldier and thereby saving his life.'[28]

The Chief Crown Solicitor, Arthur Byrne, Assistant Under Secretary Sir Andy Cope, and Mr Egan, CI, were present when all the new evidence was investigated. Private Snelling was not interviewed and there is no evidence in the file that he returned to Dublin on foot of the telegram sent requesting his presence there. The report of the investigation was sent to Sir John Anderson by the chief crown solicitor on 13 March 1921. It said that Sergeant Nixon, the police officer present at the identification parade where

Paddy was picked out, Colonel Browne, Major Carew, Captain Perdue, Snelling's superior officer, and Mrs McLaverty were interviewed. Sergeant Nixon and Colonel Browne were present at the identification parade when Paddy was picked out; they stuck to the story that Snelling and Lawrence picked him out independently. Major Carew testified that he saw Snelling on the afternoon of Sunday 21 November, and that he was quite possessed and clear, that he told him much the same story as he told at the court-martial. (Yet Major Carew had said in the statement he gave for the court-martial that he did not see Snelling until he met him at the identification parade at Arbour Hill).

Mrs McLaverty was interviewed and the report states that she 'is very positive' that Snelling assured her that he could not remember anything on that day. 'Is very positive' is crossed out in the report and written over it is 'she was at first positive'. It states that Mrs McLaverty said that Snelling phoned the Castle (in her statement she says the maid phoned for him) and had said that he had been pushed into No. 38 Mount Street, and that two officers had been murdered there. Captain Perdue was also interviewed. He said that he interviewed Snelling on the afternoon of Sunday 21 November, and while Snelling did not point out to him that he could identify the man who held him up and covered him with a revolver at No. 38 Upper Mount Street, he did mention that he was sure he could identify several of the men he saw. The crown solicitor asked Captain Perdue if he had ever heard that Snelling was inventing evidence? Colonel Browne had brought an army sergeant with him who said that Snelling was telling inconsistent stories about Sunday 21 November. Captain Perdue said he never heard anything of the kind. The conclusion was that if Snelling could remember the house number and the number of officers killed then the rest of his evidence was reliable.[29]

On Friday 11 March, Joseph Devlin, MP for West Belfast, tried to put a question in the House of Commons to the chief secretary or the attorney general for Ireland about the Prerogative of Mercy in the cases of Patrick Moran and Thomas Whelan. The speaker would not permit the question because it was not a matter which could be discussed in the house. Devlin objected because the very same question had been allowed in other cases. The speaker then explained that the question had to be a direct one 'whether or not the Prerogative of Mercy had been exercised'. Devlin then asked that question and received the one word reply, 'No'.[30] Joseph Devlin met Prime Minister Lloyd George on the same day and was asked by him to place any evidence in his possession before the Irish authorities.[31] The prime minister did not give any personal assurance that his intervention would lead to a reprieve, but he promised that the cases would be carefully reviewed in light of the new facts. Devlin's efforts to raise the matter at the highest level were appreciated by the Moran family. Paddy's sister, Mary (Cissie), wrote to Devlin on 26 March 1921:

> My father wishes me to thank you in his name, for your unstinted efforts on behalf of my brother Patrick Moran.
>
> We are fully aware of the deep interest you took in the case, and we thoroughly appreciate what the sacrifice of so much time means to a public man like yourself.
>
> I saw my brother and undoubtedly the victory was his. May God Bless you always.
>
> Yours gratefully,
> Mary Moran[32]

She received this reply written on 30 March 1921:

> It is very good of you to write [to] me and I appreciate your kindly thought in doing so. I was only too happy to do what I did, and indeed I did a great deal more than most people know, but there is no need to talk of that now since my efforts were unavailing. I was shocked at your brother's execution and was so angry that I could

barely contain myself at what I regard as a cruel crime of infamy. My
heart goes out to you and to your family but I am glad to know that
they and you have borne this sorrow so bravely. That you have taken
the sacrifice in such a fine spirit is indeed another inspiring example
of that courage and unselfishness which makes a Cause enduring. I
shall always treasure your good wishes.

Yours sincerely,

Joseph Devlin[33]

Paddy's links with the trade union movement also came into play.
The Dun Laoghaire branch of the National Union of Railwaymen
telegraphed J.H. Thomas, MP, their parliamentary representative,
to ask him to intercede on Paddy's behalf to obtain the Royal
Prerogative of Mercy.[34] The vice-president of the 800-strong Union
of Grocers' Assistants protested in the strongest manner against
the sentence of death passed on their president, Patrick Moran,
in the face of overwhelming evidence for the defence, and called
on all lovers of justice to stop judicial murder.[35] The Secretary, Mr
Turner, of the National Amalgamated Union of Shop Assistants,
Warehousemen and Clerks in Dilke House, Malet Street, London,
advised P. Hughes, Secretary of the Irish Grocers' Assistants,
Parnell Square, Dublin, that he had sent a wire to Sir Hamar
Greenwood strongly urging 'respite of death sentence on Patrick
Moran, president, Grocers Assistants' Union, Dublin, pending
further enquiry and civil trial, believing same would prevent grave
miscarriage of justice'.[36] Mr Turner did not receive a reply and at a
full national executive meeting held on the weekend of 11 March
1921, he was instructed to write again to Sir Hamar Greenwood.
In a letter to Hughes, Turner says, 'unfortunately we did not know
on Sunday that a decision had been hastily come to on Saturday,
fixing the execution for Monday morning. This rather looks as if
they feared the growing feeling against the executions. We only
learned of the decision simultaneously with the execution.'[37]

Lord Justice O'Connor, who was in discussion with Fr Michael O'Flanagan at this time about a peace settlement, phoned general headquarters from Kilkenny and wanted to wire the prime minister on 13 March to give his view that if the executions went ahead then all chance of settlement of the Irish question would be seriously jeopardised or practically destroyed. His concerns were instead communicated by letter to the Irish authorities by Sir John Anderson, who referred Lord Lieutenant French to the files of Moran and Whelan which were attached. Anderson added his own note which stated, 'There is nothing in my opinion to alter the decisions arrived at.'[38] The fate of Paddy Moran and Thomas Whelan was sealed.

Arthur Griffith, writing from his prison cell and quoted in the *Irish Independent*, warned that 'the fact that the British government proposes to kill six of my fellow prisoners in this jail early tomorrow indicates that it desires no peace.'[39]

In the same paper, the celebrated Dublin-born author, George E. Russell (Æ), asked the British people:

> … to consider with the utmost solemnity the effect on the Irish people of the execution of the six men. If these penalties are allowed to be indicted, if the evidence of dozens of witnesses is to be set aside, the soul of Ireland will grow as far apart from possibility of friendship with Great Britain as Earth is from the Polestar. Humanity is judging the character of British justice by its actions in Ireland today. Take heed what its verdict will be. There is nothing humanity abhors more than a vacuum in itself.[40]

Michael Collins is recorded as saying after the executions, 'We know who did those jobs and neither Whelan nor Moran were guilty. When the British government puts to death men like these it is one of the reasons we have no faith in such a government.'[41]

The men who were to be executed spent their last days in

Mountjoy receiving visits from family and friends and writing messages on the reverse of prayer leaflets. Despite Paddy's earlier suggestion that they should not come, his sisters travelled from England to say goodbye. Michael Noyk requested permits for Annie, Bridget and Clare Moran and for Paddy's brothers James and Batty Moran. Mary (Cissie) Moran asked for a visit for herself and her sister Lena. Margaret Doyle, a cousin, asked to visit him with his sister.[42] They visited him on 12 March 1921. His girlfriend, Bea Farrell, also visited and they exchanged a gold locket and a cross.

His parents did not make the journey from Crossna to Dublin to be with him. His father was an old man; he was seventy-seven in 1921 and his mother had a serious operation in the Mater Hospital, Dublin, in 1912 and was frail for years following her illness. It must have been difficult, especially when Mrs Whelan visited her son, Tommy, his friend and cellmate. Mrs Whelan, in a last minute bid to save her son, sent this telegram to Queen Mary: 'My innocent boy is being hanged on Monday in Mountjoy Prison, Dublin, and I implore you to save him.' The telegram is marked 'not acknowledged'.[43]

Paddy's brother, Jim, spent the evening with him on the eve of the execution. Uncle Jim never talked about that evening but it was a difficult last evening for both of them. It was on this visit that Jim learned of Paddy's involvement in the action at the Gresham Hotel and of his worries that Mr McCormack might have been shot in error.[44]

Paddy asked to see his confessor, Fr Patrick O'Byrne, who visited him on Saturday and Sunday.[45] Fr O'Byrne said that he had the consolation of preparing and making him happy for the journey to Heaven and that he found him in wonderful spirits for a young man in his position. Paddy asked Fr O'Byrne to give his love and best wishes to the people of Dun Laoghaire and to tell them that 'with the help of God, I will face the execution bravely in the morning and die like a true Irishman'.[46] Paddy told Fr O'Byrne he was innocent of the charge against him, for which he was wrongly convicted. 'In perfect peace with God, he bears no hatred or ill will towards anyone and is prepared for the supreme sacrifice, to meet his God and offer up his young life for his country as he believes he is doing'.[47]

Paddy McGrath, quartermaster of his Volunteer company, went to see him with a plan in mind. The Auxiliary who was guarding him moved to the far end of the cell and turned his back. Paddy McGrath was wearing a heavy overcoat and a hat, and he proposed to Paddy Moran that he should put these on and walk out. In the dimly lit cell the swap would not be noticed. Paddy agreed that it could work but was worried about the consequences for McGrath and for the officer guarding him who had been 'very decent to him'. When McGrath later reported to his commanding officer what he had proposed, the officer said that because he had acted without orders he should be court-martialled. McGrath asked that the court-martial be held immediately, and the result of this was that he was asked to go in and try again, but Paddy Moran would not hear of it.[48]

This story is told slightly differently in the Christmas edition of *The Nation*, 14 December 1929, when a photograph showing Paddy Moran, Thomas Whelan and the Auxiliary, Lester Collins, was reproduced for the first time. The negative was smuggled to Arthur Griffith who was in another wing of the prison at the time of the execution. He preserved it until his release and gave it to P. Moylett who concealed it so carefully that it was not found until 1929. In the article Oscar Traynor described the exploit to effect an escape:

Paddy Moran was one of the most efficient and fearless officers of the Dublin Brigade. We decided to get him out if at all possible. The plan eventually decided on was that someone resembling him in stature and build should go on a visit to Moran and, while the guard's attention was held by someone else, effect a slight change of clothing with him. Moran was then to walk out and his substitute to remain behind. The man who volunteered for this hazardous job – for it is obvious what would have happened when the Auxiliaries had discovered the substitution – was Patrick J. McGrath. He and Dan O'Carroll went into Mountjoy as visitors. While Dan beguiled the guard, McGrath informed Moran of the plan, and prepared to exchange clothes with him. Moran, however, refused. He said he had hoped to die fighting, but now that he had made up his mind to face the gallows, he did not want somebody else to be sacrificed for his liberty. McGrath and O'Carroll came from the jail despondent. But headquarters decided to make one other effort and next day, Sunday, McGrath was again sent into the jail, this time to endeavour to bribe the guard to allow Moran to escape. That also Paddy Moran refused to allow. 'The fellows minding me have been too decent,' he said. Next day he and his five gallant comrades were hanged.[49]

Paddy had made friends with the warders and wrote final messages to some of them. On the back of a picture of St Joseph he wrote 'to my friend Warder Daly'.[50] He gave a similar picture card to Warder Wheeler.[51]

The Sisters of Charity from Gardiner Street were allowed to visit the condemned men each day from 12 March. One of the sisters wrote to Paddy's parents after the executions and described the 'boys' as 'bright and cheerful' to the end.[52] Fr Michael O'Flanagan visited and he too found him in very good form. Paddy asked him to shake the hand of the officer guarding him because 'he is one of the best'. He told him to tell the people of Roscommon that they would have no reason to feel ashamed of how a Roscommon man met his death.[53]

The Lord Mayor, Alderman O'Neill, made official enquiries to the authorities at 6 p.m. on Sunday evening and was informed that the government had decided that the law must take its course. He called to see Paddy who gave him, as a souvenir, a card of Saint

Christopher with the words 'Intercede for us in the hour of danger' printed on it. Paddy wrote on the back, 'Good-bye loved Ireland and You. Patrick Moran, sentenced to death, Mountjoy Prison, Dublin. March 1921.'[54]

Arthur Griffith, TD, Michael J. Staines, TD, Eoin Mac Néill, TD, and E.J. Duggan, TD, who were prisoners in another wing of Mountjoy, sent a message to the condemned men: 'Your fellow prisoners, like all men and women of Ireland, are thinking of you always, and especially in their prayers. All recognise the death to which you are doomed is an honour to you, and we know that you are going to that death in the spirit of the best and bravest of your race'.[55]

The condemned men spent their recreation period on Saturday, 12 March, in a rather unusual way for men who were facing the gallows two days later. They recorded their activities on and inside an envelope belonging to Tommy Whelan. They had a syndicate of the six and placed an anti-post bet in the Lincolnshire Handicap, run at 3.00 p.m on Monday, 14 March 1921. They bet two shillings and six pence each way on Pirseus at 33–1 and five shillings to win on Poltova at 4–1. They were executed before the race was run but as Pirseus finished twenty-first and Poltova seventeenth, their investment yielded nothing.

Inside the same envelope were cigarette packets, a red scapular, a holy picture and a poem from Thomas Whelan to his girlfriend, Pauline. Each of the six men wrote his name and sentence on the inside of a cigarette packet. On another someone recorded the results of a 50 yard sprint race run on Saturday, 12 March 1921 in the prison yard: Moran 1st, Bryan 2nd, Doyle and Ryan – dead heat. The holy picture had a message for Warder Wheeler, one of the auxiliary soldiers guarding them in Mountjoy. Warder Wheeler brought the envelope and its contents from Mountjoy after the executions. The scapular belonged to Paddy Moran.[56]

When the Sisters of Charity visited the men on Sunday they

joked about their places in Heaven. All agreed that Tommy Whelan would get the highest place. Paddy Moran said he would not be satisfied to be away from Whelan and asked, 'Will not you come down and stay with us, Tommy?'[57] Tommy Whelan entertained the men with a rendition of 'The Shawl of Galway Grey', a song that evoked raw emotion in my father whenever he heard it sung afterwards.

Ellis, the executioner, with three assistants, arrived in the prison on Saturday in a tank, and all were accommodated in the prison hospital.[58] A plan to execute Ellis was in place but the information on his lodging arrangements was incorrect. He was expected to stay in the Gresham Hotel and be collected from there about an hour before the executions. Members of the Squad met at Oriel House on the morning of the executions to get final instructions from the headquarters intelligence officers, Cullen and Tobin. However, the plans never came to fruition because Ellis was already in Mountjoy and under police protection.[59]

Crowds gathered outside the jail on Sunday to pray for the condemned men and to convey sympathy to the relatives as they emerged from their final visits. They remained outside until curfew.[60] Remembering the scene afterwards the poet, Thomas MacGreevy, wrote:

THE SIX WHO WERE HANGED

The sky turns limpid green.
The stars go silver white.
They must be stirring in their cells now –
Unspeaking likely!
Waiting for an attack
With death uncertain
One said little.
For there is no certainty.

The sun will come soon,
All gold.
'tis you shall have the golden throne –

It will come ere its time.
It will not be time,
Oh, it will not be time,
Not for silver and gold,
Not with green,
'Till they all have dropped home,
'Till gaol bells all have clanged,
'Till all six have been hanged.

And after?
Will it be time?

There are two to be hanged at six o'clock.
Two others at seven,
And the others,
The epilogue two,
At eight.
The sun will have risen
And two will be hanging
In green, white and gold,
In a premature Easter.

The white-faced stars are silent,
Silent the pale sky;
Up on his iron car
The small conqueror's robot
Sits quiet.
But *Hail Mary! Hail Mary!*
They say it and say it,
These hundreds of lamenting women and girls
Holding Crucified Christs.

Daughters of Jerusalem …

Perhaps women have Easters.

There are very few men.
Why am I here?
At the hour of our death.
At the hour of youth's death,
Hail Mary! Hail Mary!
Now young bodies swing up.
Then
Young Souls
Slip after the stars.
Hail Mary! Hail Mary!

Alas! I am not their St John
Tired of sorrow
My sorrow, their sorrow, all sorrow,
I go from the hanged,
From the women,
I go from the hanging
Scarcely moved by the thought of the two to be hanged,
I go from the epilogue

Morning Star, Pray for us!

What, these seven hundred years,
Has Ireland had to do
With the morning star?
And still I too say,
Pray for us.

Mountjoy, March 1921[61]

Do cum Glóipe Dé ⁊ onópa
na hÉipeann.

Guiḋ ap anamnaċaiḃ áp mbpáiṫpeaċa
a ḟuaip báp ap ron na hÉipeann
Mápta 14aḋ, 1921.

Páopaig Ó Mópáin.

Tomár Ó Faoláin.

Ppóinpiar Ó Maoltuile.

Dpian Ó Riain.

Tomár Ó Dpiain.

Páopaig Ó Duḃgaill.

" Why cut off in palmy youth ?
    Truth they spoke and acted truth.
" Countrymen, Unite," they cried,
    And died for what our Saviour died."

Memoriam card in Irish for the six men
executed on 14 March 1921

CHAPTER 9

THE EXECUTIONS
AND THEIR AFTERMATH

MOUNTJOY – 14 MARCH 1921

Forgive us this tense hour, our brothers brave,
If we who stay less courage show than you
Who face the lonely highway of the grave
Unawed, to all high promptings grandly true.
Forgive us, should our anguish break your peace
Or darker thoughts our prayers for you disturb;
Still fettered we for you the Great Release;
Your courage shall our grief's fierce tumult curb,
What though the felon's hemp they round you cast:
One waits who well knows how the matter passed.

Maeve Cavanagh[1]

Monday, 14 March 1921 was a wretched morning. Thick, forbidding clouds hung overhead, a wetting mist soon gave way to a choking fog and the cold was intense.[2] The Irish Transport and General Workers Union called for a general stoppage of work from 8 a.m. to noon as a protest against the executions of their six fellow-countrymen. The public complied with a request from the national executive of the Labour Party to observe these hours as a time of mourning.

Thousands knelt in prayer outside Mountjoy Jail. Masses were offered in many of the nearby churches. Relatives of the condemned men were among the first to arrive. Paddy Moran's three sisters, Mary, B and Annie, and his brother Jim were there. Many of those outside the prison were workers who would normally be on their way to work. Some knelt on the damp ground, 'the thin morning breeze sweeping along the broad thoroughfare', and prayed the rosary.[3]

The crowd expected that a bell would ring at 6.00 a.m. when the first of the executions was due to take place. When there was no such indication from inside the prison, they thought that perhaps there had been a last minute reprieve for the men. They continued to pray and when at 7 a.m. the outer gates of the prison opened, the people surged up the lonely avenue. Another hour passed without any word from inside the prison, then at half past eight the door opened and a note was posted on the gate. It read:

> The sentence of law passed upon Thomas Whelan, Patrick Moran found guilty of murder and Francis Flood, Thomas Bryan, Patrick Doyle and Bernard Ryan found guilty of high treason by levying war, was carried into execution this morning.[4]

Paddy Moran and Tommy Whelan were the first to be hanged. They went to the gallows at 6.00 a.m. Sister Patricia, one of the Sisters of Charity from Gardiner Street, described what happened inside the prison:

> Mass commenced at 5.15 a.m. Paddy and Tommy Whelan prayed with wonderful fervour during mass. They got absolution, received holy communion and made their thanksgiving in a kind of ecstasy of prayer. When the prayers were said, Paddy walked without faltering to the scaffold. Tommy took his place beside him.[5]

Canon Waters, the prison chaplain, celebrated that mass. Patrick Doyle and Bernard Ryan attended the second mass said by Fr

MacMahon and then went calmly to their deaths at 7.00 a.m. Thomas Bryan and Frank Flood had mass said for them by Dr Dargan before they were executed at 8.00 a.m.

Those three priests were present at the executions. Canon Waters said that all 'died beautiful, Christian deaths as became good Catholics and good Irishmen. Their thoughts were wholly occupied with the next world and with their immortal salvation. The chaplains who prepared them for their end were edified by their resignation, their calm and their charity towards all.'[6] Canon Waters had got Paddy Moran and Tommy Whelan to sign a prayer book for him on the eve of their execution.[7]

In Paddy's native place, where there was no curfew, the community held a night vigil in Crossna church. A large congregation prayed all night for him; they all hoped that he would be reprieved. Paddy's mother stood up just after 6 a.m. and told them to go home, the execution was over.[8] She told her other son, Tom, afterwards, that she heard a loud knock, as if the door was rapped, at the time of the execution and she knew in her heart that it was all over.

Another Crossna son, Patrick Skeffington, was in Mountjoy at that time and he recorded his thoughts in this poem:

In Memory of the Mountjoy Martyrs

God give you rest brave comrades,
God grant you peace today.
Yours was the work right hard to do,
To mark our Freedom's way.

You did your best, sleep among the Bless'd,
Then justice held its sway.
Adding another debt which we'll pay yet,
In our own Republican way.

Seán Kavanagh was also a prisoner in the jail and he described that March day as 'a very black day', one which he would never forget. One of his most poignant recollections was seeing through the spy hole in his cell door 'six empty coffins being brought from the workshop in the basement of C wing'.[9]

Shortly before he went to the gallows, Thomas Whelan wrote a letter to the lord mayor of Dublin:

Your Honour,

Will you permit me to thank you for your kindness to my mother during her stay in Dublin in her sad trouble. This is the 14th. It has come at last, to find us ready. We were always ready, like Irishmen, to die for our old cause. I am in the best of spirits now, as ever. An Irishman's honour is a great pledge, so, like men, we must meet our doom this morning. It is now 4.40 a.m., so I have not long. I wish to thank you again, and all the citizens of Dublin, for your kindness to me.

Sincerely yours, Thomas Whelan.[10]

The kindness extended to his mother did not endear Dublin to Mrs Whelan: 'When all is over, I will return to my native Clifden and never see Dublin again. Perhaps it would have been far better if poor Tom had never seen it.'[11]

In a final attempt to pay their last respects to their loved ones, Frank Flood's father, Bernard Ryan's mother, Thomas Bryan's father, Tommy Whelan's mother, Patrick Doyle's wife and Jim Moran, Paddy's brother, each sent a requisition to the governor for the bodies to be handed over to them for burial. That did not happen.

Crowds lingered in the precincts of the prison hoping to get some information as to how the men had met their fate. They went away quietly when a contingent of soldiers under a military officer marched into the open space in front of the main door and told them to disperse.[12]

Ellis, the hangman, and his assistants were driven in an armoured car to the boat in Dun Laoghaire on Monday evening. They were accompanied by a large force of Auxiliaries and the entrance to Dun Laoghaire pier was guarded.[13]

The Freeman's Journal gave an account of the reaction in Dun Laoghaire and Blackrock:

Patrick Moran was well known and extremely popular in Dun Laoghaire and Blackrock. Yesterday a day of solemn mourning was observed. Business was at a standstill, all of the establishments, including the banks, being closely shuttered. The municipal flag in each township was floated at half-mast, while all the offices were closed. Masses were celebrated from 6 o'clock each hour until midday in the Catholic churches, and the congregations were enormous. While the incoming mail service was handled as usual, there were no mails sent on the outward journey to Holyhead, as no train service left Westland Row for the boat. All the schools were closed, and the children attended masses. With the exception of the train and tram service, which resumed at 11 o'clock, the townships were completely closed down all day. It was a day of mourning unprecedented in its solemn observance.[14]

The Dublin correspondent for the *Daily Mail* said that Dublin on 14 March was 'a city of snow and sorrow. The women of Dublin gathered in their thousands in the murk of morning drizzle to give a maternal benediction to the passing of the six young Irishmen. The members of Cumann na mBan marched in procession to Mountjoy Jail that morning.'[15]

After the executions, the British press condemned the British government's policy in regard to Ireland and expressed concern that a peace settlement under the prevailing conditions would be impossible. The editorial in the *Daily News* said:

Even the soldiers seem to have been moved by the extraordinary scene which took place yesterday outside Mountjoy Prison while the six Sinn Féiners, who had been sentenced by court-martial, were being hanged within. It is a pity that neither the British prime minister nor the Irish chief secretary could have been present in person, disguised very completely as harmless citizens, to mark the meaning of this deeply impressive spectacle. They might have hardened their hearts, but surely the old phrase about having 'murder by the throat' would not have passed their lips without an effort. The vast crowd [the newspaper estimated it at 20,000] of men and women had not met to pay its tribute of sorrow and admiration to six murderers. It was there to express its profound belief in their innocence, to protest with deep religious fervour against the persecution of what the greater part of Ireland regards as a tyrannous government and to show with dramatic emphasis how the fate of these men symbolises the spirit of Irish resistance … The manner of their death will go forth to the rest of the world, giving other nations fresh opportunity to scoff at the pretentious hypocrisy of Great Britain as the 'self-styled protector of little peoples'.[16]

The *Westminster Gazette* added its voice to the criticism of government policy and said it was enough to make anyone despair of an improvement in the Irish situation: 'It is useless to pretend that these men belong to a small gang of desperate criminals. Their deaths are regarded by the mass of the Irish as martyrdoms, and when executions become martyrdoms they cease to act as a deterrent.'

Sir William Watson summed up the feelings of many in Britain in this sonnet:

IRELAND'S MADNESS

Is it all folly, yonder, hour by hour,
To choose, not peace, but strife, and there to dare
The lion couched in his unnative lair,

The world-famed lion, mighty to devour?
Oh, that some folly as splendid were a flower,
Not on all shores but those, so wondrous rare!
Common as weed in Ireland everywhere
That splendid folly blooms, and hath the power
To make a mere slight boy not only face
Death with no tremblings, with no coward alarms,
But like a lover woo it to his arms,
Clasp with a joyous and a rapt embrace
Death's beauty, death's dear sweetness, death's pure grace,
And count all else as nought beside death's charms.[17]

Yet despite this outpouring of grief and anger, the British authorities stood by their decision. An unsigned letter from police headquarters in Parkgate Street, Dublin, to Sir Hamar Greenwood on 16 March 1921, refers to allegations in the press that the court, in Paddy Moran's case, had rejected the evidence of a large number of witnesses who provided an alibi. There was, it said, only one witness, Miss McGough, the housekeeper at Magees', whose evidence was inconsistent with Paddy having been at the murder scene. Three other witnesses had breakfast with him and the police had in their possession statements by two of these, Doyle and McCourt, supporting a completely different alibi. Even if all the other alibi witnesses could be believed, it continued, it was possible that he could have been at 8.00 a.m. mass, have been present at the murder scene at about 9.00 a.m. and returned to catch the 9.30 a.m. tram if he had a motorcycle or even a bicycle.[18]

The *Weekly Summary* from the police referred to the executions:

The executions of six Sinn Féin prisoners on the 14th were attended by a remarkable but orderly public demonstration. Two of the condemned men were convicted of complicity in the assassination of British officers in their beds on morning of 21 November 1920, and although the evidence produced at the trial was conclusive of their guilt and was not shaken by any event subsequently brought forward, the suggestion of their innocence was deliberately worked up day by day in the anti-government press with the result that many public appear to have come to the belief that a miscarriage of justice was perpetrated for political purposes. The other four men were convicted of high treason on the charge of levying war against the crown by taking part in an ambush on a party of Auxiliary police in Dublin. The decision to enforce the capital penalty in those cases was based upon the necessity of employing the strongest measures available to put down the practice of attacking military and police lorries in the streets of Dublin, a practice which in spite of disregard for public safety has within the past few weeks formed a regular part of the general plan of the campaign of guerrilla warfare waged by the so-called Irish Republican Army.[19]

A military court of inquiry, in lieu of an inquest, assembled at Mountjoy on 14 March 1921. Major Langley, Lieutenants Pavey and Pritchard of the Welch Regiment and Captain Brink, Royal Army Medical Corps, were present. Charles A. Munro, Governor of Mountjoy, said that he was present at the execution of Paddy Moran with the provost marshal who was there in place of the sheriff. He said that the deceased was attended by chaplains of his own persuasion. He identified the body as that of Patrick Moran, aged 26 (he was actually 33), single, grocer's assistant, of 5 Main Street, Blackrock, County Dublin. Dr Hackett, the medical officer for Mountjoy Jail, said that he saw Patrick Moran executed by hanging at 6.00 a.m. In his opinion, death was instantaneous and due to fracture of the cervical vertebrae.[20]

Frank Flood's parting words to his parents were, 'I hope there will be no trouble over us. Let us rest in peace.'[21] His request was not heeded. According to witness statements, the first reprisal for the executions was carried out by the IRA in Brunswick Street at about 8.00 p.m. on Monday 14 March.[22] An armoured car and two tenders full of police left Dublin Castle to raid No. 144 Great

Brunswick Street, the headquarters of the Dublin Brigade IRA. They were fired on by members of the IRA from the doorway of No. 145, the windows of No. 144 and from the roof of a house opposite. Three civilians were killed, three wounded and five Auxiliary cadets were injured, two of them seriously.[23] Cadet Francis Joseph Farrell later died. Thomas Traynor was arrested at the scene and was subsequently court-martialled and found guilty. He was executed by hanging on 25 April 1921.[24]

It did not take long for the IRA in north Roscommon to take revenge for Paddy Moran's execution. Just a week after the execution, two policemen were killed and a third policeman injured when the police were ambushed on the road between Keadue and Ballyfarnon, not far from St Lasair's Holy Well and Kilronan graveyard. Two units of the IRA, one from the North Roscommon Brigade and the other from the Leitrim Brigade had planned to ambush a military patrol at Tarmon on the Roscommon-Leitrim border between Drumshanbo and Drumkeerin, but when word came that the patrol was not going out, the North Roscommon unit decided instead to stage a robbery at the post office in Ballyfarnon in order to lure a police patrol out of Keadue. Three of the men went to the post office and demanded that the proprietor give them £5. The remainder of the men took up an ambush position at Kilronan on the Keadue to Ballyfarnon road. The police patrol came out from Keadue on their bicycles on the morning of 22 March 1921 to investigate the robbery. As they reached Kilronan a single shot was fired and that was the signal for a full onslaught of firing. Two policemen, Constables Dowling and Devereaux, were shot dead and one, Sergeant Reilly, was wounded. Three rifles, five revolvers and some ammunition were captured before the ambushers made a hasty retreat.[25] Michael Dockery, the O/C of the North Roscommon Brigade was a participant in the ambush. British records describe Dockery as a leader who had taken part in several attacks on the crown forces and who was probably the leader of the Keadue ambush, which took place twenty-two miles from his home.[26]

Captain Jenkins, the military doctor, left Boyle in the Red Cross car to travel to Keadue as soon as he received word of the ambush. He had only his military driver in the car with him. The roads were trenched and blocked but the doctor managed to make the twelve-mile journey in twenty minutes. On the way he stopped near Ballyfarnon to ask an old woman if the road was clear or if it was trenched and blocked with stones. She had watched open-mouthed the car bounding and swaying and coming down the narrow road at break-neck speed and her answer to the doctor amused himself and his driver: 'Divil the stone in Ireland would stop you, Doctor!'[27]

A military court of inquiry, in lieu of an inquest into the deaths of the constables was held on 22 March 1921. Constables Frizzell and Tully gave evidence. Constable Frizzell said he was the fourth and last man in the convoy of police headed by Sergeant Reilly (there were actually five men in the convoy). When they were just about a mile from Keadue, he heard a shot, followed by several more. He saw Constable Dowling fall to the right-hand side of his bicycle and lie there. He took cover and fired about ten shots. He saw a horse and cart pass but did not know who was driving it. Constable Tully gave similar evidence but he knew that the driver of the horse and cart was John Conlon, a worker at M.J. McManus, Keadue. Constable Tully saw Constable Devereaux go over to the wall on the left-hand side and look over it. He heard a shot and saw Constable Devereaux dump his bicycle, raise his hands and shout. A shot rang out about forty yards behind Constable Tully and several volleys were fired from both sides of the road. Tully took cover on the right-hand side and fired all the rounds he had in his magazine. He ran up the hill and got into a corner in the rectory yard where he reloaded his gun. He met Canon Boyd and went with him to the rectory. Inside he saw Sergeant Reilly and he was badly wounded. Constable Tully and Canon Boyd then went down the road to where Constable Dowling lay dying. Having assisted the canon to move Constable Dowling to the side of the road, Tully cycled for assistance. He did not see any of the attackers. Captain Jenkins, the military doctor, said that Constable Devereaux had a bullet wound in his left jaw and one through the chest, which caused his death. Constable Dowling had a large wound to the head and a number of pellet wounds on his left leg. Despite witness statements to the contrary, he said death in his case was instantaneous.[28]

Sergeant Michael Reilly gave his account of what happened, when he appeared at the Boyle quarter sessions on Thursday, 2 June 1921, before the County Court and Judge Wakely, KC, during the hearing of a claim for £4,010 compensation for his injuries. He said that he and four other policemen were cycling towards Ballyfarnon on 22 March at about 9.30 a.m. He was leading and on reaching a hill about a mile from Keadue he dismounted his bicycle. As he walked up the hill he heard shooting and saw Constable Devereaux, who was behind him, fall dead. Sergeant Reilly threw his bicycle on the side of the road and crossed a gate into the nearby churchyard. As he did so he was wounded in the head. There was a man standing inside the gate. Sergeant Reilly spoke to him by name and asked him, 'Is this the work you are at now?' The man replied, 'Don't shoot me.' As Sergeant Reilly was drawing his revolver, another man jumped on his back and caught his arms behind him. The first man then grabbed the lanyard of his revolver and pulled it away; another man fired two shots which just missed the sergeant's head. He came back onto the road and had to travel a distance of about 100 yards to get to the clergyman's house. He was wounded twice in the head while he was getting to the gate. The man who had taken his revolver came and stood in front of him, told him to stand and not to move. Two other men came running down the road, one with a shotgun and another with a revolver. The sergeant opened the gate and while he was going up the avenue to the house, he was shot at again and was wounded in the back of the head, knocked down and wounded again. He had a wound in the left shoulder and one on the spine as well as wounds in his head by the time he reached the clergyman's door. When the ambushers were gone he and the clergyman came out to find Constable Devereaux dead and another constable (Dowling) dying on the road. The latter died a few minutes later. The doctor from Keadue, Dr Rodden, took Sergeant Reilly back to Keadue where he dressed his wounds. That evening he was taken to Carrick-on-Shannon and from there to Steven's Hospital in Dublin where he spent eight weeks. Sir Arthur Chance, a surgeon in Steven's Hospital, said he examined Sergeant Reilly on 22 March and found six wounds scattered on the side of his head; there was gritty matter in the wounds and in the operation to get these cleaned he found all the layers of the scalp cut down to the bone. He did not recollect seeing wounds in the sergeant's back but they might not have needed attention. While his physical condition was now good, he complained of headaches and nervousness.

J.J. Kearney, District Inspector, RIC, Boyle, testified that the sergeant had a very high character in the force and he was aware that he was at the top of the list for promotion to head constable. He was a very intelligent man. The sergeant was forty-four years old and was twenty-three years in the force.[29] Sergeant Reilly's son, Michael, in conversation with me recently, said that his father knew Michael Dockery, having played cards with him while he was in Elphin. When Dockery held him up in Keadue, Sergeant Reilly asked if he was going to shoot him; Dockery said he was not but he would give him a good kick up the ——. Sergeant Reilly remained in the force until its disbandment on 12 May 1922. He lived in Drumcondra, Dublin, for the remainder of his life.[30]

At the Boyle quarter sessions of Friday, 18 June 1921, Mrs Maria Devereaux, wife of Constable Devereaux, was awarded £3,000 with costs for the loss of her husband. He was from Wexford, fifty-eight years old and had been in the force for thirty-one years; he had one son who was twenty-three years old at the time.[31] He and the other members of the police patrol were sent out because of their knowledge of the Ballyfarnon area. Mrs Devereaux asked the *Roscommon Herald* to publish a message of thanks to her many kind friends who had sent messages of sympathy to her.[32]

Constable Dowling must have had a feeling he would be killed that day; he is reported to have suggested that they should not take that particular road to Ballyfarnon. He was stationed in Croghan and Boyle before going to Keadue and he was very popular.[33] People who knew him said he was one of the most decent policemen ever stationed in Keadue.[34] He was twenty-nine years old, unmarried and was the son of an ex-RIC sergeant from Wicklow.[35] Constable Dowling's brother, a railway worker, was shot dead by crown forces in Arklow, County Wicklow, a few months earlier and the two brothers lie side by side in a Wicklow grave; one ambushed in Keadue, the other shot in his home town.[36]

The monthly report from the 4th Battalion, IRA, Crossna area, for March 1921, to the Chief-of-Staff, Richard Mulcahy, outlines a series of activities in the area and concludes with the Keadue ambush: 'ten men attacked a police patrol from Keadue on 21 March [it actually happened on 22 March]; two constables were shot dead, a sergeant was seriously wounded and the following items were captured, one Lee Enfield rifle, one shotgun, two hand grenades, three Webley revolvers, seventy-five rounds of .303 ammunition, three bandoliers and three bicycles.'[37]

After the Keadue ambush the surrounding area was combed for suspects by British forces. A convoy of lorries and cars left Boyle on Thursday 23 March, carrying military and police, proceeding to Keadue where local forces joined it. It went to Arigna and there all the male inhabitants of the surrounding districts who could be found were rounded up. Many, hearing the lorries approach, took to the hills and remained hidden in the ravines and gorges, which are a feature of the Arigna mountains, while the raid was in progress. Only one prisoner, Owen Cull, was taken back to Boyle. Thomas Gaffney was arrested on 24 March at his home in Derreentawney, Ballyfarnon and Paddy Gannon was arrested on 26 March as he ran from his home in Arigna. He was shot in the legs and suffered permanent disability.[38]

On Saturday, 26 March, another contingent of crown forces came upon a local family, the Molloys, working on their farm in Aughnafinnegan, Knockvicar, Boyle. Joe Molloy, a young lad of fifteen, was shot. He died shortly afterwards:

A party of military from Drumdoe, Ballinafad, who were guarding Lord French, the Lord Lieutenant's [country] residence, were carrying out operations in the districts around Lough Key. It seems the military party were divided up into four or five sections and were advancing across in extended formation. At about 3.15 p.m. they arrived at Aughnafinnegan [about two miles from Crossna]. Joe Molloy and his three brothers were at work in a field. They were engaged in spreading manure or 'top dressing' as the operation is termed in agricultural circles. The eldest of the brothers is about eighteen years of age and the youngest about ten years. Armed soldiers suddenly appeared passing in extended formation along by a wall on one side of the field. It seems that the boys stopped working and went towards the wall to look at the soldiers, as they, like most boys, had their interest awakened by military display. On the opposite side of the field to where the soldiers were is Molloys' house and the military state that firing broke out from this direction as the boys advanced. The soldiers near the wall, it appears, came to the conclusion that this fire was being directed at them by parties in ambush and they promptly replied. None of those who were involved in the sad affair are clear as to how it actually occurred, but Joe Molloy fell mortally wounded. He was caught in the fire directed by the soldiers from near the wall. He received three bullet wounds. The other three brothers threw themselves flat on the ground. When the youngest boy was afterwards asked what he had done when the firing started, he replied, 'I said an act of contrition'. Some of the bullets fired hit the walls of Molloys' house. When the excitement had subsided somewhat the soldiers ran to the wounded boy and rendered all possible aid. When the boy's parents came to the scene their distracted cries of grief were pitiable. The military had the wounded boy conveyed with the least possible delay to Boyle Military Hospital, where Major Jenkins, the kind-hearted military doctor, made an examination. It was found that life was extinct. A pathetic coincidence was that the boy's birthday was on Saturday 26 March. The soldiers are emphatic in their assertions that they saw at least seven men at the side of the field near the house from where the firing came. They stated that these parties got away. Some of the boys state that a party of soldiers were also at that side of the field. A military court of inquiry into the circumstances attending the death of the deceased was held in Boyle Military Barracks on Easter Monday. The military and the next of kin were represented by solicitors. The proceedings were open to the press.

The inquiry opened at 3 p.m. on Monday and continued until 7 p.m. The court sat to complete the taking of evidence at 10 a.m. on Tuesday, and the inquiry closed at 1 p.m on that day. Military and civilian witnesses gave evidence. A verdict was returned to the effect that the death of Joe Molloy was due to shock and haemorrhage, earned by gunshot wounds, and that he met his death from being accidentally caught in the fire directed by the military at some unknown persons who were behaving in a suspicious manner.

At about 6.30 p.m. on Easter Monday the funeral of the deceased boy left Boyle Military Barracks. Relatives of the deceased were allowed unrestricted admission to where the remains were in the barracks, and the officers and soldiers were most courteous and sympathetic. They saluted as the remains were borne out. The funeral cortege was of huge dimensions. Up to eighty horse-drawn vehicles were in it, as well as a considerable number of horsemen and pedestrians. When Killeelan [sic] cemetery, where the internment took place, was reached, darkness had fallen and the deceased was laid to rest there amid every token of sincere sorrow and sympathy. Rev C. Clyne, Crossna, officiated at the graveside. R.I.P.[39]

Thus the execution of Paddy Moran was directly responsible for the deaths of the two constables near Keadue and the death of Joe Molloy. The finding that there were 'unknown persons, who were behaving in a suspicious manner' was hotly disputed locally; there was no evidence that anyone was firing on the crown forces and it is believed that Joe Molloy was an innocent victim who was shot and killed by an enraged military.

The military continued to comb the area for suspects for the Keadue ambush. Thomas Lynham and Patrick McLoughlin were arrested on 1 May 1921; James Conlon and Patrick Daly were also arrested; Thomas Lavin, who had injured himself with a bomb at his own home on 29 April 1921, was arrested at the Sligo Infirmary; Michael Dockery was arrested in O'Hara's Public House in Cootehall on 17 May 1921, along with John Glancy and Joseph and Willie O'Hara.[40] Dockery and Glancy were taken across the road and put standing against the wall surrounding the church grounds. Dockery tried to make a dash for it but was shot and wounded in the leg as he tried to scale the wall fronting the priest's residence.[41] Two rifles were captured during the raid; one was the rifle (described as a revolver in Reilly's account) that Dockery had taken from Sergeant Reilly during the Keadue ambush and the other, a lancer, was traced to a raid on Longford Military Barracks.[42] The prisoners were taken to Boyle Barracks and were beaten there. Dockery and Glancy were charged with the murder of the police in Keadue, though Glancy was not there. Dockery later escaped with the help of a friendly soldier, Corporal George Meadlarkin, who facilitated him by procuring the key to his cell and opening the door. In the early hours of a June morning Dockery slipped from his cell, climbed out through a washhouse window, lowered himself into the Boyle river and waded across it to freedom.[43] The two O'Haras and James Conlon were released by order of the deputy adjutant general on 15 July 1921. Patrick Daly was released in August 1921, because the witness who identified him decided not to give evidence. Owen Cull, Thomas Gaffney, John Glancy, Thomas Lavin and Paddy Gannon were due to be tried by court-martial but the trial could not proceed while Lavin and Gannon were in hospital.[44] By the time Gannon and Lavin were fit to be tried the Truce had been called and there is no evidence that these men were ever tried. They were released in 1922.

In Clifden, County Galway, the home town of Tommy Whelan, who was executed with Paddy Moran, the local IRA also carried out a reprisal. On the evening of 16 March 1921, at 7.30 p.m., four constables under the command of Constable Charles Reynolds left the barracks in Clifden. Later, two of the constables moved down Main Street and rounded Eddie King's Corner into Market Street; some distance behind Constables Reynolds and Sweeney followed. Three or four men wearing trenchcoats approached and opened fire and the two constables fell. Constable Reynolds lay dead and Constable Sweeney was badly injured. He died from shock and haemorrhage two days later.

The crown forces took revenge for those killings in the early hours of Thursday, 17 March 1921. In a rampage by the Black and Tans, John J. McDonnell, a civilian, was killed, Peter Clancy, a civilian, was seriously injured, fourteen houses were burned and several others were damaged. The people of Clifden ran in fear as their homes blazed and all their personal belongings went up in smoke. Some took refuge in the convent and others went to the workhouse. The Whelan family home on the Sky Road was raided and photographs were taken, but since Tommy's brothers were not there, the cottage was left standing. Monsignor McAlpine, the parish priest in Clifden, spoke in very strong terms about the events of that week: 'I never for a moment thought that I would witness such calculated bloodshed or such terrible scenes in

Catholic Ireland. The crime by which he [Constable Reynolds], lost his life was a dastardly murder, just as was the shooting of poor McDonnell a brutal murder.'[45]

One reprisal was followed by another; the tit for tat killings went on and on. It is little wonder that negotiations were intensified between the two countries, through intermediaries, to try to achieve a settlement. King George V came to Northern Ireland on 22 June 1921, to open the parliament formally and concluded his speech with the following words:

> I speak from a full heart when I pray that my coming to Ireland today may prove to be the first step towards the end of strife among her people, whatever their race or creed. In that hope I appeal to all Irishmen to pause, to stretch out the hand of forbearance and conciliation, to forgive and forget, and to join in making for the land they love a new era of peace, contentment and goodwill.
>
> It is my earnest desire that in Southern Ireland, too, there may, ere long, take place a parallel to what is now passing in this hall; that there a similar occasion may present itself, and a similar ceremony be performed. For this the Parliament of the United Kingdom has in the fullest measure provided the powers. For this the Parliament of Ulster is pointing the way.
>
> The future lies in the hands of my Irish people themselves. May this historic gathering be the prelude of the day in which the Irish people, north and south, under one parliament or two, as those parliaments may themselves decide, shall work together in common love for Ireland upon the sure foundation of mutual justice and respect.[46]

A truce was agreed between the British army and the Irish army (IRA) and it came into effect on Monday, 11 July 1921.

On behalf of the British army it was agreed as follows:

1. No incoming troops, RIC, and Auxiliary police and munitions,

and no movements for military purposes of troops and munitions, except maintenance drafts.

2. No provocative display of forces, armed or unarmed.

3. It is understood that all provisions of this truce apply to the martial law area equally with the rest of Ireland.

4. No pursuit of Irish officers or men or war material or military stores.

5. No secret agents, noting description or movements of Irish persons, military or civil, and no attempts to discover the haunts or habits of Irish officers and men.

   Note: This supposes the abandonment of curfew restrictions.

6. No pursuit or observance of lines of communication or connection.

On behalf of the Irish army it was agreed as follows:

(a) Attacks on Crown Forces and civilians to cease.

(b) No provocative displays of forces, armed or unarmed.

(c) No interference with government or private property.

(d) To discountenance and prevent any action likely to cause disturbance of the peace which might necessitate military interference.[47]

The Truce came three months too late for Paddy Moran and Tommy Whelan, for Constables Devereaux, Dowling, Sweeney and Reynolds, Joe Molloy and John J. McDonnell. It came too late for the four men executed with Paddy and Tommy on 14 March, for Thomas Traynor who was executed on 25 April, and for Edmond Foley and Patrick Maher, who were executed on 7 June 1921. Those nine men were buried in Mountjoy beside Kevin Barry who was executed on 1 November 1920.

The Truce did help others, including the men who were held in Mountjoy awaiting trial for the Keadue ambush; they were released without trial.

CHAPTER 10

FAMILY AND FRIENDS

After his death, Paddy's brothers continued to fight for the Republic he had died for and so did his girlfriend, Bea Farrell.

My father, Tom (Paddy's brother), hadn't even the consolation of seeing Paddy for one last time or of standing outside the jail on the fateful morning. He was the officer commanding the Crossna Battalion at the time. He was arrested without charge on 1 February 1921 after the burning of Cootehall Barracks and was taken to Boyle Military Barracks.[1] Boyle Military Barracks was not a pleasant place to spend six weeks. The prisoners, as many as fifty, were housed in a low lean-to shed, with a door at one end, two windows in the roof and a trench across the clay floor. There were about four cells partly underground in which selected prisoners were housed. The food was scarce and of poor quality. The prisoners were given tea in a jam pot, two to each pot, and at dinner four men had to eat from one plate. The dinner consisted of mashed potatoes, a few peas, small scraps of beef and on Sunday a salt herring. Each prisoner was given a small bundle of straw in a sack to lie on and two or three worn army blankets, which were fumigated occasionally. The toilets were at a distance from the shed and a prisoner had to have an escort of two soldiers to take him there. The sentries resented having to accompany the prisoners so they broke a hole in the concrete wall near the door and ran a piece of piping through it into a bucket which nearly always overflowed before it was emptied. Not surprisingly there was an outbreak of typhoid in the summer of 1921 and the prisoners were moved to other jails.[2]

Tom wasn't a stranger to incarceration. He and his brother Batty had spent two months in Mountjoy Jail in 1918. They were arrested and charged with unlawful assembly when they intervened in a local dispute about land distribution. They refused on principle to pay the fine imposed and were sent to jail.[3] Tom was moved to Athlone on 15 March and as we can see from this letter to his parents, he too had hoped for a reprieve for his brother. He was not officially told of Paddy's execution but read about it in the daily paper:

My Dear Parents,

I suppose you will be surprised to see that my address is changed. I was brought here yesterday.

I postponed writing last week thinking there might be some improvement, but I see by this day's paper that we must resign ourselves to the will of God. It is hard to think that we are parted from one we all loved so well, but in God's name let us accept it in the spirit Paddy would wish.

It is a hard trial for all of us, but we have a lot to be thankful for. He died a glorious death in a glorious cause. Although I feel his death keenly I am proud to be his brother. He lived a man and he died a man.

I am anxious to hear from my Father and Mother so as soon as you receive this write at once as I am not sure how long I will be left here. I got a letter from Cissie last week which I did not answer and as I have not her present address I would ask you to forward this one to her.

I don't intend to let this letter through the censor's hand. The fellows here tell me I have a chance of getting it out tomorrow with a visitor so you need not make any reference to this letter when answering. I will write another asking for some things I want.

Don't fret for me, I am doing splendidly and I know we are all of same metal and even under those trying circumstances we won't give way. I will be anxiously awaiting a reply. Hoping you are all well.

I remain,

Your fond son,

Tom Moran

The address given was Detention Room, Military Bks, Athlone.[4]

Tom spent six weeks in Athlone before he was moved to 'The Rath Camp' in the Curragh, County Kildare. My father didn't talk much about his time in the Curragh but he did say that he was glad that he was not around home for the Keadue ambush. He knew the policemen who were shot and did not approve of their killing. He believed that the ambush was ordered by Michael Collins and that Collins had said that no member of the Moran family should be involved.[5]

With little or nothing to do all day, Tom had plenty of time to think about his brother and the effect the execution had had on his mother and father and his siblings. He was probably also thinking of Seán Connolly from Longford, a good friend of his and the man who appointed him battalion commandant.[6] Seán had been sent to North Roscommon by GHQ in October 1920 to help organise activities there. He planned an attack on Keadue RIC Barracks and to this end he sent six revolvers, ammunition and bombs to Tom Moran, O/C in Crossna. When the cache arrived at 6.00 a.m. Tom went to the nearby bog and hid it. The house was raided at 9.00 a.m. The Volunteers had suspected that information was being passed to the police in Boyle and this surprise raid confirmed their suspicions. The raid on Keadue Barracks was called off.[7]

On Friday 11 March 1921, Seán Connolly had been wounded and five men shot dead when they were surprised by a patrol of the Bedfordshire Regiment from Carrick-on-Shannon, at Selton Hill, County Leitrim. Seán died from his wounds the following day. The five other men who lost their lives were Brigadier Seamus Wrynne, Commandant Joseph Beirne, Captain Michael E. Baxter, Captain John O'Reilly and John Joe O'Reilly.[8]

The Truce, when it came into effect in July 1921, did not improve the lot of the internees at the Curragh; they continued to be held in 'The Rath Camp'. When Tom wrote to his sister in August, he was thinking of possible pastimes and also keeping an eye on the more serious issues of the peace talks:

> Sometime that it would be convenient to the people at home, they ought to send me some money, as the nights are getting long now and we have a game of cards an odd time.
>
> As Bruen [Charlie, the local wit] said, the peace confidence is going on well! I suppose another month will see it one way or the other.
>
> All the boys from around there are in the best of form. Hoping you are all the same.
>
> I remain,
> Your fond Bro,
> Tom

The prospect of escape consumed much of the internees' time and energy. A few attempts were made over the summer months of 1921. The first escape took place towards the end of April. There were workmen engaged in completing the construction of the camp and they came in and out daily. Rory O'Connor and a man named Ryan walked calmly out one day at dinnertime dressed in workmen's overalls, which had been smuggled in by other workmen.[9]

Joe Galvin, Mount Talbot, County Roscommon, got the idea of digging a tunnel under the huts and the barbed wire fences and he discussed it with a few trusted prisoners. James Brady of Cavan had worked in the Arigna mines in County Roscommon, and with his experience of digging underground he became the chief strategist. Implements for digging were in scarce supply, but anything that could be used was picked up from workmen on the site. Spoons were hidden at meal times and they were used also. The workmen supplied another piece of essential equipment: a wire cutter. The huts were standing on concrete blocks about two feet off the ground. That gave the men room to dig and sufficient space under the huts to spread the soil that was removed from the tunnel. Things were progressing well until a letter that was being smuggled out by a visitor was found by the authorities. It contained a lot of detail about the plan that was afoot:

A Chara

There is a chance of a number of men escaping from here. There is a tunnel dug under the wires. There is double barbed wire round this camp at 13ft in height. The tunnel goes beyond that all right, but about 30 yards further out a fence has recently been erected. This is a simple wire fence as for a sheep pen, but barbed wire is now being passed about this. This only gives a short time to get out, as it is impossible to carry the tunnel that far out.

The arrangement is that at night a number of men will pass through the tunnel which will be opened into the field that the Rath is in (to the east of the camp). It is doubtful if this can be done without their being seen coming out of the earth by the sentries. But it is possible. After that the trouble will be to get away. As it will have to be at night, the motors are hardly feasible. Would it be possible to get a goods train going to Dublin? Or can you offer any other suggestions? At least those escaping should be told the direction to go in and the places to avoid. There is also the question as to who should go. Can you send a list of those you want to get out? You might send instructions as soon as possible. There will also be the question of money for the men who do get out; money is taken from us here.

The boys who are working on the tunnel say they have gone nearly as far as they can. They will have reached the limit in a few days.

You understand that the men will appear in the field where The Rath is. There is something there that looks like a dug out. They may have a guard there at night as well as the sentries in the boxes at the corner of the camp.

I think that if assistance cannot be got from the outside, it would be better for you to say that the whole thing should be called off. It will be necessary for the men not only to get out but also to get far away, as they have so many troops here that they could comb out any place nearby thoroughly, if they had an idea that the men were there.

Do Chara

D.F.[10]

The tunnel was discovered and the prisoners were punished. They were deprived of all privileges and rights and they responded by refusing prison food for nine days. Privileges were then restored. The British army dug a trench four foot deep and four foot wide on the inside of the boundary wire all around the camp in an attempt to prevent any further such attempts. However, the prisoners decided to make another escape attempt on 9 September 1921, and they proceeded to dig another tunnel this time under hut no 37.[11] (Other accounts say the number was 31). They dug a hole two feet square and four feet deep and then outwards and downwards. Eighteen days later their fellow prisoners watched from the hut while a piece of paper was pushed up from the tunnel. The exit had to be clear of searchlights. The paper showed that it came up too near the compound so they laboured for another day and decided to go that night. Time was of the essence; they knew that the intention was to fill the trench around the camp with water as an extra security measure.

At 11.30 p.m. Joe Galvin and Jim Brady slid into the tunnel and asked the others to give them about an hour to open the outer end and cut the wires surrounding the camp. The two men crawled to the outer end and opened the shaft to the surface. The light from the arc lamp shone straight into Joe Galvin's face. The men climbed out of the tunnel and moved towards the wire fence twenty yards or so away. They had only gone a few yards when the sentry on the elevated post shouted twice: 'Halt, who goes there?' They heard him load his rifle. They lay motionless and then they heard an officer, an NCO and six men doing their rounds. The sentry was distracted by them and probably thought it was their approach he had heard. The two men were in luck. They continued to the wire, cut a way through, crawled to the next fence and cut it. They knew the direction they wanted to follow was down towards the stand on the racecourse. A thick fog came down and it was difficult for them to see where they were going, but their sense of direction was good and eventually they found themselves on the Newbridge, County Kildare, road.[12]

About seventy prisoners followed through the 'Brady Tunnel' before it was discovered. Selected Dublin prisoners were the first group out; they were followed by the Roscommon prisoners and finally the Longford men. Todd Andrews was one of the Dublin group. He was seized by a fit of terror when he went inside the small passage. It was about three feet wide and two feet high. As he wriggled along his shoulders touched the sides. He was afraid the roof would collapse and he would be smothered. It took him about fifteen minutes to reach the end of the tunnel and his instinct was to get up and run but he resisted. He crawled on his belly out to the wire fence where his two companions Jack Knowthe and Myles Ford were waiting for him. They crawled towards the Curragh Racecourse and from there started on a long and hazardous journey to Dublin.[13]

Not all the men who intended to escape broke out. John Joe Gavagan from Westmeath was about to emerge from the tunnel when he heard a sentry shout, 'Halt there!' A shot was fired and the sentry shouted for the guard to come out but got no response. He then yelled out, 'If you don't come quick, there won't be a "Shinner" in the camp, they are going out like rabbits.' John Joe had to go back. At roll call next morning, those who were left behind answered

'Gone through the tunnel' when an escaped prisoner's name was called. A few days later, John Joe Gavagan and Joe Duffy did escape from the isolation hut at the camp. They had noticed that the hut was never searched so they hid in it until the early hours of the morning and then boldly went out the window of the hut and crept through the barbed wire to freedom.[14] No wonder a bard wrote:

> They smash my jails to scrap!
> They'll wipe them off the map, boys!
> There's no place I can keep them safe,
> In air or land or sea.
> The whole wide world is chaffing:
> Its sides a'shake with laughing.
> From pole to pole Sinn Féiners make
> An awful ass of me.[15]

Tom Moran was one of the Roscommon group that escaped. He told us about the thick fog that hampered his group. When they thought they were well clear of the camp they found themselves back at the wire. They turned and walked in the opposite direction but they knew they were lost. They knelt and prayed that they might find their way to safety. As they finished the rosary they heard rooks cawing in nearby trees; they knew that the only trees anywhere near the Curragh were behind the grandstand on the racecourse. Guided by the rooks they found their bearings and hurried away from the camp as quickly as they could. With only socks for footwear they found it hard to make haste and when they reached a group of houses they took a chance and knocked on a door. There they found a friendly family; they were fed and when they had eaten, they were taken across fields to Reverend Smith's house in Rathangan, County Kildare. They rested in this house during the daylight hours and when they set out again they had fresh clothes and shoes on.

Local Volunteers conveyed them by horse and trap to Weymes's Hotel in Carbury village, County Kildare. There the proprietor put his car at their disposal and told the driver to drive them as far as they wanted to go. They had to be careful not to fall foul of a police patrol; when they reached the strongly garrisoned town of Athlone, it was close to midnight so they decided that the car might arouse suspicion and they sent it back. Mick Murphy knew his way around Athlone and he got a lorry from Mr Fitzpatrick of Connaught Street to bring the twelve men to Kiltoom, where they dropped Mick Murphy and Dick Mee. Pat Tennant lived in Knockcroghery; when they reached his house the remaining nine rested while a messenger was sent to the South Roscommon IRA brigade staff. Pat Madden and Frank Simons arrived with two cars and drove the men on from there. Jim Farrell, Pat McNamara, Pat Beirne, Paddy Barry and Tom Moran were brought to Strokestown. Paddy Duffy of Elphin provided the last car to take these men to their homes.

The men had escaped in the early hours of Friday morning.[16] Tom Moran arrived in Crossna on Saturday night. He did not go straight to his home but went into Crossna Hibernian Hall where he met his youngest brother, Joe. He sent Joe home ahead of him to announce his arrival to his parents in case his sudden appearance would give them a shock. The joyful homecoming was tinged with sadness for all of them. Tom had not seen his parents since his brother's execution six months previously. He found them in good shape as we see from his letter to his sister Mary (Cissie):

Crossna,
Boyle.

Dear Cissie,
I had a letter written to you on Thursday last ready to post it on Friday morning if our plans did not work to our satisfaction. But as Maggie has

already told you, they did work and I am back again in dear old Crossna. I could not believe until I saw them that my Father and Mother could be so good. Thank God it is nothing short of being a miracle.

We left the camp at about 2.30 a.m. on Friday and arrived home on Sat. night about 9 p.m. J. Doyle did not come yet but he was ready to leave when I was leaving and I cannot believe but he came out. It may have taken him longer than it took us to find the right road.

When Barry and myself came to the hall on Saturday night there were a few of the youngsters in it, our Joe among them. We walked in and stood in the centre of the floor, and for about five minutes they could not speak a word, you would think it was two ghosts that appeared to them. When they came to they gave us a hearty welcome and we had to answer some hard questions from Freddie [Doyle] and the rest of them.

I sent Joe down then to have the news broken gently to them at home. I was afraid that a delightful surprise might give them as big a shock as anything else. I did not believe they were so strong. They are certainly proving themselves worthy of the son they reared.

Tiernan [the postman] is just after passing. He had your letter for Joe. He also had one for the Doyle's with John's handwriting from the Curragh so it seems he did not try the tunnel.

Aunt Anne and Baby were here until today. They left this morning in great form. So I had an opportunity of thanking her for all the parcels she sent me. The Leigh family sent me a parcel some time ago. In the letter that went to Mary Kate in America I had asked you to thank them.

I had a very nice letter about a month ago from Miss Kelly, B's friend. When you see her again say hello for me to her.

There came a memory card here from the Gurteen boys to be sent to you. I am enclosing it. The composer of the verses deserves to be congratulated.

Write soon as I may be going into another camp next week.

I remain,

Your fond Bro,

T. Moran[17]

Tom continued his work with the IRA, serving at Sinn Féin courts and at a training camp in Kilronan, near his home. When the Treaty was signed he took the anti-Treaty side and during the Civil War he was with C Company, 4th Battalion, 2nd Sligo Brigade. He fought with the anti-Treaty forces in Ramsey's Hotel in Sligo against Free State troops on 16 April 1922. He was also involved in blocking roads and blowing up bridges in the Crossna, Woodbrook and Knockvicar areas.[18]

Two of his brothers, Jim and Joe, were also active in the IRA during the Civil War. They both joined the anti-Treaty Arigna flying column. Joe was arrested at his digs in Ballaghadereen, County Roscommon, on 8 September 1922. No charge was made against him or the others who were taken prisoner with him; instead they were offered forms to sign declaring allegiance to the Free State government. Joe didn't sign and he was taken to Boyle Military Barracks and moved from there to Athlone Detention Centre two days later. He was held there in the gymnasium where there were 150 other prisoners.[19] He wrote to his sister Cissie on 18 December 1922 and told her that Paddy Doyle and himself had come to the conclusion that there was no chance of them being home for Christmas. But Joe arrived home unexpectedly as the family were about to sit down to their Christmas Eve supper. He had a particular way of opening the front door and when his sister Annie heard it opening she said, 'That sounds like Joe'; he had escaped from Athlone by scaling a wall when the guard had his back turned.

Jim Moran was arrested on 1 February 1923, the day after the barracks in Ballinamore, County Leitrim, was attacked. The Arigna flying column, of which he and his brother Joe were members, attacked the barracks in the early morning and called on the occupants to surrender. There were no casualties on either side, but the attackers captured a Lewis gun, twenty-four rifles and 400 rounds of ammunition. The occupying forces were taken prisoner, brought by train to Drumshanbo and released. The following day Captain Moore and a cycling column from Boyle captured Jim Moran and four others, Frank Barlow from Keadue, John Doyle from Dereenaseer, Crossna, Thomas Treacy from Cootehall and Patrick McGearty from Arigna.[20]

Jim was taken to Boyle Military Barracks and was removed from there to Athlone Detention Centre on Monday, 3 February 1923. He wrote to his sister in England and told her that he and John Doyle were arrested while taking charge of two prisoners at Kilmactranny, County Sligo; 'So', he said, 'that's what we got for keeping law and order in that part of the country'.[21] He was in fact found in possession of a gun, an offence that carried the death penalty. Andy Lavin, a Sinn Féin TD for Roscommon, went to the Minister for Defence, Richard Mulcahy, to plead for him. He was told that the case would have to be dealt with by the army council. Lavin then went to the army council and made a case for him, saying that Jim's brother, Paddy, had already paid the ultimate price at the hands of the British and the last thing that was needed now was another Moran martyr. It is interesting that Lavin chose to plead for Jim as he had been arrested shortly before Jim's incarceration for taking the pro-Treaty side. He was brought to Keadue by the Moran brothers, Tom and Jim, but was immediately released by Jimmy Cull of the anti-Treaty Arigna flying column.[22]

On 8 August 1923, Richard Mulcahy, Minister For Defence, signed an order under the Public Safety (Emergency Powers) Act, 1923, detaining Jim Moran in military custody; he was sentenced to five years penal servitude.[23]

The Civil War began in June 1922 and ended in April 1923. The prisoners were not released immediately on its cessation for fear of reopening hostilities and in case links would be established between disaffected Free State soldiers, republican units and neutral IRA members. It was decided to release the prisoners in stages, according to the danger they were considered to represent.[24]

Jim Moran was moved to B wing in Mountjoy Jail and was there when Michael Kilroy, the officer commanding the prisoners, announced a hunger strike in protest against the treatment of the prisoners, the conditions in the prison and their continued incarceration. The strike started in Mountjoy on 13 October 1923 and ended on 23 November 1923. Prisoners in other camps joined the strike and at one stage more than 7,000 prisoners were on hunger strike, 462 of them in Mountjoy.[25] Among them were Austin Stack, Seán Buckley, Gerard Boland, Daniel Corkery, Charles Murphy, Ernie O'Malley, Barney Mellows, Paddy McGarville, Michael Kilroy, Peadar O'Donnell, Jim Moran and Seán Milroy.[26] The Free State government announced that from 26 October, no prisoner taking part in the strike would be released.[27] The prisoners in some prisons were refused absolution by the jail chaplains and a telegram was sent to the Pope from Sinn Féin headquarters in Cork, appealing to his holiness for speedy justice for prisoners who were very weak and asking for the sacraments.[28]

The prospect of being set free was attractive and many prisoners came off the hunger strike; some signed the pledge to be loyal to the government and were released, others began taking food and the number on hunger strike was considerably reduced. The government refused to give concessions to the prisoners. Two hunger strikers died: Commandant Denis Barry from Cork in Newbridge on 20 November, and Captain Andrew Sullivan, Mallow, County Cork, in Mountjoy on 22 November 1923. The IRA leaders within the prisons decided that a further sacrifice of lives could not be justified and called off the hunger strike.[29] Jim Moran participated in the strike to the end. Like many prisoners at the time he kept an autograph book and there is an entry from a fellow occupant of 'D' wing in that book that indicates that he was on hunger strike for thirty-nine days:

14 Oct–22 Nov.

The foreign and domestic enemies of the Republic have for the moment prevailed – But our enemies have not won! Neither tortures nor firing squads nor a slavish press, can crush the desire for freedom out of the hearts of those who fought for the Republic, or out of the hearts of our people.[30]

Jim wrote to his sister Annie on 29 November 1923, from Cell 4, D Wing, Mountjoy Jail, a few days after the ending of the strike:

Dear Annie,

Just a few lines to say I am doing fine T. God. I got your letter on Tuesday and I needn't tell you how delighted I was to know how well everybody is. It was the only thing that gave me any little trouble during the strike. I knew perfectly well they would be prepared for the worst news and that they would rather see me standing the test than to hoist the white flag – which I hadn't the least notion of doing. The fight was not an easy one, but it was made harder by false comrades than by anything our captors could do. A less brutal government than the present could not give us a win. We have far too many singing 'Kevin Barry' but when they are up against it, it's a different matter. Up to the present we have been getting cream crackers and milk with an odd cup of Bovril. We got tea and brown bread today for the first time. I will not shower praise on you, I know you don't want it, but I must say I was very fortunate to have you here. I got your parcel of underclothing (minus the pair of socks), Bovril, biscuits, etc. Saturday evening, tea, sugar etc. on Monday, pipe, cigs etc. yesterday. There are some complaints about things being missing but as long as you put the list in it's fairly safe. I hope you got my letter all right. I am sending this through a chap from 'Farrell's town'. I cannot say what I want in the line of food, you should know yourself. Send a stick of shaving soap and shaving brush, toilet soap, brilliantine and a towel. When writing mention the other letter but not this, just ask me how I liked the pipe, then

I'll know if you get this. Send me some stamps and I'll write to Ciss and home and Lena. There were no stamps here when yours came so I had to lend. We are feeling quite happy here now, although I'd welcome release, I'm not worrying about it so long as all is well.

Your affectionate brother,

Jim

P.S. Butter is the only thing I'm badly off for!

Jim was moved from Mountjoy to Hut 18, C Line, Hare Park, the Curragh, on Thursday, 3 January 1924. The conditions there were grim; the men were housed in huts that were draughty and overcrowded. Sanitation consisted of four open latrines with buckets and while these were emptied each day, they were seldom disinfected. The daily food ration was sixteen ounces of bread, twelve ounces of meat, a half pint of milk, two ounces of butter, half an ounce of tea, two and a half ounces of sugar, eight ounces of fresh vegetables and twelve ounces of potatoes. The men got a few very small, thin blankets and a thin mattress to lie on, and they were often cold at night. There were twenty-seven patients in the camp hospital where conditions were even worse. Rain poured in on one side of the hut so the beds had to be arranged on the other side.[31]

The Free State government released the prisoners gradually after the hunger strike and, by the summer of 1924, all except those with criminal convictions were set free. Judges Doyle and Dromgoola considered the cases of all political prisoners still held on 29 May 1924 and recommended that the remainder of their sentences be remitted and the prisoners be released. The director of intelligence of the army said that he had no military objection to their release as there was no possibility of civil charges being brought against them. Jim Moran was released on 6 June 1924.[32]

Tom, Joe and Jim Moran were very strong characters, hard-working, upright and faithful men, all very gentle in nature, very good-humoured and they commanded great respect in Crossna. All were advocates of democratic politics in later life.

Tom lived on the small family farm. He took it over when his father died in 1928 and he took care of his mother until she died in 1941. He was married to Agnes Killoran, Ballindoon, Boyle, just a few days before his mother died. The land he farmed was bad and it was a struggle for him subsequently to keep his wife and seven children. He applied for an Old IRA pension in 1935 but was denied it for years. I still remember the upset that this denial caused him. He asked for a reinvestigation of his case in 1953 on the grounds that he was in a position to prove facts sufficient to establish that he was a person to whom the pension act applied. The statement outlined the facts regarding the parcel of arms sent by Seán Connolly, the raid on the house in Crossna and the conviction that the raid was a 'direct result of spying … I could quote incidents by the dozen where we were fooled by the people we looked up to in the IRA and I was arrested through the same spy system.' Finally, in July 1955, he was awarded his pension of £25 per annum.

Tom and my uncle Jim were both awarded War of Independence service medals in 1958. Jim Moran didn't apply for a pension. Joe Moran was refused an Old IRA pension and he did not apply for a service medal. Paddy Moran was posthumously awarded that medal and a 1916 medal. Both his medals are now held in Kilmainham Gaol Museum.

Tom was described as an 'unassuming man of a quiet disposition' when he died in 1969.[33] He was eighty years old.

Joe emigrated to England and trained as an electrician. He was called up by the British army in the Second World War and was stationed on the Isle of Wight. He remained single and returned to live in Crossna in the early sixties. He died in September 1972, aged sixty-nine.

Jim became a commercial traveller and worked for Denny's

Bacon products. He was interested in greyhounds and was the owner of a dog called Yorick which won a race in Shelbourne Park, Dublin. Jim was described as 'the well-known and popular commercial traveller' in the newspaper report of the victory.[34] He retired to live in Crossna with his three sisters in 1957 and died in 1984 at the age of ninety-one. The long hunger strike he endured had obviously done him no lasting damage.

Bea Farrell, Paddy's girlfriend, was active in the Civil War too. She was arrested on 7 November 1922, by Free State troops at a house in Grove Avenue, Blackrock, and taken to the naval base in Dun Laoghaire. She escaped from there on Christmas Day, 1922. While there, she was questioned by Captain Kane, an intelligence officer with the Free State. She alleged in a briefing note sent to the director of intelligence, IRA, 2nd Dublin Brigade, that it was Miss Róisín O'Flanagan who gave information about her to Captain Kane. She blamed Róisín for telling the captain that the Farrells had a Thompson gun, for passing on dispatches meant for officers of the brigade, for giving him information about trouble the brigade was having with the Irish Republican Prisoners' Dependants Funds and for relaying to him the happenings at brigade meetings. She warned that Róisín knew the haunts of some of the men on the run and that she might give them away to be murdered at the hands of the enemy. She finished by asking that some action be taken against Róisín, describing her as 'a wrong one'.[35]

Róisín O'Flanagan wrote a letter to the secretary, Cumann na mBan, in December 1922, pleading for immediate action against a malicious rumour that she was a spy. She added a postscript: 'The hard part of this business is that I know there has been no misapprehension whatever, and that it has been set afoot from purely personal evil motives.'

Bea Farrell wrote to the quartermaster, Dublin 2 Brigade, in February 1923, asking for information on another individual who was considered suspicious. He was calling on members of the

South Dublin Company of the IRA and was planning to shoot three spies in Blackrock. She mentioned that this individual said that all communications from GHQ came to the Technical School in Blackrock, the address of the O'Flanagan family.[36] Róisín was a sister of Margaret (Peg) O'Flanagan, the lady who organised the alibi evidence for Paddy Moran. Because of this or for some other reason it seems that there was a certain vindictiveness against the O'Flanagan family on the part of Bea Farrell.

Margaret O'Flanagan had joined Cumann na mBan in 1918. She collected and distributed the Irish Republican Prisoners' Dependants Fund, she helped to raise funds for elections, canvassed, distributed leaflets and helped to sell Dáil Bonds. During the War of Independence she arranged safe custody of arms and delivered them to Volunteers as required. She had to renounce her membership of Cumann na mBan for three months to give evidence for Paddy Moran. She took the anti-Treaty side in the Civil War and was arrested and held in Kilmainham Gaol in February 1923, for having in her possession a document detailing the movement of Free State troops.[37]

The Moran brothers sided with de Valera when he formed Fianna Fáil in 1927, but Bea Farrell, remained a sympathetic member of the IRA. One day, while I was waiting for a file to be brought to me in the Military Archives at Cathal Brugha Barracks, I picked up a book called *Spies in Ireland* by Enno Stephan. Opening it at random on p. 144, I saw a picture of Bea and Mary Farrell with a German, Dieter Gaertner. I verified with the archives staff that the ladies in the picture were the Farrell sisters from 7 Spencer Villas, Glenageary, County Dublin. I knew Miss Farrell's address because when Bea died in 1966 her sister sent Paddy's sister, Annie, a box which contained Paddy's scarf, the collar with the message that he sent out from Kilmainham Gaol, a locket that Paddy gave Bea dated 14 March 1921, and a few other artefacts belonging to him. Stephan described the Farrell sisters as 'angry old ladies' who felt that Ireland's fight for freedom did not end with the Treaty or with the lost Civil War; they regarded themselves 'as guardians of an historical inheritance'.

During the Second World War, the Farrells provided assistance to the new IRA and to the man who was sent from Germany to collaborate with that organisation.[38] The IRA began a bombing campaign in England in January 1939 and the Germans were anxious to establish links with them as possible allies against the British. The Germans sent a number of agents to Ireland to establish contact with the IRA in order to further Germany's war aims. The agent who operated in Ireland for the longest period was Hermann Goertz. While incarcerated in Parkhurst Prison in England for spying, Goertz came in contact with members of the IRA who were serving sentences for their part in the bombing campaign in England. On his release in 1939 Goertz returned to Germany, but was quickly sent to Ireland as an intelligence officer. His presence was discovered by the Irish government, who were taking a strictly neutral stance in the war, when the house of Stephen Held where he had been staying was raided. Goertz escaped over the garden wall but he left behind a typewriter, a file with information about Irish harbours, a wireless, money, German war medals, and a black tie with 'Berlin' inscribed on it. Goertz spent the next nineteen months sheltered and protected by a number of elderly ladies who could be best described as die-hard republicans. Among these were the Farrell sisters, Mary and Bea.

Goertz was finally arrested in November 1941, spent some time in Mountjoy and was transferred to Athlone Internment Camp, where he stayed until Germany's surrender in May 1945. After the war ended, he again went to stay with the Farrell sisters, but when informed he was to be deported he took his own life. Mary and Bea Farrell attended his funeral in Deansgrange Cemetery, Dublin.[39]

Bea Farrell lived with her sister Mary, next door to Seán MacBride. Her neighbours, Paddy (now deceased) and Rose

Richardson, gave an account of the Farrells when I visited them. Bea dressed very well and was quite class conscious and she worked for Stokes Kennedy Crowley until her death in 1966. In contrast, her sister Mary was a chain smoker and was not very clothes or class conscious. Mary often hopped across the wall between the two back gardens to visit the Richardsons. She was clearly the less formal and more popular of the two! Bea had a gun which she kept hidden underneath the seat of a dining-room chair. The house was raided on several occasions by the Gardaí but the gun was never found.[40]

Two of Paddy Moran's sisters wrote to Bea Farrell after their brother's execution. Annie, having sympathised with her, referred to the fact that she only knew her for a few months but that she was the strongest earthly tie she had with Paddy. She looked forward to seeing her often. Bridget Moran thanked her for taking Paddy's place at the pier when his two sisters were returning to England. She regretted that Bea would not be a dear relation but hoped that their affection would be none the less sincere and lasting. However, the friendship does not seem to have endured. When Bea Farrell died in 1966, Mary returned the articles that Bea had belonging to Paddy Moran, to his sister, Annie Moran. It was a generous gesture on her part.

Chapter 11

Sympathy and Remembrance

It is often said that Paddy Moran and his comrades were forgotten very soon after they made the supreme sacrifice. It is true that these men never became household names in the way that Kevin Barry did, but there were various commemorations in memory of Paddy Moran in Crossna and in Dublin over the years. His brothers and sisters kept his memory alive in their devotion to organising an anniversary mass for him annually. His anniversary notice stood side by side with that of Thomas Whelan in the *Irish Press* until that paper went out of business in 1995.

Following his death, letters of sympathy came not only from relatives and friends of the family but also from various trade unions, and from some of those he had encountered in the Volunteers. The Irish National Union of Vintners', Grocers' and Allied Trades Assistants, passed a resolution at a special committee meeting that was held on Sunday 20 March, expressing 'unutterable sympathy with the family in the terrible bereavement which they have sustained through his brutal but glorious death. A high-souled Christian, a true patriot, a loving comrade whose life was devoted towards doing good for his fellow workers and his country, he has gone to reap a noble reward.' Mr Hughes, the General Secretary, conveyed the resolution in a letter to Paddy's father. He also attached copies of letters of sympathy he had received from John P. Candon, the

Clerk of the Dublin Union, a resolution passed by the Rathdown Board of Guardians, a letter from the Liverpool Branch of the Shop Assistants' Union and a letter from John Turner, General Secretary of the Shop Assistants' Union in London:

It is impossible for me to attempt to convey in ordinary language, the feelings of horror and detestation that these executions have raised in the hearts and minds of the workers on this side. May I however say that the same government which is meeting, with such brutality, the resistance of the Irish people to their authority, is the same body which is betraying every promise made to the workers on this side during the war. It is also meting out terms of imprisonment to any workers who dare speak too freely, whether it is on behalf of their unemployed fellows, or the hopes expressed for a better social order. The fact that Patrick Moran was of the same class as our members undoubtedly appealed strongly to the national executive committee, though I know that a similar miscarriage of justice in connection with anyone would have aroused feelings of sympathy.

It is probably because the big mass of the workplace here are treated from a 'class' point of view, that makes the political Labour Party the only one which sincerely and honestly desires a just settlement of the Irish question. When men can die as bravely as those six did last Monday, for any cause, it means it is bound to succeed eventually. Even papers politically opposed to the Irish cause, had to pay homage to their courage.

I can only hope that these terrible sacrifices on the part of brave young men will hasten the day of understanding, and that the workers of both countries will, perhaps through the International Labour Movement, yet join together against those who oppressed them so far.

I feel my letter very inadequately conveys all that is felt by my executive and myself on this question, and can only regret that the little efforts we made were of no avail.

With every good wish, mingled with feelings of shame at what has occurred.

Believe me,

Fraternally Yours,

John Turner

General Secretary[1]

The first annual delegate meeting of the union after Paddy's execution was held on 30 November 1921. Vice-President Joseph Garry said it was his 'painful duty to refer to a tragic event since their last meeting which caused great sorrow to every member of the Union, namely the death of their late president, Patrick Moran. It was not necessary for him to remind the delegates of all that Patrick Moran had done for the Labour movement in general and his own union in particular, sufficient to say that their late president was equally true to his Labour principles as he was to the great principles for which he had laid down his life. While they all deeply mourned his loss they felt proud that such a man had been a member of their union, and his memory would serve as a noble example to his comrades for the furtherance of their cause.'[2]

The union honoured Paddy by placing a portrait of him in Banba Hall, Parnell Square, Dublin, once headquarters of the union and now the Hugh Lane Gallery. That portrait of Paddy remained in Banba Hall until the location of the head office of the union changed to Cavendish Row, Dublin. The portrait was presented to the Moran family by the president of the union, Mary Larkin, at a commemorative mass in Crossna church in 2002, and John Douglas said that it was 'as a small token of the appreciation of the union and of the Labour movement for the work of Patrick Moran'.[3] The inscription on the portrait reads: 'Presented to the Moran family in memory of Captain Patrick Moran, D Company, 2nd Battalion, Dublin Brigade IRA and President of INUVG&ATA (now Mandate Trade Union). Executed 14th March 1921, Mountjoy Prison'.

A plaque on the wall of Banba Hall still commemorates the Grocers' Assistants who died in the period 1916–1923. Capt. P. Moran's name heads the list and is followed by that of Lieutenant Martin Savage. Martin Savage was killed at Ashtown in December 1919, when an attempt was made to kill Lord French, Lord Lieutenant and Governor General of Ireland, as he returned from his country home at Drumdoe, near Ballinafad, County Sligo. The attempt failed but Martin Savage was shot dead. Paddy Moran was his company captain. Henry Kelly is remembered on that plaque too; he was killed in Banba Hall in November 1920 when crown forces raided it just after Bloody Sunday. He worked in Grogan's grocery at North Wall Dublin.[4]

The Sisters of Charity, Gardiner Street, Dublin, who had visited the prisoners, were among those who wrote to Paddy's mother and to his girlfriend, Bea Farrell. Sister Patricia told Bea that Paddy was very fond of her and felt the parting hard. She told his mother that the boys were always bright and cheerful when the sisters visited and although the nuns sometimes went in weeping they always came out laughing. Fr Dominic O'Connor, the Franciscan Capuchin Friar from Church Street, who had been Paddy's 'next door neighbour' in Kilmainham Gaol was in Parkhurst Prison, England at the time of the execution. He wrote to Paddy's parents following his release from Parkhurst:

> I learned to love him and admire him and have happy memories of his bright and cheery companionship. There is no necessity for me to tell you he was perfectly innocent of the charge made against him. That is a fact. He knew that someone's life would be sworn away in revenge, and he used to say to me, 'Well, Father, it is all the same what way we die if it is for the Republic and after all we might be better prepared this way than if we went down in an attack.'

Later in that letter he said, 'And he had after all a great comfort in dying to see the flag he raised or helped to raise in Easter week, 1916, still flying over brave fighting men, when he went to join Seán Mac Diarmada and his companions in Heaven. He enclosed a few lines that he wrote in Parkhurst Prison on the day he heard of the execution:

In loving memory of my fellow prisoners in Kilmainham Gaol, Capt. P. Moran (my mass server) and T. Whelan of the Army of the Republic.

> Come for them, ye Saints of God;
> Haste, Angels of the Lord,
> To welcome these Martyrs for our Land.
>
> Receive each noble soul;
> Proclaim from Pole to Pole
> Its Christlike Sacrifice of Love.
>
> At God's Eternal Throne
> With palm and victor's crown
> Surround them in Christ's bright martyr throng.

Fr Dominic
Parkhurst Convict Prison
16/3/21[5]

Fr Michael O'Flanagan wrote to Paddy's sister in October 1921. He had called to see Paddy's father and mother on the previous Monday and he told her:

I was very glad to see how well they understood and felt the splendid spirit of our time. Why should they mourn one who is more alive than the living? Life is but a fleeting breath, and nothing counts except to spend and end it nobly, which your brother did beyond all his associates. I did not go to sympathise with them, but rather to venerate the parents of one of Ireland's best. Yes, please God, the fruit of his sacrifice will come before long.[6]

Visitors to Crossna church still see 'Pray for Patrick Moran' on both confessional boxes and on two of the statues in the side aisles. The candelabrum is also dedicated to him. These dedications were probably the result of a meeting held in September 1921 in Crossna Hibernian Hall for the purpose of erecting a memorial to him. That meeting elected a committee under the chairmanship of Fr Clyne, CC, Crossna, with Patrick Regan, Derreenadoey, Ballyfarnon, the vice-chairman, James McLoughlin, Cleragh, and Edward Doyle, Derreenaseer, Crossna, the treasurers, and eleven other committee members.[7]

Seán Ó Riagáin honoured him in verse when he addressed these lines:

To his heroic parents on the morning of March 14, 1921:

Mother weep not for thy son,
Father proudly hold thy head,
The good fight, he has fought and won,
He is dead; aye nobly dead.
Dead for Éireann! happy death.
True to her and ye and God.
Dead for Éireann! happy fate,
Gently sleeps he 'neath the sod.

What matter if in death he rests,
Where Saxon troopers strut above,
His resting place his Country's breast
Well has he won his nation's love.
He feared not death, 'tis slaves that fear,
He faced their noose with smiling eye,

'Mother, still thy sobs and hear
This is the way a MAN can die.'

Ireland's manhood, do not dare,
Crossna's buachaills be ye proud;
Ireland's maidens breathe a prayer,
Crossna's cailíns weave a shroud.
Mothers tell your babes his name,
How he died – but did no wrong.
How Britain's hanged him – to her shame,
How Éireann holds him dear in song.

Pilate and Herod had but their day,
The rabble won on Calvary's crest,
Judas the traitor went his way,
And Mary the Mother knew no rest.
But He that died lives on today,
The rabble are forgotten – gone.
And he that died but yesterday,
In Éireann's heart shall live as long.[8]

In Dun Laoghaire, County Dublin, where Paddy worked, a proposal to change the name of Lower George's Street, Dun Laoghaire, to 'Moran Street' was put to a plebiscite issued by the Kingstown Urban Council soon after the execution. It failed on the first attempt. Some ratepayers marked the neutral box, effectively saying 'no' to the proposal. It was decided that a new plebiscite would be taken and just two options given – 'Yes' or 'No'.[9] Whether or not the second plebiscite was carried is not clear but Bea Farrell, Paddy's girlfriend, had in her possession a medal marked 16 Moran Street, Dun Laoghaire. Her address was 16 George's Street at that time. It is possible that in her fervour she decided to call the street Moran Street, without the name actually having changed.

Fr Tommy Moran blessing Moran Park in 1961.

In 1961 Dun Laoghaire did honour him when the Harbour House and grounds were renamed Moran Park. The house was built in the 1840s for Captain William Hutchison, the first harbour master of Dun Laoghaire. In July 1898, Guglielmo Marconi used Harbour House as the base for an experimental outside radio broadcast. It was also the headquarters for the local branch of the Red Cross during the Second World War. Dun Laoghaire Corporation acquired the house in 1954 with the intention of using it for the benefit of the citizens. Since 1961, when it became Moran Park House, it has had a variety of uses. It was a tea room, it housed the county council's housing department temporarily and, since 1989, it has been home to the Dun Laoghaire Rathdown Heritage Centre.[10] Fr Tommy Moran, Paddy's nephew, blessed Moran Park at the official opening in 1961. The late President Éamon de Valera unveiled two plaques to Paddy Moran in Moran Park in 1966, in Irish and English, saying:

Moran Park is named in honour of the patriot Patrick Moran of Dun Laoghaire and Roscommon: Captain D Company, Second Battalion,

Dublin Brigade, Irish Republican Army. Executed in Mountjoy Prison, 14th March 1921. R.I.P.

The invitation to attend the unveiling ceremony, on 5 June 1966, was sent to the Moran family by the Patrick Moran Memorial Committee. The chairman was Vincent Byrne, vice-chairman Charles Harkin, the honorary treasurers were Michael Fitzpatrick and Senator D. Ó Conalláin, and the honorary secretaries were Eoin O'Keeffe and Mark Hyland. The address for the committee was 21 Shaw Street, Dublin 2. The chairman of Dun Laoghaire Corporation, Norman Judd, said at the ceremony that Paddy Moran was one of those who died that the country might be free to pursue its own destiny in its own way. President de Valera said that Paddy Moran was one of the men who, in life and in death, had shown that Easter week was not enough.[11] Following the dedication ceremony the relatives met President de Valera and having shaken hands with a large number of them he remarked, 'I'm glad to see the clan is going from strength to strength.'

Paddy had spent a few short weeks in Blackrock before his arrest and execution. The second seat on the left aisle in the Roman Catholic church of St John the Baptist in Blackrock is dedicated to him. The inscription is in artistic Gaelic lettering in Irish: 'I gCuimhne Phádraig Uí Mhóráin, a crochadh 14/3/1921.' (In memory of Patrick Moran who was hanged on 14/3/1921.)

On 15 September 1963, a memorial to honour the forty Roscommon men who lost their lives in the fight for freedom in 1920–1923 was unveiled at Shankill, near Elphin, by IRA veteran Commandant General Tom Maguire. Paddy Moran is named on that memorial.

Paddy's association with the GAA was rewarded with dedications to his memory too. The football club that he founded in 1918 changed its name from Dunleary Commercials to Patrick Morans after his death. The club fielded junior football and junior hurling teams and were runners up in the Junior Hurling League in 1929. The club amalgamated with the Foxrock Geraldines in the early 1970s and became Geraldine Morans. It still exists today. The Geraldines were associated with the National Foresters, a charitable organisation that was the forerunner of St Vincent de Paul.[12]

A club named after Paddy was also formed in Belfast in 1922. At the time there were clubs named after Parnell, Kevin Barry, O'Donovan Rossa, Davitt, O'Rahilly, Emmet, O'Connell and other well-known Irishmen. However, it is likely that this club was named after Paddy Moran because his brother Jim was a barman in Belfast for many years. Its members were mostly from the bar and grocery trade. The Belfast Patrick Morans fielded football, hurling and camogie teams and competed at junior, intermediate and senior levels in football and hurling over the years. They progressed through the junior football ranks and were runners-up in the senior championship in 1926. William Ludlow of Ballymena and Patsy McGuckian of Dunloy made their senior debut for Morans. Both went on to play on the Antrim county team and McGuckian played for Ulster. Morans played in the final of the South Antrim Senior Football Championship on Sunday 29 May 1927 against O'Donovan Rossa's. They lost by three points. This was the highest point of the club's fortunes on the field of play. South Antrim was effectively Belfast; its winners played the North Antrim winners in the county final proper. When Fermanagh won the All-Ireland Junior Football Championship in 1959, John Maguire started at No. 8 and Hugh Murphy was a substitute; both were Morans' players.[13]

The Moran club organised Irish language classes in the Banba Hall, 38 King Street, Belfast, in 1934. The following year, P. McFadden, the chairman of the County Antrim GAA spoke at a meeting of the club about Gaelic pastimes. At the same meeting, Hugh S. Downey gave a lecture on the life and ideals of Patrick

Moran. Sadly the report of the meeting in the *Belfast Morning News* does not give any of the text of that lecture. The club was described as a progressive club in a report of its Annual General Meeting held in early 1942 and it continued to exist until the 1960s.[14]

In Paddy Moran's native area of Crossna, St Michael's and St Ronan's joined together to form a senior team named after him in 1956 and 1957. The team was drawn against Elphin in both years and lost to them in the Abbey Park, Boyle, in 1956 and in Carrick-on-Shannon in 1957. The late Fr Tommy Moran played on that team and scored a magnificent goal in the second match. Although there was great rivalry between those two adjoining clubs, the players jelled well and made a fine team.[15]

Paddy Moran's burial place was not in a cemetery where it could be easily visited; it was in the grounds of Mountjoy Jail, alongside nine others, the five men executed with him, as well as Kevin Barry, Thomas Traynor, Edmond Foley and Patrick Maher. The first memorial gravestone was erected in Mountjoy Jail in November 1934 and was unveiled by Seán Fitzpatrick of the National Graves Association at a ceremony attended by the men's relatives, among them three of Paddy's sisters, Annie, Lena and Cissie, his cousins from South Circular Road, Mr and Mrs Dunne, Mr and Mrs Aughney, and his girlfriend's sister, Mary Farrell. Mrs Traynor, mother of Thomas Traynor is photographed in the press on that occasion, placing a wreath on her son's grave.[16] Paddy Moran's mother wrote to the treasurer of the National Graves Association in January 1935 and she sent a subscription of one guinea towards the funds and expressed heartfelt gratitude for the work of the association. She enclosed a further subscription of ten shillings from a cousin of Paddy's, Miss K. Mattimoe of Derrynarry, Kilmactranny, Boyle.[17]

The memorial stone erected in 1934 was replaced in 1961 by four granite slabs and a twelve-foot High Cross. That was sponsored by the Irish government and was unveiled by President de Valera. The four slabs represented the four days of executions in Mountjoy Jail. One was placed on Kevin Barry's grave, a second slab on the graves of the six men executed on 14 March 1921, a third slab on the graves of Edmond Foley and Patrick Maher, and the fourth slab on the grave of Thomas Traynor. This enduring and very beautiful memorial was preserved when the bodies of the ten men buried there were exhumed in 2001, and it now covers their graves in Glasnevin cemetery.

Paddy's comrades in the IRA also remembered him. Members of the 2nd Battalion, D Company, Dublin Brigade went annually to pay homage at Paddy's grave in Mountjoy Jail. Mass was celebrated in St Joseph's church, Berkeley Road, for all the deceased members of D Company. A march to Mountjoy followed and a wreath was laid, a decade of the rosary was recited in Irish and the Last Post was sounded. A report from one of those ceremonies says there was almost a full attendance of old 2nd Battalion members including Oscar Traynor, then Minister for Posts and Telegraphs, Senator Matt Stafford, Frank Henderson, Leo Henderson, James Foley, Jim Kirwan, Seán Farrelly and Paddy McGrath.[18] Another report describes a march to his grave in Mountjoy Jail by members of the 2nd Battalion and members of the Paddy Moran Fianna Fáil Cumainn (Dun Laoghaire and North City).[19]

The fiftieth anniversary of his death in 1971 was celebrated in Crossna. The church was full for the commemoration mass, which was celebrated by four priests. Fr Tommy Moran was the chief celebrant; Fr T. Conroy, Fr Raymond Browne and Fr Peadar Lavin were the other concelebrants. Speaking at that mass, Fr Tommy Moran said, 'If there is a lesson to be drawn from the lives and activities of my uncle and those who shared his ideals it is surely this. They showed a selflessness and a spirit of dedication in working for the good of others and for the good of their country which we of this generation might well imitate.'[20]

The Roscommon Association in Dublin organised a ceremony

in 1991 to remember the seventieth anniversary of his death. The current generation of the Moran family attended a mass celebrated by his nephew, Fr Tommy Moran in Berkeley Road church and then went to the grave in Mountjoy. Rita Dorr, then president of the Roscommon Association, laid a wreath and in keeping with tradition a decade of the rosary was said in Irish and the Last Post was sounded. Tom Maye, a native of Croghan, Boyle, hosted a reception afterwards for all those present at Mayes Tavern, Dorset Street, Dublin.

The Roscommon Men's Association sponsored the restoration of Paddy Moran's cell in Kilmainham Gaol in 1962.[21] Paddy's sister, Bridget, responded to an appeal for donations of artefacts to Kilmainham Gaol in 1971 and presented Paddy's copy of a letter written by fellow prisoners at the time of the execution of the six men. It was signed by Arthur Griffith, Eoin Mac Néill, M.J. Staines and E. Duggan:

> Your fellow prisoners, like all the men and women of Ireland, are thinking of you always, and especially in their prayers. All recognise that the death to which you are doomed by the tyrant and oppressor of our nation is an honour to you and we know that you are going to that death in the spirit of the best and bravest of your race.
>
> The sacrifice you have made will pledge the men and women of Ireland to be faithful as you have been even unto death in the cause for which your lives are given.
>
> Go neartaigh Dia sibhse agus sinne agus go dtuga Sé saoirseacht agus sonas d'Éireann. Céad moladh agus glóire dá thoil ró naofa.[22] [May God strengthen you and us and may He give freedom and happiness to Ireland. Praise and Glory to God and Blessed be His Holy Will.]

The tour guides in Kilmainham Gaol tell Paddy's story daily when they conduct tours of the gaol and museum.

Chapter 12

The State Funeral, October 2001

The men who were executed on 14 March 1921, were buried side by side in twos in individual graves, beside Kevin Barry who was executed by hanging on 1 November 1920. He was convicted for his involvement in an attack on a military van in North King Street, Dublin, on 20 September 1920. Kevin Barry's name is better known today than any of the others; he was the first to be executed by hanging during the War of Independence, he was just eighteen years old and he is immortalised in the well-known ballad 'Kevin Barry'. Thomas Traynor was hanged on 25 April 1921 – he was convicted of the murder of Cadet Farrell, RIC, on 14 March 1921, in Brunswick Street (now Pearse Street), Dublin. Edmond Foley and Patrick Maher were hanged on 7 June 1921 – they were convicted for involvement in the rescue of Seán Hogan at Knocklong Station, County Limerick on 13 May 1919. They were in prison for twenty-one months and during that time were the subject of two jury trials that failed to convict them. After the Restoration of Order Act of 1920, it was decided to court-martial them and they were found guilty and sentenced to death.[1]

Requests from the relatives of the men at the time of their deaths to have their bodies given to them for burial were refused on the grounds that, under the Capital Punishment Act, the body of an executed person had to be buried in prison grounds.

Immediately after the Treaty was signed, some relatives of the men buried in Mountjoy requested that the remains be removed from prison grounds. Emmett Dalton wrote to Michael Collins on 27 January 1922, saying that Mrs Quinlan, a relative of Patrick Maher, had written to him asking for his remains to be removed. Dalton was told that the whole matter of the remains of the men executed would be taken up at some time in the future and a public announcement would be made. Collins observed that it would be a very big task.

In February 1922, Michael Collins wrote to Seán Ó Muirthile suggesting that a meeting of the Wolfe Tone committee should be called to organise the disinterment of the men shot in 1916 and those executed since then. Richard Mulcahy, Minister for Defence, acknowledged in a memorandum to the Dáil cabinet on 22 February that where men were buried inside jails to which public access could not readily be arranged, it was desirable to remove the bodies. However, he thought that the matter should be left to rest until the bodies could be removed in a national ceremony to some graveyard.

Emmett Dalton wrote to the chairman of the Provisional Government again on 4 March 1922 and Michael Collins replied, saying that the whole matter was the subject of an inquiry. He asked, 'Who was buried in Kilmainham?' Dalton replied that he understood some of the 1916 men were buried there.

Relatives of men who were executed in Cork and buried in prison grounds there also tried to have their remains removed. The Minister for Justice, Kevin O'Higgins, said in December 1924, that it was impossible to accede to the request because these men were not buried in coffins and it would be impossible to distinguish individual remains because of the time lapse since the burials. But the Cork relatives persisted and wanted to exhume the remains of all the men and bury them in a single grave outside the prison.[2]

The report of the inquiry that Michael Collins had referred to was considered at a meeting of executive council members of the Dáil, on 15 June 1925: 'Having regard to the time which had elapsed since burial and the consequent difficulty of identifying the remains in most cases, the general opinion was that the bodies should not be disturbed. It was decided that the matter should be further considered at a full meeting of the executive council and the extern ministers should be asked to attend.'[3] In the case of Patrick Moran, it stated that the body was coffined and that he, and the five men executed on 14 March, were interred side by side in one grave, the precise location of which was known. The remains were placed in porous deal coffins, not strongly built and they were interred in heavy wet clay. It was considered that the practicability of exhumation would be doubtful.[4]

Following the full meeting of the council, which was held on 13 July 1925, a letter from Diarmuid Ó hÉagartaigh, secretary of the executive of Dáil Éireann, to the secretary of the Department of Justice, stated that the opinion of all was elicited and that it was decided that the exhumation of the bodies would be impractical.[5]

In 1926 the National Graves Association (NGA) was established with these aims: 'to restore the graves and memorials of our patriot dead of every generation, to commemorate those who died in the cause of Irish freedom, and to compile a record of such memorials.'[6] It was the NGA that erected the headstone in Mountjoy Jail in 1934 commemorating the ten executed men.

Dan Breen, TD, who was himself a very active participant in the War of Independence, wrote to the Minister for Defence in 1951, on behalf of a constituent requesting the disinterment of Edmond Foley. The reply from the government was that the graves were well looked after and that it would be impossible to identify the remains. Seán Kavanagh, who was in prison in Kilmainham

and Mountjoy in 1921, and who later became a governor of
Mountjoy Jail, wrote in 1960 to Oscar Traynor, Minister for
Justice, requesting permission to erect a memorial on behalf of the
prison staff. The request was refused, but the following year the
government decided that it would erect a memorial in place of
the National Graves Association memorial of 1934. Relatives of
the ten men were invited to attend that ceremony on Sunday, 8
October 1961.[7] Jim and Tom Moran and Tom's son, Paddy, hired a
hackney car and were driven to Dublin for the ceremony. My sister
Bridie and I were at boarding school in Dublin. We would have
welcomed the chance to get out for the day but it was not offered
to us. Indeed we felt a bit peeved that the men headed back home
to Crossna without paying us a visit.

Members of the general public wrote to the Department of
Justice when the remains of Roger Casement were reinterred in
Glasnevin cemetery, expressing dissatisfaction that the remains of
Kevin Barry were still buried in prison grounds. The government of
the day persisted in the view that the men were suitably honoured
in the grounds of Mountjoy Jail and that it would be impossible to
identify the individual remains.

When Máire Ní Céarnaigh became the National Graves Association secretary in 1987, she intensified the campaign to have the
remains removed from prison grounds. She wrote to the *Roscommon
Herald* and to the *Roscommon Champion* in December 1993, seeking to contact any living relatives of Patrick Moran. The *Roscommon
Herald* did not publish the letter. As the family was well known to
the management, the letter was simply passed on to Joseph Moran,
Paddy's nephew, who worked as a printer with the *Roscommon
Herald*. Bridget Moran, Paddy's sister, was a healthy ninety-nine-
year-old at the time, and did not wish to have the remains of the
men disturbed as she feared that it would be impossible to identify
the individual remains after such a long period and she felt that it
was a sensitive time in Irish history.

Bridget died on 30 December 1997, in her hundred and third year and, shortly after her death, the campaign to remove the remains of the ten men began to receive publicity again. Christy Burke, a Dublin Sinn Féin councillor, called on the Minister for Justice to liaise with prison authorities and the families so that arrangements for the reburial could be made. Headlines like 'Get Kevin Barry out of Mountjoy' and 'Row blocks bid to exhume body of Kevin Barry', appeared in the press. The Moran family were at the receiving end of veiled criticism and we decided that if all relatives of the other nine men wished to have their remains reburied, we would try to reach an accommodation.

The passing of the Good Friday Agreement in Northern Ireland in 1998 helped allay our fears on the issue of the sensitivity of the time. Sinn Féin signed up to that agreement and declared itself committed to taking the gun out of Irish politics. The IRA was on cease-fire. In the referendum that followed the signing of the agreement, it was endorsed by the majority of the people of Ireland, north and south.

I wrote to the Minister for Justice, Equality and Law Reform, John O'Donoghue, TD, in June 1998, on behalf of the family setting out the family position on the reburial of Patrick Moran. Over the following two years I met with Ruairí Gogan and Jim Mitchell, both officials with the Irish Prison Service, and through their skilful handling of negotiations, agreement was reached to have the remains removed from prison grounds. The families of the ten men were invited to meet in Mountjoy on 1 November 2000 for the unveiling of a plaque that rests on the wall of the hang house where the executions were carried out. John O'Donoghue, TD, announced the intention of the Fianna Fáil/Progressive Democrat coalition government to proceed with the reburial and said that within a matter of weeks legal documentation would be given to the relatives to facilitate them in requesting exhumation of the remains. He assured the families that the process would be dignified, respectful and appropriate. The state would accede in every possible way to the families' wishes in the manner of the reinterment of their loved ones and it would render honours at the funerals in accordance with the wishes of the families. He continued:

> It is a great honour and privilege, on behalf of the government, to unveil the plaque to commemorate all who died in this prison place down the years. I do so with the formal assurance that no development at Mountjoy Prison will ever erase the history which this chamber symbolises. It will be preserved in memory of those brave young men and in recollection of harsher times.

The plaque, as well as mentioning by name the ten men, states: 'We remember with respect all who died here and celebrate the social progress in Ireland which has consigned the gallows to history'.

Jim Mitchell of the Irish Prison Service wrote in March 2001, setting out two options for burial places for the remains:

1. Burial together in a new, specially dedicated plot, which would in future be maintained by the National Graves Association and in which no further burials would take place.
2. Burial in any other place in Ireland chosen by the family.

It was at this stage that the Moran family made a family decision not to separate Patrick Moran from his comrades. He was with them for some time before his execution and he was beside them in the grave for eighty years. The new grave would be a sealed plot so they would continue to rest together.

Representatives of the ten families were invited to Government Buildings, Dublin on 1 May 2001, to sign documents giving permission to exhume the remains. Paddy Moran, Bartley Moran, Mary Keegan (née Moran) and I, all nieces and nephews of Patrick

Moran, represented the Moran family. We met in Mountjoy Jail and were served lunch in the Women's Prison. This was the first chance that the relatives had to meet, chat and share stories. It was the first time that the younger generation of the Moran and Whelan families met.

During that visit to Mountjoy, John Lonergan, the prison governor, showed us the book that contained the record of the executions. It gave each man's name, age, the time of and the reason for execution. Paddy Moran's stated age, 26, is actually incorrect. His birth certificate confirms that he was born in March 1888, so he was 33 at the time of his execution.

After lunch in the prison we visited the graves of our relatives in the grounds of the prison and were given the option of going inside the hang house. The execution chamber is preserved exactly as it was all those years ago. The door on which the condemned prisoner stood, the large bolt that was used to drop the door downwards and the hanging rope are all there. Seeing it was a chilling experience. It was eerie; one could almost hear the door drop in the stillness. When the thick black bolt was drawn noisily back and one looked down into that abyss and saw the strong, rough rope with the noose on the end hang threateningly down, it was hard to think that anyone, least of all a family member, would have to make that cold, lonesome journey to death.

That afternoon we viewed the proposed location for the graves in Glasnevin cemetery. Consensus on its location, close to the National Graves Association plot, but not in it, was secured. But shortly before the state funeral, Seán Sherwin, a member of the ad hoc committee that organised the funerals, contacted the relatives' representatives to say that a more easily accessible and more suitably sized plot was available. The Moran family considered the plot eminently suitable, located as it is inside the main gate, beside Roger Casement's grave and in the shadow of the Daniel O'Connell monument.

We also went to Government Buildings at five o'clock on 1 May, to meet the Taoiseach, Bertie Ahern, TD, and the Minister for Justice, Equality and Law Reform, John O'Donoghue, TD, and to sign the documents giving the family's permission for the exhumations.

Another meeting at City Hall on 28 June 2001, saw family representatives gather again to witness the handing over of the licence to exhume the bodies to Seán Aylward of the Irish Prison Service by the City Manager, John Fitzgerald, in the presence of the Lord Mayor of Dublin, Maurice Ahern. At the reception that followed the formal ceremony, we, the relatives, had another chance to get to know each other.

On 27 August 2001, the first formal meeting of relatives' representatives was held in Government Buildings. My sister Rita and I attended for the Moran family. The ad hoc committee set up under the chairmanship of Brian Ó Cléirigh was there and also Peter Ryan, Brian Collinge and Síle de Búrca from the Taoiseach's department, Nick Reddy from Government Information Services, Jim Mitchell from the Irish Prison Service and representatives of the NGA. The artist, Robert Ballagh, distributed photographs of the monument stone that he had designed for the graves. Lt Colonel Conor O'Boyle outlined and circulated the proposed military ceremonies. The draft epitaph was circulated by Brian Ó Cléirigh.

The original date for the state funeral was 7 October 2001, but we were told that the President of Ireland, Mrs Mary McAleese, would not be able to attend if the funerals were on that date and a new date, 14 October 2001, was agreed. It was reported at this first meeting that the exhumations of the remains of the ten men from their graves in Mountjoy were underway.

The lists of names of those wishing to attend the funerals provoked some discussion. The ad hoc committee had envisaged that each family would have about fifty names. There were great variations in the numbers from family to family, the largest having 200 plus names on their list and the smallest twenty-five. The organising committee was anxious to accommodate as many family members as possible but, because it was felt that the pro-cathedral was the most appropriate venue for the solemn requiem mass and because the cathedral would have limited accommodation, families were asked to try to reduce the numbers.

It was agreed that the pro-cathedral choir would be asked to provide the music, the families would provide lists of relatives and nominate people to take part in the readings, prayers of the faithful, the bringing of gifts to the altar, the lifting of the coffins into the hearses at Mountjoy Jail and the taking of the flag and laying of the wreath at the graveside. The state would handle the arrangements for engaging undertakers, providing mourning cars, coaches for relatives, and providing wreaths and flags. Because of the close involvement of the Capuchin order with the prisoners during the War of Independence, the families requested that they should be invited to concelebrate the mass.

Another meeting was held on 7 September 2001. Rita, my sister, and her son Paul, represented the Morans on that occasion. Dr Máire Delaney, anatomist, Trinity College, and Tom Conditt, archaeologist from Dúchas, the heritage service, reported on the exhumations. Tom Conditt said that the remains of the ten Volunteers had been identified and he outlined how he conducted the search. He stressed that at every point in the operation due respect and dignity was afforded to the dead. Dr Máire Delaney confirmed that she was satisfied that she could identify each of the remains. Both agreed that they regarded it a great privilege to have been involved.

The fears that the bodies had been buried in quicklime and that it might be impossible to know which was which, were allayed when the men's bodies were found in exactly the locations given on the map left by the British military. The bodies were found with arms folded in individual coffins. The fact that they were treated with respect and dignity at the time of burial is a great source of consolation to the families.

It was agreed that family members eligible to attend should be confined to brothers/sisters, nephews/nieces, grandsons/grand-daughters, grandnephews/grandnieces and great grandnephews/ great grandnieces. Each family was asked to provide a list of relations within these criteria. The Moran family list now stood at fifty-nine. From within that number the family was asked to nominate seven members for the mourning car, six pall bearers, one to read or bring up a gift, one to accept the Tricolour and one to lay a wreath. All relatives could not be accommodated at every venue so it was agreed that those in the mourning cars and the pall bearers would be the only relatives allowed into Mountjoy Jail on the morning of the funerals. To accommodate other relatives wishing to visit Mountjoy Jail and see the coffins laid out, a service was organised for Saturday evening, 13 October 2001, at 7 p.m.

As the day, 14 October 2001, drew near, various groups of relatives, all determined to be there for this historic day, arrived from different locations in Ireland, England, Sweden, Denmark, America and Saudi Arabia. My brother, Seán, and Thomas Whelan's sister both travelled from Saudi Arabia. Bridie, my sister and her two daughters, travelled from Rainham in Essex, England. Joe Duignan, a nephew of Paddy's, his wife, Josephine and their daughter, Claire, travelled from Wood Green, London. Pádraig Moran (a grandnephew of Paddy) travelled from Sweden. Other Moran relatives travelled from Kilkenny, Sligo, Donegal and Roscommon, some on the Saturday and some early on Sunday morning.

The prison chaplains conducted a very moving, music-filled and prayerful service at the graveside in Mountjoy, in lovely October sunshine, at 7 p.m. on Saturday, 13 October 2001, the eve of the state funeral. The soloist, Patricia Burke D'Souza, accompanied on the harp by Áine Ni Dhúill, gave a beautiful rendering of 'There's a place' and 'May the songs of the Angels welcome you'.

Approximately 600 relatives met at Dublin Castle on the morning of 14 October 2001, for what proved to be a very special day. A steady stream of cars and buses filtered into the Castle yard by the Ship Street entrance. This was the entrance that Uncle Paddy asked his girlfriend to use when he wrote a rushed note on an envelope to her just after his court-martial. Groups of relatives made their way to the conference centre and greeted each other with a mixture of joy and sadness. Different coloured badges were allocated to the relatives going to the different locations, green for those going into Mountjoy and gold for those joining the cortege in College Green and thence to the pro-cathedral and Glasnevin cemetery.

A buffet breakfast was served in the Castle and the relatives had an opportunity to meet and mingle. Taoiseach Bertie Ahern came and met informally with the families in the conference centre at Dublin Castle before addressing the assembled crowd. He expressed his delight at being able to join us on what would, he said, be a long but historic day. He thanked the families and their representatives, particularly those who had been involved with the organising committee and with his own department over a number of years, for their assistance in making the day a reality. He welcomed those who had travelled from the Middle East, Saudi Arabia, the United States, Great Britain and all other places, and people from all over the island of Ireland who had come to be present on this day. We would, he said, all go through the day remembering days and times past. Despite some problems with the logistics of organising such a big occasion, he hoped that things would run as smoothly as possible at every location.

It was now time for proceedings to begin. The mourning cars and the buses to transport the family members to Mountjoy Jail awaited us in the Castle yard. Seven of Paddy Moran's nieces travelled in the mourning car and six nephews in the coach with the pall bearers. These thirteen people accounted for all his nearest next of kin able to be present on the day. It was humbling and gratifying to see people gathering silently at the top of Whitworth Road and around the entrance to Mountjoy Jail even at this early stage in the day. It was a day for the families but the presence of so many people on the streets indicated to us that it was also a day for the nation. In Mountjoy Jail ten coffins draped in Tricolours stood, each one over the spot where that body had been buried. It was a very moving scene. John O'Donoghue, TD, and the Director General of the Irish Prison Service, Seán Aylward, were present. Prison officers stood in a guard of honour. The soft October rain seemed to emphasise the poignancy of the occasion.

John Lonergan said that the staff had taken great pride in maintaining the graves: 'A big part of the history of Mountjoy, a chequered history maybe, will be leaving it today. The dead men were very much part of the history of Mountjoy and they will be missed in the context of Mountjoy.' However, he expressed total agreement with the principle that these and other remains should be removed from prison grounds to more suitable resting-places. He expressed sadness that there are a number of unmarked graves in the grounds of the prison and that nobody knows who, or exactly where, they are. Referring to the 'many rumours' about the way the men had been treated before burial, he said it was important for him, representing the governor of the time, to say now that there was evidence to indicate that they were buried 'in a civilised and decent fashion', and he continued, 'I think that's important in the context of the history of Mountjoy.'[8]

Fr Declan Blake, the head chaplain, conducted a prayer service, and prayed for all those who had been hanged in the prison, their families, those still in prison, ex-prisoners, and all who died in the War of Independence. After the blessing, each family carried the remains of their relative to the waiting hearse. Paddy and Seán Moran, Michael and Joe Duignan, Barty Moran and Pádraig Fitzpatrick, all nephews, carried the remains of Paddy Moran. Paddy's nieces, May and Rita Moran, Bridie Plummer, Anna Sheerin, Mary Keegan, Áine Hunt and Bridie McClean, stepped forward to claim and mourn him. As the cortege left the prison grounds the relatives walked behind each hearse. It was a very poignant journey for all of us and we felt it an honour and a privilege to claim him on behalf of his parents, brothers and sisters who never got a chance to mourn him in a funeral. A guard of honour of prison officers lined the route out of the prison. The prison bell tolled as the cortege came out the gate. Traditionally, the bell had tolled fifteen minutes after an execution.

The defence forces took over once the cortege had left the prison grounds. At the first glimpse of the hearses, the resounding applause of the crowds outside signalled for the first of many times that day that the people were standing solidly with us in appreciation of the sacrifice of these men and of the decision to remove them from prison grounds. Scenes such as this were repeated on the route down Phibsboro Road. Paddy Moran knew this route well, having lived and worked as a barman at the well-known landmark, Doyle's, 160 Phibsboro Road. The cortege continued down Broadstone and Constitution Hill and along through Church Street. Paddy was associated with the church here through his contact with Fr Dominic, the Capuchin who was his friend in Kilmainham Gaol. The cortege continued along Bridge Street, High Street, Lord Edward Street, past Dublin Castle where Paddy had made his statements and spent the days following his court-martial at City Hall. The cortege continued down Dame Street and when it reached College Green it stopped. The relatives that were not in Mountjoy joined the cortege here and all walked with the hearses through Westmoreland Street and O'Connell Street

At the General Post Office, scene of much of the fighting during the Easter Rising of 1916, the cortege stopped. Full military honours were rendered. A lone piper played a lament. The Irish state was formally recognising that these men were soldiers who had fought and died for Ireland. This would have meant so much to Paddy's mother, his father and his siblings. I remember how upset my father was that his brother did not even get 'a soldier's death'.

A large crowd had gathered in O'Connell Street and there was much cheering and clapping. The cortege continued down O'Connell Street, turned right into Cathal Brugha Street and into Marlborough Street, where it arrived at the pro-cathedral. The left aisle of the church was already filled with public representatives, members of the council of state, the Dáil, the Seanad and the European parliament. I remembered a little incident that happened the evening before when I was in the pro-cathedral for a practice for the readings at the mass: an old lady with a strong Dublin accent approached me, asked who I was and which Volunteer's family I belonged to. She shook my hand vigorously when I told her and was loud in her praise for what the ten men had achieved. Then she said, 'Now tomorrow do not let them politicians take the front seats in this church, put them down the back and ye be sure and get the front seats.'

When the relatives were in place on the right-hand side and in various aisles, the Tánaiste, Mary Harney, the Taoiseach, Bertie Ahern, the Lord Mayor of Dublin, Michael Mulcahy, and finally the President of Ireland, Mary McAleese, joined the congregation. The coffin-bearers from Athlone's Custume Barracks, carried each coffin into the pro-cathedral for mass. The bearer party that carried Patrick Moran's coffin was led by Sergeant Declan Dowling of Cartron Drive, Athlone. As the coffins were being carried to the altar the choir sang the 'Kilmore Carol' alternating with 'Ag Críost an Síol'.

The former Primate of all Ireland, Cardinal Cathal Daly, was the chief celebrant of the mass. Dr Daly and his concelebrants were joined on the altar by representatives of the Church of Ireland, and the Methodist, Lutheran, Jewish, Coptic and Greek Orthodox churches. Dr Daly spoke of the ideals of these men and said that the true inheritors of these ideals are those who are 'explicitly and visibly' committed to implementing all aspects of the Belfast Agreement:

> There is no other basis on which Northern Ireland can enjoy peace, prosperity and normal life. The only legitimate struggle in Northern Ireland is an unarmed struggle for justice, equality and human rights for both of its political traditions and for peace, reconciliation and co-operation between them. Some groups will claim that they and they only are the inheritors of the ideals of these men. Some will claim that the mantle has passed to them of being the men and women whose duty it is to complete the unfinished business of 1916. Freedom for the sake of justice was the all-absorbing national aim in 1916; these men died in the belief that their deaths would bring into being an independent Ireland, an Ireland of freedom, of justice, an island in which people would never again resort to violence in order to secure human rights and equal opportunities for all its citizens.

Relatives participated in the mass: the first reading was given by Elizabeth Smith, grandniece of Thomas Bryan. Seán Óg Ó Ceallacháin, representing Bernard Ryan's family, gave the second reading in Irish. Lt Col Danny Flood, nephew of Frank Flood, read two prayers of the faithful and I, representing the Moran family, read two prayers, one in English and one in Irish. The gift offerings were carried to the altar by Irene Whelan, niece of Thomas Whelan, Geraldine Quinlan, grandniece of Patrick Maher, Bernadette Shanahan, grandniece of Edmond Foley, Michael Barry, grandnephew of Kevin Barry, and two children Sarah and Jack Whelan great, great grandchildren of Patrick Doyle.

This participation by the relatives added to the sense of ownership that we, the families, had on the day. When the ceremonies were finished, the bearer parties carried the coffins to the hearses and the cortege moved toward the Garden of Remembrance on Parnell Square. It stopped here for a minute's silence to pay tribute to these soldiers who were part of the struggle for freedom that is commemorated in this spot. The cortege moved on again through North Frederick Street, Dorset Street, Whitworth Road, Prospect Road and Finglas Road to Glasnevin cemetery, the route all the way lined with people who had come to pay their respects.

Nine of the men were buried side by side in Glasnevin cemetery in a simple grave. The granite memorial designed by artist Robert Ballagh was already in place. At the head of each grave is each man's name. They lie in the order of execution, Kevin Barry, Patrick Moran, Thomas Whelan, Patrick Doyle, Bernard Ryan, Thomas Bryan, Frank Flood, Thomas Traynor, Edmond Foley and, although Patrick Maher is buried in Ballylanders, County Limerick, his name is also on the gravestone. The ceremony of the undraping of the coffins took place when the coffins were placed by the bearers at each resting place. Paddy Moran, Patrick's nephew and namesake, was presented with the Tricolour that draped his coffin and it is now a treasured possession of this family. A wreath-laying ceremony followed the burial. Barty Moran, another nephew, laid the wreath on behalf of the Moran family.

Taoiseach Bertie Ahern gave the graveside oration. He spoke of the pride felt by the state in these men and in all those who fought for freedom and lost their lives doing so:

> Their sacrifice is not being forgotten by the people of Ireland and it never will. In the war they fought they had one support that could not be ignored. That was the mandate for independence from the general election of 1918. When the Declaration of Independence was passed, the Ceann Comhairle of the first Dáil said to the deputies present

that they all understood that war would be the consequence of the Declaration.

The Taoiseach went on to say that, in honouring the men, the Irish state was:

> ... discharging a debt of honour that stretched back eighty years. The ten men died defending and upholding the independence proclaimed by Dáil Éireann on 21 January 1919. The Dáil took formal responsibility for the actions of the Volunteers and recognised them as its army. They explicitly acknowledged the democratic legitimacy of the campaign they had fought and accepted accountability for it. So those of us who are proud of our national independence should have no reservations about honouring these Volunteers. It would be quite wrong, however, to apply without distinction, any such presumption to other times and circumstances, and to a quite different situation, or to stretch the democratic mandate of 1918 far beyond its natural term. Conversely, the memory of the Volunteers of 1920 and 1921 does not deserve to be burdened with responsibility for terrible deeds or for the actions of tiny minorities that happened long after their deaths. People of common sense and goodwill understand all that perfectly ... there is neither need nor excuse for the extra-judicial use of force by anyone today ... We all look to a future in which the people of Ireland can conduct warm and friendly relations with each other and with our neighbours in Great Britain on a basis of equality and partnership, in an atmosphere free of force and coercion in which people of all traditions can live and co-operate together for the common good.

A volley of shots and the playing of the Last Post brought the day's ceremonies to a fitting end.

The people of Ireland showed the understanding and goodwill that the Taoiseach spoke of by coming out in such large numbers on the streets of Dublin, to share this occasion. It was particularly heartening to see the faces of friends and neighbours in the crowds and to hear shouts of 'Up Crossna' as we came down O'Connell Street. The presence of so many young people and the dignity of it all was truly impressive and it proved they were there standing with us and with the state in removing these ten men's bodies from prison grounds and in according them high honours. Those at home had the opportunity of being part of the celebration through the compelling coverage of it on RTÉ. The sadness of the occasion was compounded for the Moran family by the fact that one of Paddy's nephews, Joseph, was too ill to be present, although he would have dearly loved to be there. He had taken a great interest over the years in the life of Uncle Paddy and was always able to offer good advice within the family through the negotiations that led up to the decision to go ahead with the reburial. He watched the funeral on television and was touched by the mention of him by Tim Carey during his commentary. Joseph died in April 2002.

I found it a very emotional day. Although Uncle Paddy died eighty years ago, there were many times during the day when I felt the overwhelming sadness that is part of the everyone's experience at any funeral for a person close to us. It was a proud day too; one that will never be forgotten by those of us who had the privilege of taking part in it. It was the day that the Irish state recognised Uncle Paddy for his contribution to its formation.

CHAPTER 13

CONCLUSION

Paddy Moran's story is the story of an individual participant in the events that are part of the history of Ireland between 1916 and 1921. He was just one of a handful of people that were executed by hanging during the War of Independence, yet his story has never before been told. How was it that he found himself addressing cards to friends and family with the words 'Goodbye Loved Ireland and You' on the eve of his execution in Mountjoy Jail? What motivated a young man from a small farm in the west of Ireland to devote his life to the cause of Irish freedom and to pay the ultimate price for that cause?

Paddy was motivated by a conviction that Ireland should be a free and independent nation and the causes he espoused all marked out a path towards that objective. He was a member of the Gaelic League, the Gaelic Athletic Association, the trade union movement, Sinn Féin, the IRB, the Volunteers and the IRA.

Paddy was not just motivated by a desire for Irish freedom; he spent much of his time fighting against the social conditions that prevailed at that time and particularly those for shop assistants in the licensed trade. The injustices that Paddy saw around him drew him into the trade union movement in 1913, where his leadership qualities soon came to the fore. He was elected chairman of the Dun Laoghaire branch of the Grocers', Vintners' and Allied

Trades Assistants' Union and was its delegate on the national executive. Paddy was involved in the campaign for an across the board increase in wages, shorter working hours, more holidays and changes in the 'living in' system throughout a period of great unrest in his union between 1918–1920. The ten-week strike in 1920 was the culmination of that period of unrest and the workers gained many of the concessions they had looked for. During the strike, Paddy went to prison rather than pay a fine for preventing a breach of the strike. He was elected president of his union in 1920 in recognition of his organisational and leadership abilities and, no doubt, his involvement in securing the settlement terms of the strike in 1920. That dispute was a watershed because it laid the foundation for the consolidation of trade unionism in the Licensed and Grocery Trades.[1]

Paddy Moran's work on behalf of his fellow workers has never been forgotten by his union (now Mandate) which has always recognised that he was a key figure in the labour movement during those turbulent years of 1913–1920. Jack Cagney is one of the older living members of the Barmen's Union (Mandate) and he recalled the esteem in which Paddy Moran and his union were held when he began working in the licensed trade in the 1940s.

Paddy Moran pursued other interests too; not only did he play football and hurling himself, he encouraged those around him to play. He took the initiative in founding a club in Dun Laoghaire in 1918 and used every opportunity to pass on the skills he learned in Dublin to the young men in Crossna.

Those leadership qualities helped Paddy play an important role within the Irish Volunteers in the period 1914–1921. The men of D Company, Dublin Brigade IRA, recognised those qualities when they elected him adjutant on the formation of the company and again when they elected him captain after the 1916 Rising. Those qualities of trust and leadership were recognised in his native place where Paddy was active in recruiting members for the Volunteers and establishing companies in Crossna and its environs. Michael Collins placed his trust in Paddy when he asked him to meet men who travelled between Dun Laoghaire and Holyhead on secret missions for him. It was his ability and leadership that prompted Michael Collins and the GHQ staff to place him in charge of the operation planned for the Gresham Hotel in O'Connell Street, Dublin, on Bloody Sunday.

Bloody Sunday, November 1920, was the culmination of a series of events over the years that preceded it. At the general election of 1918, Sinn Féin, the political standard bearer for revolutionary nationalism, won comprehensively at the expense of the Irish Parliamentary Party, which represented constitutional nationalism. The newly elected Sinn Féin MPs refused to take their seats in Westminster and in January 1919, set up a rival Parliament, Dáil Éireann, in Dublin. Dáil Éireann set about winning international recognition for the right of Ireland to its independence, but its representatives were denied a hearing at the Peace Conference held in Paris in 1919, a conference convened in the wake of the 1914–1918 War to discuss the rights of small nations to govern themselves. The Dáil responded by pressing ahead with efforts to make an alternative government a reality for the Irish population; it introduced Dáil courts, issued Dáil bonds, took over local government and established a republican police force. However, there were within the Volunteers many who, like Paddy Moran, did not see any hope of gaining independence through political means and who were prepared to continue with a military campaign. The British reaction to the Easter Rising, the threat to impose conscription into the British army, the refusal to recognise Dáil Éireann and the denial of a hearing at the Peace Conference helped to convince the Volunteers and their supporters of the necessity and legitimacy of the use of violence to achieve independence.

That campaign of violence intensified between the British military and the IRA. The IRA targeted and shot several policemen and burned barracks in several towns. The security forces responded by burning houses and killing many civilians. Ambushes, reprisals and counter-reprisals were regular occurrences. The British government responded by giving the RIC better weapons and equipment and extra personnel in the form of the Black and Tans and Auxiliaries. The RIC was reorganised into divisional areas and high-ranking British army officers were appointed to the commissioner posts. The Restoration of Order in Ireland Act, passed by the British parliament in August 1920, gave the military authorities in Ireland extensive powers; they could imprison without charge, try a prisoner by secret court-martial, without the presence of a person with legal knowledge, unless the case was liable to the death penalty. Even in those cases the legal person was nominated by the crown. The lord lieutenant was empowered to suppress coroners' inquests and substitute military inquiries so the police no longer feared being exposed in an independent coroner's court. Sixteen British intelligence officers under Sir Ormonde Winter were sent to Ireland to locate and destroy Collins and his organisation. According to Dorothy Macardle:

> Seventeen Irishmen were murdered in October 1920, in circumstances which confirmed Michael Collins's suspicion that 'shooting by roster' had been officially organised. He was aware that the English secret service in Ireland was, as General Crozier (the commander of the Auxiliary police) afterwards affirmed, no secret service but a mere gang of *agents provocateurs* and the like, while the secret service department and the propaganda department of the police was a camouflaged institution having as its avowed object the extermination of Sinn Féin extremists.[2]

The action ordered by Collins and GHQ on Bloody Sunday, which resulted in the deaths of twelve men suspected of being secret agents, and two cadets, was a response to these policies and events. Many of the Volunteers who were involved in the action of Bloody Sunday were uncomfortable with being asked to go into the various houses where the listed men lodged and shoot their targets.[3] They preferred, as Simon Donnelly put it, to meet the enemy in the open where all had an equal chance. However, the men who carried out the operation did so because it was organised by GHQ and sanctioned by the Dáil, and Paddy Moran did what he had to do and took charge of the action in the Gresham Hotel that morning. He agonised afterwards about the innocence or otherwise of Captain McCormack but McCormack's name was on the list, which Paddy had no responsibility for drawing up.

The actions of the military in Croke Park on the afternoon of Bloody Sunday succeeded in galvanising public support for the actions of Michael Collins' men earlier that day just as effectively as the execution of the leaders of the Rising had done in 1916. Dick McKee, Peadar Clancy and Conor Clune were murdered in the guardroom of Dublin Castle on Monday, the day after Bloody Sunday. To this day Bloody Sunday is associated with the killings in Croke Park and the deaths of those three men, much more than with the loss of fourteen of the crown forces earlier that morning.

The IRA claimed that the assassinations in the morning were justified and that the shootings in Croke Park in the afternoon were a reprisal. The Castle claimed that the British officers were murdered and that the mayhem in Croke Park was caused by unidentified men shooting at the military who were there to search for arms. Arthur Griffith, the founder of Sinn Féin, had difficulty in coming to terms with the actions of the IRA; he thought the actions in Croke Park were terrible but that was a British crime, and so beyond his control.

There were wholesale arrests of nationalists after Bloody Sunday; some had been involved, others were completely innocent. Most of those who had been involved were released because they were not identified by any of those who witnessed the action.

The manager of the Gresham Hotel said that several members of staff were called to various identification parades but identified nobody. The risk of the consequences of informing no doubt prevented witnesses from identifying any of the participants, even if they wanted to. Unfortunately for Paddy Moran, the encounter with the batman to Major Carew on Saturday night in Mount Street meant that the batman was able to identify Paddy and he undoubtedly told Private Snelling and Major Carew to pick him out at the identification parade in Arbour Hill. This and the fact that a photograph of Paddy, in uniform and holding a gun, was shown at the court-martial, although not admitted in evidence, was enough to secure his conviction. The military authorities may have suspected that Paddy was involved in the action somewhere on Bloody Sunday but they knew very well that he was not in Mount Street.

The only other man executed for Bloody Sunday, Tommy Whelan, was also framed. He was falsely convicted of the murder of Captain Bagally at 119 Lower Baggot Street, Dublin. The only witness for the prosecution in Tommy's case was a British army officer, who was in a room next door to Captain Bagally. Paddy and Tommy were both identified by members of the British army only. Tommy Whelan was not involved in the actions on Bloody Sunday.

The IRA did its own share of inventing evidence and managed to get an array of witnesses who were prepared to testify to an alibi for Paddy. Margaret O'Flanagan, who organised the alibi, was ordered to resign from Cumann na mBan so that she could say, if asked, that she did not belong to any political organisation. Unfortunately Doyle and McCourt were known members of the IRA and were interned, on suspicion of involvement in Bloody Sunday, in Ballykinlar Camp, County Down, in December 1920, so Margaret O'Flanagan probably did not have a chance to brief them before their arrest and internment and was unaware that they had already made statements to the police in December that would conflict with the alibi arranged.

There is some misinformation regarding Paddy Moran's case in print. Sir Ormonde Winter, clearly referring to his case, later wrote that a shop assistant, who was supposed to have sold Paddy a glass of milk on Bloody Sunday morning, was asked what Paddy was wearing. She was said to have replied that he was wearing a dark blue coat and a dark blue hat. Winter claimed that witnesses behind Paddy at mass in Blackrock church had testified that he was twisting a grey hat between his fingers. The shop assistant was not called at all to give evidence at his trial and the only witness who said anything about what Paddy was wearing referred to a fawn coat and a fawn hat. Winter says that eight men were tried and convicted and seven of them were hanged. Again he is wrong; only two men were hanged for Bloody Sunday: Paddy Moran and Thomas Whelan.

The IRA leadership knew that Paddy was not in Mount Street, but to admit that he was in the Gresham Hotel or anywhere near the other scenes of action on Bloody Sunday was not an option. The men who were in Mount Street could hardly be expected to own up either – some of them were involved in organising the escape from Kilmainham Gaol and it must have been a disappointment to them that Paddy chose not to take part. The success of the venture clearly depended on a small number, two or three, attempting it, and getting out in less than five minutes. IRA GHQ seemed to have decided who should take part and while Paddy Moran was the third man on the list, it seems that he gave his place to another man. He did not do that because, as has often been said, he believed in British justice, which he most certainly did not, but because he did not put his own interests first. He showed that same lack of self-interest when he refused to allow Paddy McGrath to exchange places with him, or to allow Dan Carroll to involve the warder who was guarding him, when both men were trying to find a way of getting him out of Mountjoy Jail just before his execution. It is said that Paddy organised a concert in Kilmainham to divert the warders' attention while the escape was taking place, but I did not find any written evidence to support that claim, even though my father often told us that story.

While more than 1,700 survivors of the War of Independence made witness statements in the 1950s, not everybody who participated in that war agreed to make a statement. These statements add to the sum of our knowledge about events during that time, but they should be viewed with caution; they were made more than thirty years after these events and human memory can be coloured by experience, it can be selective and it can be faulty. Nowhere did I notice this more than in the recollections of witnesses to the same event, the escape from Kilmainham Gaol, where there are several differences between witness accounts.

Equally the extensive records held in the British National Archives have to be viewed with some degree of scepticism, in the light of what General Crozier and others have said. Tom Bowden, when he was researching his article 'Bloody Sunday – a Reappraisal', found an official Public Record Office note entitled 'Revision of Records – Second Weeding – items for destruction', on the back of which was written in longhand 'Croke Park'. He observed that it vindicated Disraeli's remark that, 'generally speaking all great events have been distorted, most of the important causes concealed and some of the principal characters never appear'.[4]

A great deal of propaganda surrounds the War of Independence on both sides. *The Irish Bulletin* was the chief organ of the IRA during that war and it listed atrocities committed by the British and was circulated at home and internationally five times a week. The British government set up a publicity department in Dublin Castle to counter Sinn Féin propaganda and it was from there that 'official reports' were circulated. These reports often contained the 'vilest stories against Irish insurgents', accusing them of mutilitating bodies and killing men with hatchets.[5] They defended the actions of the police and military with gross distortions of the truth. The British Labour Party called for an independent inquiry into the conduct of the forces in Ireland and when that was refused it set up its own commission of inquiry. It reported, 'that reprisals by members of the Crown Forces fell under six main heads: general terrorism and provocative behaviour, arson and wilful destruction of property, looting, cruelty to persons, and shooting.'[6]

Before Bloody Sunday, tentative moves for peace in Ireland were being made. After Bloody Sunday these initiatives were intensified and on Monday, 11 July 1921, a truce was called. The Truce paved the way for the negotiations that led to the signing of the Treaty on 6 December 1921 but Bloody Sunday had other consequences. Two policemen lost their lives in the Keadue ambush and Joe Molloy was shot by Auxiliaries in Aughnafinnegan, while in Tommy Whelan's home town of Clifden two policemen and a civilian were killed in reprisal.

Historians have argued about the necessity for the use of violence as opposed to constitutional politics to achieve independence for Ireland. Ronan Fanning has argued that 'there isn't a shred of evidence that Lloyd George's Tory-dominated government would have moved from the 1914-style niggardliness of the Government of Ireland Act of 1920 to the larger, if imperfect, generosity of the Treaty if they had not been impelled to do so by Michael Collins and his assassins.'[7] Roy Foster, on the other hand, has written of the eventual offer of Dominion Status and observes, 'whether the bloody catalogue of assassination and war from 1919–1921 was necessary in order to negotiate thus far may fairly be questioned.'[8]

Certainly, the price paid for the establishment of an independent twenty-six county state was a high one. Many civilians, Volunteers and security force personnel lost their lives. For the Moran family the price was the loss of a beloved son and brother.

APPENDIX 1

THE GARRISON IN JACOB'S FACTORY

Thomas MacDonagh, Major John MacBride and Michael O'Hanrahan were in command.

There were about 150 Volunteers altogether and among them were the following: Vincent Byrne, Joseph Lawless, James Carbury, William Byrne,[1] Paddy Moran, Seosamh De Brún, Con Colbert, Miss Conroy, Dick Cotter, Pádraig Ó Ceallaigh, Louise Gavan Duffy, John MacDonagh, Mick McDonnell, Dick McGee, John O' Grady (the man who was shot),[2] Sonny O'Brien, Eily O'Hanrahan, Michael Hayes, Tom Hunter, Peadar Kearney, Sarah Kealy, Kathleen Lane, Michael Molloy, Captain Meldon, Seán Murphy, William Oman,[3] Thomas Pugh, Séamus Pouch,[4] Mrs Maud Price (Máire Ní Shíubhlaigh), Éamon Price, Tommy O'Riordan, Tom O'Reilly, Thomas Slater,[5] Jack Twomey,[6] Séamus Ó hAodha, Pat Callan, Eamon Comerford, Patrick McDonnell, Hannraí Ó hAnnracháin, Joe Thunder, Mrs O'Daly, Séamus Ó Maolfhainn, Mick Slater, Micheál Ó Caomhanaigh,[7] Derry O'Connell,[8] William James Stapleton,[9] Phil Shanahan, Patrick Sweeney, Michael Walker,[10] Gerard Boland,[11] Charles Goulding, James Cunningham, John Furlong, Richard Davy, Andy Comerford, Matthew Furlong, Terry Simpson, Joseph Vize, Dan Kavanagh, Michael Fitzpatrick, Paddy

Walsh, Patrick Callan, Hugh O'Hagan, Peadar Christie, John Joyce, Patrick Lanigan, Owen McDermott, Martin Mullen, James Barrett, James Cassells, Michael Colgan, Liam Daly, Tom Drum, James Kenny, Thomas Losty, Seán Lynch, William Lynch, Joseph O'Hanrahan, Seán O'Rourke, Kathleen McDonald (nee Pollard), Josephine Daly (née Pollard), Patrick Rooney, James Shields, Denis Shelly, Thomas Shelly, James Slattery, Michael Smyth[12] and Christopher McEvoy.[13]

Appendix 2

The total casualties of the 1916 Rising

Killed:
Military: officers – 17, other ranks – 99; RIC: officers – 2, other ranks – 11; Dublin Metropolitan Police – 3; civilians and insurgents – 318.

Wounded:
Military: officers – 46, other ranks – 322; RIC officers – 0, other ranks – 22; Dublin Metropolitan Police – 7; civilians and insurgents – 2,217.

Missing:
Soldiers – 9

Total: 450 people were killed, 2,614 were wounded and 9 were declared missing.[1]

Appendix 3

Volunteer casualties in 1916

A file in UCD archives, containing lists of republican soldier casualties, names the following Volunteers killed in action in 1916:[1]

Charles Corrigan, age 34, from North Frederick Street – died in Henry Street.

John Corrigan, age 21, from Swords – died in Ashbourne.

John Cromean, age 23, from 13 Fingal Place – Not known where he died.

Andrew Cunningham, age 24 – no address given – died in Ringsend Road.

Patrick Farrell, age 19, from Parnell Street – died in Church Street.

John Hurley, age 29, from Clonakilty, County Cork – died in Richmond Hospital (wounded in the head at the Four Courts and died later in hospital).

Thomas O'Reilly, age 21 – address and place of death not known.

Thomas Rafferty, age 24, from Lusk, County Dublin – died in Ashbourne.

Daniel Sheehan, age 30, from Ballytubrid, County Limerick – drowned when the car he was in went off pier at Killorglin.

Charles Monaghan of Na Fianna – drowned when the car he was in went off pier at Killorglin.

Edward Walshe, age 43 from 8 Lower Dominic Street – died in GPO, having been wounded in Parliament Street.

Peter Wilson, age 40, from The Green, Swords – died in the Mendicity Institute.

Henry Coyle, age 28, from Leinster Avenue – died in Henry Place.

Patrick Stortis, age 25, from Ballybough Road (originally from Kerry) – died in Moore Street.

John Adams, age 40, Irish Citizen Army (ICA) – died in St Stephen's Green.

James Byrne, age 46, from 23 Summerhill Place, member of ICA – died in City Hall.

Philip Clarke, age 36, from 109 Cork Street – died in St Stephen's Green.

Seán Connolly, age 33, from 108 Philipsburg Avenue, Fairview, ICA – died in City Hall.

James Corcoran, age 30, from Gorey, County Wexford, ICA – died in Stephen's Green.

Charles Darcy, age 21, from Summerhill, ICA – died in Parliament Street.

John Divan, from Gardiner Street – died in the Four Courts.

James Fox, from 74 Thomas Street – died in St Stephen's Green.

George Geoghegan, age 38, from Cork Street – died in the College of Surgeons.

James McCormack, from Railway Cottages, Ballydoyle – killed somewhere on the northside of the city.

John O'Reilly, age 30, from 14 Lower Gardiner Street – shot after the surrender in City Hall when another man bent down to tie his shoelace. A British officer opened fire (possibly he thought he was reaching for a weapon) and killed this man.

Fred Ryan, from 4 High Street – died in Harcourt Street.

Arthur Weekes (Néill) from Norwich England – died in Moore Lane after the evacuation of the GPO.

John Healy, age 15, from 188 Phibsboro Road – wounded by shell fire at Phibsboro Corner on 25 April and died at the Mater Hospital on 27 April. He was a member of Na Fianna for three years.

APPENDIX 4

LOCATIONS OF THE BLOODY SUNDAY KILLINGS BY THE IRA

The eight locations where officers, cadets and a civilian were killed on Bloody Sunday were:

1. 38 Upper Mount Street: Lieutenant Peter Ashmut Ames and Captain George Bennett were both killed.
2. 28 Upper Pembroke Street: Major Dowling was killed, Captain Leonard Price, Captain Kennlyside, Colonel Montgomery and Lieutenant Murray were wounded. Colonel Montgomery died later.
3. 117 Morehampton Road: Lieutenant D. McClean and T.H. Smith were killed and a civilian, Mr Caldow, was wounded.
4. 92 Baggot Street: Captain W.F. Newberry was killed.
5. 119 Baggot Street: Captain G.T. Bagally was killed.
6. 28 Earlsfort Terrace: Captain Fitzgerald was killed.
7. 22 Lower Mount Street: Lieutenant Angliss (worked under assumed name McMahon) was killed. Lieutenant Peel escaped by stacking furniture against his room door. The chance arrival of a lorry carrying enemy troops forced the men to retreat and he was saved. Two auxiliary cadets, F. Carniss and C.A. Morris, were attempting to return to Beggar's Bush Barracks to get reinforcements and ammunition, when they ran into the covering IRA force. They were taken to the back of number 16 Mount Street and were shot dead.[1]

8. The Gresham Hotel, O'Connell Street, Dublin: Captain McCormack and Mr L.A. Wilde were both killed.[2]

APPENDIX 5

DETAILS OF THE DEAD AND WOUNDED IN CROKE PARK, BLOODY SUNDAY

Details from WO 88/B court of inquiry in lieu of inquests into deaths in Croke Park.

James Matthews, age 48. Labourer. 32 North Cumberland Road, was married to Kate Matthews. Doctor Robert Vincent Monaghan (Mater Hospital) said he had a round bullet wound on one side of his leg and a large ragged one about eight inches long and three inches wide on the other leg. He said that was an exit wound.

John William Scott, age 14. Schoolboy. 15 Fitzroy Avenue, Drumcondra. Dr Monaghan said he had a round wound on his back and a large triangular one on his front. He was dead on admission.

Patrick O'Dowd, age 58. 18 Buckingham Street Buildings, Dublin, was a builder's labourer. Doctor Monaghan said he had a circular bullet wound on the top of his head and death was due to laceration of the brain destroying vital centres.

Jeremiah O'Leary, age 10. 69 Blessington Street. Schoolboy. Doctor Patrick Moran (Mater) said he died from shock and haemorrhage about an hour after admission. He had a bullet wound, an entry wound, on the right side of his head and an exit wound a few inches above that. Brain matter was coming out from both wounds.

Jane Boyle, age 26. 12 Lennox Street, Dublin, she was a charge hand to a pork butcher. She was dead on admission. Her brother, James Boyle, 4 Somerset Street, South Lotts Road, Dublin identified her. Doctor Monaghan said she had a bullet wound on her back. Her jaw, her right clavicle and a rib were fractured.

William Robinson, age 11. 15 Little Brittain Street. Schoolboy. Dr Henry Stokes, Drumcondra Hospital, said he had a gunshot wound that caused his death on morning of 28 November 1920.

Thomas Hogan, age 19, unmarried, he was a mechanic. Miss Maggie Hogan, Kilmallock, County Limerick, identified him. Dr Patrick Moran, Mater Hospital, said he had a small wound under his spine and an exit wound in front. He had two other wounds that he thought might have been caused by bone splinters. He was not dead on admission. His right arm was amputated on Monday 22 November 1920. Gas gangrene set in after the operation and the patient died on 26 November at 18.30 p.m. Joseph Connolly from Tara Street Fire Station took him to hospital in the ambulance.

Joseph Traynor, age 21. Ballymount, Clondalkin. County Dublin. Date of death: 21 November 1920 at Jervis Street Hospital. Patrick J. Cassin, House Surgeon at Jervis Street, described his wounds. He had two wounds in the small of his back; the one on the right led into the abdominal cavity and it was full of blood. He had a large laceration on the liver and a large hole in the right kidney. He found a bullet in a muscle. He died about an hour after admission.

James Teehan, age 26. 5 Green Street, Dublin. Date of death: 21 November 1920. He was dead on admission. Doctor William Hanway said that he had a small skin wound behind his left ear, that he had bruises on his right elbow and on both knees. His lungs were congested and the walls of his heart were thin and dilated. He died of shock and heart failure.

Michael Feery (age not known) was dead on admission to Jervis Street Hospital. Doctor Cassin said he had a gash about four inches long on the outside of his left thigh and a similar gash on the inside of that thigh. The femoral vessels were severed and from these wounds a large laceration passed upwards towards the peritoneum to the pelvic bones which were shattered.

Dan Carroll, age 30, was employed in the licensed trade. He received bullet wounds in the thigh and many blood vessels were severed. Doctor Cassin found a piece of metal in a lower fragment of bone. He was operated on but died on 23 November. His employer, Martin Kennedy, visited him and Dan told him that he was on his way home when he was shot from a lorry.

Michael Hogan, age 24. Grangemockler, County Tipperary. Doctor Cassin said he was dead on admission. He had three bullet wounds on the left side of his back, his left lung was perforated by a shattered rib and he had a pint of blood in the left cavity. His second cousin, Fr Patrick Browne, Maynooth, County Kildare, identified him.

James Burke (age not known). 293 The Cottages, Windy Harbour, Dundrum, County Dublin. Doctor Cassin said he was dead on admission. His wife Annie identified him. He was employed at the Terenure Laundry. He had a small wound on his right knee. Both lungs were congested; the right chambers of the heart were engorged with blood. His death was due to shock and heart failure.

Thomas Ryan, age 27. Doctor William Hanaway described his wounds. He had a circular wound in the abdominal wall, a circular wound in his right leg just below his knee and a small wound in his back. The abdominal cavity was full of blood. He died two hours after admission.[1]

The *Dublin Evening Mail* listed the wounded and where they were being treated:

Mater Hospital:

A. Doyle, 3 Erin Terrace.

P. Gunney, 36c Corporation Buildings.

Jos. Wiseley, 10 Hardwicke Place.

Thomas Pollard, 3 Anne's Cottages.

Thomas Hogan, 130 James Street. (The address on his death certificate is given as 24 James Street).

James O'Doherty, 10 Gracepark Road, Drumcondra.

Tim McGrath, 130 James Street.

Jervis Street Hospital:

Christopher Duffy, 60 Lower Ship Street, Dublin.

Thomas O'Connor, 103 Bride Street.

James Fagan, 15 Dominick Street.

Michael Curley, 4 Morville Place.

Patrick Caulfield, 25 Corporation Street.

Patrick Connolly, 541 North Circular Road.

Laurence Flynn, 37 North Great Charles Street.

Patrick Lacey, 5 South Lotts Road.

Matthew O'Keeffe, 10 Lower Gloucester Street.

Daniel Carroll, James Street.

Patrick Howard, 11 Blessington Street.

William Banahan, 91 Stella Gardens.

James Flood, 11 York Street.

Joseph Farrell, 38 James Street.[2]

APPENDIX 6

OFFICERS ELECTED TO PATRICK MORANS, BELFAST, IN 1942

President: Séamus Dowling.

Vice-presidents: Messrs M. Mooney, M. Duffy, J. Crumlish, J. Kelly and P. McLaughlin.

Secretary: George Branagh.

Assistant Secretary: William Phoenix.

Committee: Messrs P. Murray, G. Duffy, T. Deegan, P. McCorry, B. McGoldrick, H. Matthews, F. McDonald, P. Carey and S. McDonald.[1]

ENDNOTES

Chapter 1

1   Poem given to a comrade-in-arms who asked him for a message on the night before his execution, probably written by Maeve Cavanagh McDowell. Published in *The Catholic Bulletin*, 1923, p. 231. Every effort has been made to establish the copyright holder of this poem. If the copyright holder contacts me, the necessary acknowledgement will be made in future editions.

2   Crossna, Boyle, County Roscommon. The Irish form of the name is *Crosná*. Versions of the name Kearehowecrossnawe, Crossnagh and Crosna are mentioned in the Jacobean Calendar of Patent Roll (1603) and in a manuscript in the Royal Irish Academy (1718–31c).

3   Letter from Paddy Moran, Kilmainham Gaol, 1921, Moran family papers.

4   *Our Boys*, vol. 8, no. 8, April 1922, pp. 263–264.

5   The shop was between two arched doors in Main Street, Boyle. See photograph in the Lawrence Collection, NLI.

6   *The Bible War in Ireland*, Irene Whelan, pp. 148–9.

7   Letter from Maguire's, Moran family papers.

8   1911 Census returns.

9   A postcard written to his sister in Lancashire, England, and posted in Ballyfarnon, Boyle, on 9 October 1910 tells that he is bound for Dublin on 10 October.

10 'Eye on the past', *Kildare Nationalist*, 20 February 2003.

11 *A Short History of the Irish Revolution, 1912–1927*, Richard Killeen, p. 34

12 *Ibid.*

13 *Lockout Dublin 1913*, Pádraig Yates, Prologue p. xxi.

14 Letter from Mr Glynn, Moran family papers.

15 'Our Irish Heroes' (author unknown), *Our Boys,* Volume 8, No. 8, April 1922, p. 2.

16 Oral evidence from Paddy's sister B. Moran.

17 *The Gaelic Athletic Association in Dublin,* William Nolan, Vol. 3, p. 1245.

18 Dublin county board minutes, 27 July 1915.

19 *Ibid.,* 17 October 1915.

20 *Ibid.,* 2 November 1915.

21 'Private Patrick Moran, The Sigerson Winner hanged for Ireland', Dónal Mac An Ailin, Sigerson programme 2002. Institute of Technology, Sligo.

22 Recounted by Seán O'Mahony, Dublin county board, Parnell Park.

23 Letter from Jeremiah O'Carroll, Knockanure, Newtownsandes, County Kerry, Moran family papers.

24 Oral testimony of Joseph Duignan, nephew of Paddy Moran.

25 'The Early Days of the GAA in the Area', in *St Michael's GAA Club, Ardcarne Park, Official Opening Souvenir Programme,* pp. 13–14, 19–20.

26 Micheál Shivnan, 'Memories of the Fifties' in *St Michael's GAA Club, Ardcarne Park Official Opening Souvenir Programme,* pp. 23–6.

27 Folklore submission from Bridgecartron School by Estie Fleming. Date of fishing trip 21 July 1914.

28 The book is part of the Moran family papers.

29 *The Capuchin Annual,* 1966, article by Pádraig Ó Ceallaigh.

30 *The Irish Republic,* by Dorothy Macardle quoting from the *The Irish Volunteer,* 7 February 1914, p. 61.

31 *The Irish Republic,* by Dorothy Macardle, p. 73.

32 *Irish Independent* 1 January 1936.

33 CO 904/31 British National Archives, p. 79

34 Witness statement by Bulmer Hobson No. 51, Bureau of Military History.

35 *The Irish Republic,* by Dorothy Macardle, p. 67.

36 *Ibid.,* p. 99.

37 *With the Dublin Brigade,* Charlie Dalton, p. 34.

38 Witness Statement (henceforth WS) 1387 Hugh Maguire, Bureau of Military History.

39 MS 901/59 National Library of Ireland.

40 *They Have Fooled You Again: Michael O'Flanagan (1876–1942)*, Dennis Carroll, p. 35.

41 *Ibid.*, pp. 35–6.

42 PRO CO 903/19 p. 26, British National Archives.

43 *They Have Fooled You Again: Michael O'Flanagan (1876–1942)*, Dennis Carroll, p. 37.

44 *For Ireland and Freedom: Roscommon's contribution to the fight for independence, 1917–1921*, Micheál O'Callaghan, based on testimony of Paddy's brothers, Tom and Batty, pp. 75–6.

45 Statement by Tom Moran to the Military Service Pensions Board 1937.

Chapter 2

1 WS 1746 Matthew Connolly, Bureau of Military History.

2 *The Irish Republic*, Dorothy Macardle, p. 163

3 'Jacob's Factory Area', Padraig Ó Ceallaigh, *Capuchin Annual*, 1966, pp. 214–87.

4 WS 1387 Hugh Maguire, Bureau of Military History.

5 WS 1746 Matthew Connolly, Bureau of Military History.

6 WS 1387 Hugh Maguire, Bureau of Military History.

7 *Ibid.*

8 WS 263 William Slater, Bureau of Military History.

9 WS 267 Seamus Pouch Bureau of Military History.

10 WS 263 Thomas Slater, Bureau of Military History.

11 WS 532 John McDonagh, Bureau of Military History.

12 'Our Irish Heroes', *Our Boys*, Volume 8, No. 8, April 1922, pp. 2–3.

13 *W&R Jacob: Celebrating 160 years of Irish Biscuit Making*, Seamus Ó Maitiú, www.nationalarchives.ie.

14 WS 312 Séamus de Brún, Bureau of Military History.

15 *Ibid.*

16 WS 267 Séamus Pouch, Bureau of Military History.

17 WS 263 Thomas Slater, Bureau of Military History.

18 WS 139 Michael Walker, Bureau of Military History.

19 WS 822 William J. Stapleton, Bureau of Military History.

20   WS 263, Thomas Slater, Bureau of Military History.

21   WS 204 Seán Murphy, Bureau of Military History.

22   WS 200 Fr Aloysius, OFM, Bureau of Military History.

23   WS 995 Éamon Price, Bureau of Military History.

24   WS 204 Seán Murphy, Bureau of Military History.

25   WS 995 Éamon Price, Bureau of Military History.

26   WS 200 Fr Aloysius, OFM, Bureau of Military History.

27   *W&R Jacob Celebrating 150 Years of Irish Biscuit Making*, Séamus Ó Maitiú; account of occupation of Jacob's; Web article.

28   WS 995 Éamon Price, Bureau of Military History.

29   Monthly Police Reports CO903/19, British National Archives, p. 28.

30   WS 423 Vinnie Byrne, Bureau of Military History.

31   WS 267 Séamus Pouch, Bureau of Military History.

32   WS 312 Seosamh de Brún, Bureau of Military History.

Chapter 3

1   WS 1768 Andrew McDonnell, Bureau of Military History.

2   *Ibid.*

3   WS 421 William Oman, Bureau of Military History.

4   WS 822 William J. Stapleton, Bureau of Military History.

5   WS 532 John MacDonagh, Bureau of Military History.

6   WS 822 William J. Stapleton, Bureau of Military History.

7   Paddy Moran's written account of where he was in 1916.

8   HO 144/1455/313106 (1–277), British National Archives. Paddy's registered number in Knutsford was 1538D and his address was recorded as 160 Phibsboro Road, Dublin.

9   *Richard Mulcahy (1886–1971), A Family Memoir,* Risteárd Mulcahy, p. 30

10   Skilly was a kind of gruel or thin broth.

11   *Under the Starry Plough*, Frank Robbins, Chapter 6, Knutsford Prison.

12   *Richard Mulcahy (1886–1971), A Family Memoir,* Risteárd Mulcahy, p. 33.

13   *Ibid.*, p. 35.

14 *Under the Starry Plough*, Frank Robbins, Chapter 6, p.158.

15 *Richard Mulcahy (1886–1971), A Family Memoir,* Risteárd Mulcahy, p. 30.

16 *Fron-goch and the Birth of the IRA,* Lyn Ebenezer, p. 80.

17 WS 397 Thomas Pugh, Bureau of Military History.

18 *Joe Stanley: printer to the Rising,* Tom Reilly, pp. 59–60.

19 *Fron-goch and the Birth of the IRA,* Lyn Ebenezer, p. 100.

20 WS 397 Thomas Pugh, Bureau of Military History, p. 11.

21 *Fron-goch and the Birth of the IRA,* Lyn Ebenezer, p. 101.

22 *With the Irish in Frongoch,* W.J. Brennan Whitmore, p. 63.

23 *Fron-goch and the Birth of the IRA,* Lyn Ebenezer, p. 128.

24 *Joe Stanley: printer to the Rising,* Tom Reilly, p. 85.

25 Moran family papers.

26 WS 585 Frank Robbins, Bureau of Military History.

27 *With the Irish in Frongoch,* W.J. Brennan Whitmore, p. 53.

28 WS 397 Thomas Pugh, Bureau of Military History.

29 *Joe Stanley: printer to the Rising,* Tom Reilly, p. 101.

30 HO 144/1455. List of 176 internees released on 24 July 1916. British National Archives.

31 Moran family papers, copy in Kilmainham Gaol Archive.

32 Moran family papers. Thomas O'Dea wrote again to Paddy in January 1917 from Stradbally, Kilcolgan.

33 1911 Census returns for Kingstown.

34 Seamus O'Connor on 'Lynch and O'Brien', Dun Laoghaire Borough Historical Society, *Dun Laoghaire Journal,* No. 3, 1993, pp. 6–7.

35 WS 397 Thomas Pugh, Bureau of Military History.

36 *Joe Stanley: printer to the Rising,* Tom Reilly, p. 83.

Chapter 4

1 *The Four Glorious Years, 1918–1921,* Frank Gallagher, p. 24.

2 '8000 attend as President unveils plaque', *Irish Press,* 6 June 1966.

3 MS 901, National Library of Ireland, p. 56.

4 *For Ireland and Freedom,* Micheál O'Callaghan, p. 76.

5 The History of the Irish National Union of Vintners', Grocers' and Allied Trades Assistants (Mandate web article)

6   'Was Paddy Moran judicially murdered?' *Irish Press,* 25 March 1971, article by Ross M.Connolly

7   'Foundation and growth', Bray and District Trade Union Council. Copy of article given to me by John Douglas, General Secretary, Mandate Trade Union.

8   Oral Testimony from Joe McKiernan, Manorhamilton, County Leitrim, who experienced the 'living in' system.

9   *Watchword of Labour,* 21 February 1920.

10 *Ibid.,* 20 March 1920.

11 *The Irish Times,* Monday, 8 March 1920.

12 *The Irish Times,* 20 January 1920.

13 Prison Registers MFGS 51/128, National Archives. His register number was 39.

14 Minute Book of Trade Union held in Mandate Trade Union Offices, Cavendish Row, Dublin.

15 The reference to the 'Bungs' is interesting. Guinness' Brewery did not support the strike in 1920 and when the delivery men came to deliver barrels of Guinness, the striking assistants pierced the 'bung' on the bottom of the barrel and let porter flow all over the street. Jack Cagney explained the reference to the 'Bungs' for me.

16 Moran family papers.

17 'Was Paddy Moran judicially murdered', article by Ross Connolly in *Irish Press,* 25 March 1971.

18 WS 569 John Anthony Caffrey, Bureau of Military History.

19 *Roscommon Herald,* 17 June 1917.

20 WO 904/157/1 Intelligence Notes 1917.

21 Oral evidence from Larry O'Hara, RIP, of Cootehall in conversation with me.

22 *The Irish Republic,* Dorothy Macardle, pp. 216–19.

23 Micheál O'Callaghan, For Ireland and freedom p. 8.

24 Letter from Mrs Kitty O'Doherty, Moran family papers.

25 Dan Breen, *My fight for Irish freedom* p. 8.

26 Michael Kevin O'Doherty, *My parents and other rebels* p. 100

27 *Four Glorious Years,* p. 27. De Valera speaking at a conference in the Mansion House, Dublin.

28 *The Irish Republic*, Dorothy Macardle, p. 252.

29 *Ibid.*, p. 254.

30 Copy in the Moran family papers.

31 POS 912 A/0229/A, Collins Papers, NLI.

32 *The Irish Republic*, Dorothy Macardle, p. 272.

Chapter 5

1 *Michael Collins and the Troubles*, Ulick O'Connor, p. 127.

2 *The Irish Republic*, Dorothy Macardle, p. 304.

3 MS 739 General Orders – Circulars and Memorandum of IRA 1920–21, NLI.

4 *Police casualties in Ireland*, Richard Abbott, p. 7.

5 *Bloody Sunday*, James Gleeson, p. 98.

6 *The Irish War of Independence*, Michael Hopkinson, p. 99

7 *The Irish Republic*, Dorothy Macardle, quoting from the *Morning Post*, 3 April 1920, p. 340.

8 *The Irish Republic,* Dorothy Macardle, p. 340.

9 *Theatres of War*, Seán McConville, p. 689.

10 'Bloody Sunday – a Reappraisal', T. Bowden, quoting from *Fortnightly Report* 1/6/1920, Chief Secretary's Office, Crime Branch Special 1920, State Papers Office, Dublin Castle, p. 34.

11 Gabriel Doherty and John Borgnovo, 'Smoking Gun? RIC reprisals, Summer 1920', in *History Ireland*, Vol. 17 No. 2, April/March 2009.

12 'Bloody Sunday – a Reappraisal', T. Bowden, p. 35.

13 *Theatres of War*, Seán McConville, p. 689.

14 *Bloody Sunday*, James Gleeson, pp. 107–9.

15 CO 904/177 Copy of article entitled 'We want no Inquiry', *New Statesman*, 28 May 1921.

16 *The Men I Killed*, F.P. Crozier, p. 120.

17 *Ibid.*

18 *Theatres of War*, Seán McConville, pp. 691–3.

19 CO 904 156 B, British National Archives, p. 10.

20 *Michael Collins and the Troubles,* Ulick O'Connor, p. 177.

21 *Michael Collins: The Lost Leader,* Margery Forester, p. 168; see 'Michael Collins' by Rex Taylor, p. 103.

22 *Michael Collins and the Troubles,* Ulick O'Connor, pp. 178–9.

23 Glanders is a contagious bacterial disease in which mucus discharges profusely from the nostrils.

24 CO 904/168, British National Archives.

25 WS 663 Joseph Dolan, Bureau of Military History.

26 *Michael Collins and the Troubles,* Ulick O'Connor, p. 179.

27 *Ibid.*

28 WS 615 Frank Thornton; also in *Dublin's Fighting Story,* p. 151; *Bloody Sunday,* James Gleeson, interview with Ben Doyle, pp. 143–4.

29 *Dublin's Fighting Story* p. 151; *The Four Glorious Years,* Frank Gallagher, p. 242.

30 *Richard Mulcahy 1886–1971,* Risteárd Mulcahy, p. 159.

31 *The Irish War of Independence,* Michael Hopkinson, p. 89.

32 *Michael Collins and the Troubles,* Ulick O'Connor, p. 179.

33 *Dublin's Fighting Story,* The Kerryman, p. 151.

34 Collins Papers P919 A/02532, NLI microfilm.

35 WS 1687 Harry Colley, Bureau of Military History.

36 WS 774 James Foley, Bureau of Military History.

37 WS 499 Paddy Kennedy, Bureau of Military History.

38 WS 774 James Foley, Bureau of Military History.

39 WS 387 Paddy Daly, Bureau of Military History.

40 WO 35/159B British National Archives.

41 CO 904/168 Dublin Metropolitan Police Report, 21 November 1920, British National Archives.

42 *Bloody Sunday,* James Gleeson, pp. 125 & 132.

43 *Roscommon Herald,* 27 November 1920.

44 Collins Papers, POS 911, A2316, NLI.

45 WS 771 James Doyle, Bureau of Military History.

46 *The Irish Times,* 24 November 1920.

47 'Bloody Sunday – a Reappraisal', T. Bowden, pp. 38–9.

48 *Ibid.,* p. 39.

49 'Bloody Sunday, Michael Collins speaks', Charles Townshend, pp. 377–382.

50 *Bloody Sunday,* James Gleeson, p. 132.

51 Ernie O'Malley notebooks, UCD Archives 17b, Charlie Dalton, p. 122.

52 CO 904/168, British National Archives. Handwritten memo from chief secretary's office on the evening of 21 November 1920, Dublin Metropolitan Police report.

53 Minute Book, Dublin County Board, 17 November 1920.

54 *The Gaelic Athletic Association in Dublin 1884–2000*, William Nolan, p. 171.

55 *Ibid.*, p. 183.

56 WO 35/88B, British National Archives.

57 *Ibid.*

58 *Kevin Barry*, Seán Cronin, epilogue, p. 42.

59 *Bray and South Dublin Herald*, 27 November 1920.

60 *Ibid.*

61 *Ibid.*

62 *Ibid.*

63 *Ibid.*

64 *Dublin Evening Mail*, 22 November 1920.

65 WO 35/88 B, British National Archives.

66 *The Four Glorious Years*, Frank Gallagher, p. 243.

67 WS 631 Bernard Byrne, Bureau of Military History; *My Fight for Irish Freedom*, Dan Breen, p. 157.

68 O'Malley notebooks, UCD Archives 17b, Moira McKee testimony, pp. 174–9.

69 *Ibid.*, UCD Archives 17b 110, interview with Pat McCrea, p. 110.

70 WS 376 Padraig Ó Ceallaigh, B Company Dublin Brigade.

71 *Bloody Sunday*, James Gleeson, p. 158.

72 *Winter's Tale, Dublin Castle 1920–1921*, Sir Ormonde Winter, p. 322.

73 *The Irish War of Independence*, Michael Hopkinson, p. 88.

74 *Allegiance*, Robert Brennan, p. 287.

75 *Ibid.*

76 Lloyd George Papers, LG/F/180/5/21, Pastoral Letter of His Eminence Cardinal Logue, 28 November 1920, House of Commons, London.

77 *Michael Collins*, Rex Taylor, p. 106, quoting from a private source.

78 *Michael Collins and the Troubles*, Ulick O'Connor, p. 179.

79　Oral testimony from Seán Moran, a nephew of Paddy Moran.

80　*Seán Lemass: the Enigmatic Patriot,* John Horgan, p. 17.

Chapter 6

1　Noyk papers, NLI MS 36224/1/4/5, item 2, statements of witnesses.

2　CO 904 156 B, British National Archives, p. 10.

3　Noyk papers, NLI MS 36224/1, item 2.

4　The collar is now in Kilmainham Gaol Museum.

5　Letter to Mary Farrell, 19 December 1920, Moran family papers.

6　Noyk papers, NLI MS 36224/1/4/5, item 2.

7　*On Another Man's Wound,* Ernie O'Malley, pp. 277–8.

8　*In the Front Gate – and Out the Back: the story of Frank Teeling,* Michael Meehan, p. 10.

9　Recorded by Fr Dominic in Parkhurst Prison in March 1921 when he heard of the executions, Kilmainham Gaol Museum.

10　WO 35/141/1, 2nd Battalion Welch Regiment, prisoners' routine, British National Archives.

11　*On Another Man's Wound,* Ernie O'Malley, p. 299.

12　*Ibid.,* pp. 293–4.

13　Noyk Papers, NLI, MS 36224/1, item 1, charge sheets.

14　*Ibid.,* item 2.

15　*Mountjoy – The Story of a Prison,* Tim Carey, p. 188.

16　*Bray and South Dublin Herald,* 7 February 1920.

17　O'Malley notebooks, UCD Archives 17b, Mick Smith interview, p. 122.

18　*Evening Herald,* 8 January 1936. Press cutting in Allen Library, Dublin.

19　*On Another Man's Wound,* Ernie O'Malley, pp. 306–8.

20　WS 642 Christy (Kit) Byrne.

21　WS 340 Oscar Traynor, Bureau of Military History.

22　Anna Kelly (née Fitzsimmons), 'Famous Jail Escapes in Ireland', *Sunday Press,* Part 1, 8 July 1956.

23　O'Malley notebooks, UCD Archives 17b, Jimmy Donnelly testimony, p. 115; WS 607 Joseph McGuinness, Bureau of Military History.

24 WO 35/141/1 British National Archives.

25 Anna Kelly (née Fitzsimmons), 'Famous Jail Escapes in Ireland', *Sunday Press*, Part 2, 15 July 1956.

26 Paper cutting in Moran family papers.

27 CO 904/229, British National Archives.

28 *On Another Man's Wound*, Ernie O'Malley, pp. 312.

29 WO 35/90 Arrests, British National Archives.

30 'First Rescue Attempt Failed', Denis Begley, undated paper cutting in Moran family papers.

31 Anna Kelly (née Fitzsimmons), 'Famous Jail Escapes in Ireland', *Sunday Press*, Part 2, 15 July 1956.

32 O'Malley Notebooks, UCD Archives, 17b, Jimmy Donnelly, p. 115.

33 WS 813 Padraig Ó Conchubhair (Paddy O'Connor), Bureau of Military History.

34 O'Malley Notebooks, UCD Archives, 17b, Jimmy Donnelly, p. 115.

35 WS 813 Padraig Ó Conchubhair (Paddy O'Connor), Bureau of Military History, pp. 17, 18; see also WS 607 Joseph McGuinness for a similar account of the escape.

36 *On Another Man's Wound*, Ernie O'Malley, pp. 303–12.

37 *Ibid.*, pp. 303-4.

38 For Escape Stories see WS 340 Oscar Traynor, WS 607 Joseph McGuinness, WS 1687 Harry Colley, WS 813 Paddy O'Connor, WS 642 Christy Byrne; O'Malley notebooks, UCD Archives 17b, pp. 115–22; Anna Kelly (née Fitzsimmons), 'Famous Jail Escapes in Ireland', *Sunday Press*, 8 and 15 July 1956; Collins Papers, P920 A 0620, Denis Begley account, NLI microfilm; letter from Sean Farrelly, *Irish Press*, 2 February 1936; response from Séamus Kirwan, undated, Moran family papers; Simon Donnelly, 'The Kilmainham Rescue', *Evening Telegraph and Press*, 8 October 1932.

39 WS 813 Paddy O'Connor.

40 WS 1687 Harry Colley, Bureau of Military History.

41 *On Another Man's Wound*, Ernie O'Malley, p. 301.

42 WS813 Padraig Ó Conchubhair [Paddy O'Connor], Bureau of Military History.

43 Anna Kelly (née Fitzsimmons), 'Famous Jail Escapes in Ireland',

Sunday Press, Part 2, 15 July 1956; see also WS 340 Oscar Traynor, Bureau of Military History, pp. 58–66.

44 *For Ireland and Freedom*, Micheál O'Callaghan, p. 77.

45 *Ibid.*

46 Anna Kelly (née Fitzsimmons), 'Famous Jail Escapes in Ireland', *Sunday Press*, Part 2, 15 July 1956.

47 Collins papers, P920 A 0620, Denis Begley account, NLI.

48 WS 707 Michael Noyk, Bureau of Military History; O'Malley notebooks, UCD Archives 17b, Diarmuid O'Sullivan interview, p. 122.

49 Letter to his sister Annie from Mountjoy, Moran family papers.

50 Undated press cutting, Moran family papers.

51 *On Another Man's Wound*, Ernie O'Malley, p. 303.

52 Noyk papers, NLI, MS MS 36223/1/2.

53 CO 904/44, British National Archives and MS 36222/1 NLI.

54 CO 904/42 British National Archives and Noyk Papers, NLI, MS 36223/1/2.

55 CO 904/188, letter from General Macready, 15 February 1921, British National Archives.

56 CO 904/188, 16 February 1921, British National Archives.

57 WO 35/141/1, British National Archives.

58 CO 904/188, British National Archives.

59 WO 35/141/1, court-martial of James Holland and Ernest Roper, British National Archives.

60 WO 35/56 B, British National Archives.

61 WO 71/363, British National Archives.

62 WS 707 Michael Noyk, Bureau of Military History.

63 CO 904/17, *The New Statesman*, 28 May 1921, British National Archives.

Chapter 7

1 *Irish Independent*, 16 February 1921.

2 WS 707 Michael Noyk, Bureau of Military History, p. 37.

3 *Ibid.*, p. 51.

4 WO 71/ 363, British National Archives.

5   WS 707 Michael Noyk, Bureau of Military History, p. 38.

6   WO 71/363, British National Archives.

7   *Irish Independent*, 16 February 1921.

8   WO 71/363, British National Archives.

9   *Irish Independent*, 17 February 1921.

10 MS 36222/3, Noyk papers, NLI.

11 WO 71 /363, British National Archives.

12 WO 71/363, British National Archives.

13 MS 36222/3, Noyk Papers, NLI.

14 WS 707, Michael Noyk, Bureau of Military History.

15 *Ibid.*

16 MS 36222/3, Noyk Papers, NLI.

17 WS 707, Michael Noyk, Bureau of Military History.

18 *Ibid.*

19 WO 71/363, British National Archives, p. 113.

20 *Ibid.*, p. 114.

21 WS 707 Michael Noyk, Bureau of Military History.

22 WS 727 Michael Joseph Lawless, Bureau of Military History.

23 WS 423 Vincent Byrne, Bureau of Military History.

24 WO 71/363.

25 MS 36224/2, Noyk Papers, NLI.

26 WS 423 Vinnie Byrne; O'Malley notebooks, UCD Archives 17b, Pat McCrea interview, p. 110.

27 Minutes of executive committee meeting dated 21 November 1920. From minute book of union held in Mandate Trade Union Offices, Cavendish Row, Dublin.

28 Minutes of executive meeting Sunday 14 November 1920, Mandate Trade Union Offices, Cavendish Row, Dublin.

29 WO 71/363, British National Archives.

30 Letter to his sister Annie quoted in Chapter 9, Moran family papers.

31 It was general practice to ask police in the local area about a convicted person.

32 WO 71/353, British National Archives, Statement of Sergeant James O'Sullivan, 8 February 1921.

33   *Irish Independent*, 17 February 1921.

Chapter 8

1   That witness was Harris, a man from Dun Laoghaire, who was taken from the Bridewell for the identification parade at Arbour Hill Prison on the same day as Paddy himself, 11 December 1920. He was again with him when they were paraded on 17 December and was one of the seven who was sent into the yard to stand with him and Halpin. Harris heard the staff sergeant say that there was doubt in Paddy's case and that he was not going for trial but only to be put beside another man at another identification parade. He could have testified that the identification was not made as independently as was claimed by the prosecution at the trial.

2   Letter to sisters Ciss and B then in England, Moran family papers.

3   *Ibid.*

4   Letter from Paddy to his sister Annie written on a Thursday but undated, Moran family papers.

5   Letter to Annie Moran, Moran family papers.

6   Materials given to me by Andy Gibbons. Copies of memorabilia brought out of Mountjoy by a warder named Wheeler after the executions.

7   Letter to Annie, 23 February 1921, Moran family papers.

8   Letter to Ciss and Bridget, Moran family papers.

9   CO 904/43, telegram to Viscount French, British National Archives.

10   CO 904/43, British National Archives.

11   *Ibid.*

12   Letter to Annie, 23 February 1921, Moran family papers.

13   *The Irish Times,* 10 March 1921.

14   *Irish Independent*, 14 March 1921, p. 5.

15   *Ibid.*, p. 6.

16   Moran family papers.

17   *Ibid.*

18   Noyk Papers, MS 36224/4, NLI; WS 707, Michael Noyk, Bureau of Military History.

19 *Ibid.*

20 *Ibid*, letter from Lieutenant Commander Kenworthy 14 March 1921, NLI.

21 The soldier referred to here is Snelling, but he the *Daily News* is incorrect in stating that he identified Whelan. *Hanged for Ireland –The Forgotten Ten*, Tim Carey, p. 59.

22 'Death Sentences – Two executions pending', *Daily News*, 11 March 1921.

23 *Evening Herald*, 14 March 1921, p. 3.

24 CO 904/43, file on Patrick Moran, British National Archives.

25 *Ibid.*

26 *Ibid.*

27 *Ibid.*, PRO ref. 104674, letter from Mrs McLaverty to General McMahon.

28 CO 904/43, file on Patrick Moran, British National Archives.

29 CO 904/43, British National Archives.

30 'The Crown's Prerogative – cases of Thomas Whelan and Patrick Moran', *The Irish Times*, 12 March 1921.

31 CO 904/43, British National Archives.

32 Copy of letter in Joseph Devlin papers, courtesy of Fionnuala Waters.

33 Moran family papers.

34 *Irish Independent*, Monday, 14 March 1921, p. 5.

35 *Hanged for Ireland –The Forgotten Ten*, Tim Carey, p. 85.

36 Letter to P. Hughes from John Turner, Moran family papers.

37 *Ibid.*

38 CO 904/43, British National Archives.

39 *Irish Independent*, 14 March 1921, p. 6.

40 *Ibid.*

41 Lloyd George Papers, LG/F/19/4/2, interview with a journalist, Carl W. Ackerman, House of Commons, London.

42 General Prison Board Correspondence Register 1921, CO/135, National Archives, Dublin.

43 CO 904/42, file on Thomas Whelan. British National Archives. London, Telegram dated 12 March 1921.

44 Oral evidence of Tom Moran.

45 General Prison Board Correspondence Register 1921, CO/135, National Archives, Dublin.

46 *Irish Independent*, 14 March 1921, p. 5

47 *Ibid.*

48 Robert Brennan, 'Mainly Meandering, Story of a Hero and a Friend', *Irish Press* cutting, n.d., Moran family papers.

49 *The Nation*, Christmas double, number 14 December 1929.

50 Undated press cutting re acquisitions by National Museum *c.*1935, Moran family papers.

51 Preserved by Mrs Maureen Flynn, Ballybrack, County Dublin.

52 Letter to Paddy's parents from Sister Patricia, Sisters of Charity, Gardiner Street, Moran family papers.

53 *Irish Independent,* 14 March 1921.

54 *Ibid.*

55 *Ibid.*

56 Materials given to me by Andy Gibbons and originals in the possession of Mrs Maureen Flynn, Ballybrack, County Dublin.

57 Papers of Seán Ó Luing, accession number 5140 NLI.

58 *Irish Independent,* 14 March 1921.

59 WS 631 Bernard Byrne, p. 28 (He called the executioner Pierrepoint), Bureau of Military History.

60 WS 631 Bernard Byrne, Bureau of Military History.

61 *Collected poems of Thomas MacGreevy,* Susan Schreibman.

Chapter 9

1 *Evening Herald,* 14 March 1921. Every effort has been made to establish the copyright holder of this poem. If the copyright holder contacts me, the necessary acknowledgement will be made in future editions.

2 *The Freeman's Journal,* 15 March 1921.

3 *Evening Herald,* 14 March 1921.

4 Copied from original of notice in the Allen Library, Richmond Street, Dublin.

5 Letter from Sister Patricia, Sisters of Charity, Gardiner Street, Moran family papers.

6 *The Freeman's Journal*, 15 March 1921.

7 Prayer book now in possession of Mealy's Auctioneers, Castlecomer, County Kilkenny.

8 Oral testimony of Micheál Shivnan, told to him by his mother Mrs Jimmy Shivnan who attended that all-night vigil.

9 Articles by Seán Kavanagh, *The Capuchin Annual*, 1965, Ref Ir 2713 c 15, NLI.

10 *The Freeman's Journal*, 15 March 1921.

11 *Irish Independent*, 14 March 1921.

12 *Evening Herald*, 14 March 1921.

13 *The Freeman's Journal*, 15 March 1921.

14 *Ibid.*

15 Quoted in *Ibid.*

16 Quoted in *Ibid.*

17 Quoted in *Ibid.*

18 WO 71/363, unsigned letter dated 16 March 1921, British National Archives.

19 CO 904/168, *Weekly Summary*, 18 March 1921, British National Archives.

20 CO 904/43, British National Archives.

21 *Irish Independent*, 14 March 1921.

22 WS 626, John Donnelly, Bureau of Military History.

23 *The Irish Times*, 15 March 1921.

24 WS 626, John Donnelly, Bureau of Military History.

25 WS 1001, Thomas Lavin Ballytore, County Kildare, Bureau of Military History, pp. 8–11.

26 CO 904/42, British National Archives.

27 *Roscommon Herald*, 2 April 1921.

28 WO 35 49A, British National Archives.

29 *Roscommon Herald*, Saturday, 4 June 1921.

30 Oral evidence of Sergeant Reilly's son, Michael, in an interview with me.

31 *Roscommon Herald*, 19 June 1921.

32 *Ibid.*, 2 April 1921.

33 *Roscommon Herald*, 26 March 1921.

34 *Ibid.,* 2 April, 1921.

35 CO 904/42, British National Archives Kew.

36 *Roscommon Herald,* 2 April 1921..

37 IE UCDA Mulcahy Papers, P7 38, UCD Archives.

38 *Roscommon Herald*, 2 April 1921; CO 904/42, British National Archives.

39 *Roscommon Herald,* 2 April 1921.

40 CO 904/42, British National Archives.

41 *For Ireland and Freedom*, Micheál O'Callaghan, pp. 100–1.

42 CO 904/42, British National Archives.

43 *For Ireland and Freedom*, Micheál O'Callaghan, pp. 100–1.

44 CO 904/42, British National Archives.

45 *Beyond The Twelve Bens*, Kathleen Villiers-Tuthill, pp. 209–13.

46 *The Irish Republic*, Dorothy Macardle, p. 466.

47 *Ibid.*, pp. 475–6.

Chapter 10

1 Tom Moran's statement to the Military Pensions Board.

2 *For Ireland and Freedom*, Micheál O'Callaghan, pp. 105–108.

3 *Roscommon Herald*, 30 March 1918.

4 Letters in Moran family papers.

5 Oral tradition handed down from my father, Tom Moran.

6 Tom Moran's statement to Military Service Pensions Board.

7 Tom Moran's statement to the Military Service Pensions Board.

8 *'Rising Out': Seán Connolly of Longford*, Ernie O'Malley, p. 169.

9 Article entitled 'The Rath Camp 1921'. Thomas Martin and Joseph Lawless left a record of their time in the camp. www.esatclear.ie/curragh/articles.htm.

10 CO 904/156 B, British National Archives, p. 45.

11 *Roscommon Herald*, 17 December 1921.

12 *For Ireland and Freedom,* Micheál O'Callaghan, pp. 81–5.

13 *Dublin Made Me,* Todd Andrews, pp. 186–8.

14 *Roscommon Herald*, 17 December 1921.

15 *Roscommon Herald,* 29 October 1921.

16 *For Ireland and Freedom*, Micheál O'Callaghan, pp. 78–80.

17 Moylan family papers.

18 Tom Moran's statement to the Military Service Pensions Board, 6 April 1935.

19 Letter to his sister, Moran family papers.

20 Internment Camp Files, Military Archives, Cathal Brugha Barracks, Dublin, F. O'Rourke O/C Cadet Company, Ballinamore Barracks.

21 Letter from Jim to Cissie, Moran family papers.

22 Oral evidence of Canon Peadar Lavin in conversation with me in August 2009.

23 *Eire, The Irish Nation*, 5 April 1924.

24 *Green against Green, The Irish Civil War*, Michael Hopkinson, p. 263.

25 *Eire, The Irish Nation*, 3 November 1923; *The Irish Times*, 23 October 1923.

26 *Eire, The Irish Nation*, 27 October 1923, has a full list of those on hunger strike in Mountjoy.

27 *The Irish Times*, 23 October 1923.

28 *Ibid.*, 27 October 1923.

29 *The Irish Republic*, Dorothy Macardle, p. 867.

30 Autograph book belonging to Jim Moran, now in Kilmainham Gaol Museum, entry from Tomás Mac Mastair, Kinsale, County Cork.

31 *Eire, The Irish Nation*, 5 April 1924.

32 Internment Camp Files, Box 1, Military Archives, Cathal Brugha Barracks, Dublin.

33 *Roscommon Herald*, 20 December 1969.

34 Clip from newspaper in Moran family papers.

35 Copies of papers given to me by Miceál Hodgins, son of Margaret O'Flanagan, Róisín's sister, from the NLI: MS 17285.

36 *Ibid.*

37 Margaret O'Flanagan's statement to the Military Service Pensions Board, given to me by her son Miceál Hodgins.

38 *Spies in Ireland*, Enno Stephan, p. 177.

39 *Dr Hermann Goertz – A German Spy in South County Dublin*, Foxrock Local History Club Publication No. 27, talk by Brian P. Kennedy Wednesday 10 May 1989.

40   Oral Testimony of Paddy and Rose Richardson 6 Spencer Villas, Glenageary County Dublin.

Chapter 11

1   Letters from Grocers', Vintners' and Allied Trades Assistants' Union, Moran family papers.

2   Minutes of INUVG Meeting 20 November 1921.

3   John Douglas speaking in Crossna church in 2002.

4   IE UCDA P156, republican soldier casualties, UCD Archives.

5   Letter from Fr Dominic, 13 March 1922, Moran family papers and now in Kilmainham Gaol Museum.

6   Letter from Fr O'Flanagan, Moran family papers and now in Kilmainham Gaol Museum.

7   *Roscommon Herald*, 17 September 1921.

8   *Ibid.* Every effort has been made to establish the copyright holder of this poem. If the copyright holder contacts me, the necessary acknowledgement will be made in future editions.

9   *Ibid.*, 14 May 1921.

10   Dun Laoghaire Rathdown County Council website.

11   *The Irish Times*, 6 June 1966.

12   Interview with Andy Gibbons.

13   Researched from papers compiled by Dónal Mac an Ailin, Cardinal Ó Fiaich Library, Armagh.

14   *Irish News* and *Belfast Morning News*, 5 February 1942; papers compiled by Dónal Mac an Ailin, Cardinal Ó Fiaich Library, Armagh.

15   Article by Michael Shivnan 'Memories of the Fifties' in *St Michael's GAA Club. Ardcarne Park Official Opening. Souvenir Programme*, 5 May 1996, p. 25.

16   Article entitled 'Mountjoy Prison Ceremony. Memorial Unveiled', November 1934, Moran family papers.

17   Copy of letter from Brigid Moran to the treasurer, National Graves Association, 8 January 1935.

18   Article entitled 'Jail Homage to Executed Patriot 1937', Moran family papers.

19 'Mountjoy Jail Ceremony', paper cutting, Moran family papers.

20 *Roscommon Herald*, 20 March 1971.

21 'Tatler's Parade', *Irish Independent*, 7 May 1962.

22 Letter to Kilmainham Gaol Museum from B. Moran.

Chapter 12

1   S4199, Department of An Taoiseach Files, National Archives, Bishop Street, Dublin.

2   *Ibid.*

3   *Ibid.* Extern ministers were appointed by the Governor General of the Irish Free State on the nomination of Dáil Éireann. They operated outside the Executive Council and had no share in collective cabinet responsibility.

4   C2/200, Department of An Taoiseach Files, National Archives, Bishop Street, Dublin.

5   S8904, Department of An Taoiseach Files, National Archives, Bishop Street, Dublin.

6   *Hanged For Ireland – The Forgotten Ten*, Tim Carey, p. 186.

7   *Ibid.*

8   All speeches quoted are from *The Irish Times*, Monday 15 October 2001.

Chapter 13

1   The history of the Irish National Union of Vintners', Grocers' and Allied Trades Assistants, Mandate Union, web article.

2   *The Irish Republic*, Dorothy Macardle, p. 397.

3   WS 481 Simon Donnelly.

4   'Bloody Sunday – a Reappraisal', T. Bowden, p. 28.

5   *The Four Glorious Years*, Frank Gallagher, p. 109.

6   *The Irish Republic*, *Dorothy* Macardle, pp. 405, 406.

7   *The Irish War of Independence*, Michael Hopkinson, p. xix.

8   *Ibid.*

Appendix 1

1   WS 423 Vinnie Byrne, Bureau of Military History.

2   WS 532 John MacDonagh, brother of Tom, Bureau of Military History.

3   WS 421 William Oman, Bureau of Military History.

4   WS 267 Séamus Pouch, Bureau of Military History.

5   WS 263 Thomas Slater, Bureau of Military History.

6   *Ibid.*

7   WS 312 Seosamh de Brún, Bureau of Military History.

8   WS 267 Seamus Pouch, Bureau of Military History.

9   WS 822 William James Stapleton, Bureau of Military History.

10 WS 139 Michael Walker, Bureau of Military History.

11 Web article on Politics.ie

12 *The Gaelic Athletic Association in Dublin,* Vol. 1, 1884–1959, pp. 149–161.

13 P156, Republican soldier casualties, UCD Archives.

Appendix 2

1   CO 903/19, British National Archives.

Appendix 3

1   IE UCDA P156, republican soldier casualties, UCD Archives.

Appendix 4

1   CO 904/189; *Bloody Sunday,* James Gleeson, pp. 128–129.

2   CO 904/189. Handwritten Report from Dublin Castle. British National Archives.

Appendix 5

1   WO 88 B, British National Archives.

2   *Dublin Evening Mail,* 22 November 1920.

Appendix 7

1   *Irish News and Belfast Morning News,* 5 February 1942; Dónal Mac an Ailin, Cardinal Ó Fiaich Library, Armagh.

BIBLIOGRAPHY

PRIMARY SOURCES

British National Archives, Kew, England:
- Colonial Office Records (CO)
- War Office Records (WO)
- Home Office Records (HO)
- Sturgis Diaries
- Lloyd George Papers

Files of newspapers compiled by Donal Mac an Ailin

Cardinal Ó Fiaich Library, Armagh

Dublin County Board Minute Book, Parnell Park

Dublin Minute Book, Mandate Trade Union Offices, Cavendish Row

Military Archives, Cathal Brugha Barracks, Dublin

Witness statements from participants in War of Independence from Cathal Brugha Barracks and National Archives

Military Archives, Cathal Brugha Barracks
- Internment Camp Files
- G2 Files
- Tom Moran: statement to Military Pensions Board

Michael Noyk papers, National Library of Ireland

Collins papers, National Library of Ireland

General Orders Circulars and Memorandum of IRA 1920–1921, National Library of Ireland

National Archives, Dublin
- General Prison Board files
- Department of An Taoiseach files

Register of Births, Marriages and Deaths, General Register Office: copies of Death Certificates

University College Dublin Archives: O'Malley notebooks

WEB

The History of the Irish National Union of Vintners', Grocers' and Allied Trades Assistants – Mandate

'The Rath Camp 1921', *History Ireland*, www.esatclear.ie/~curragh/articles.htm

Dun Laoghaire and Rathdown County Council Website, Moran Park House and Moran Park, www.dlrcoco.ie/ccda/heritage/mpkhistory.htm

NEWSPAPERS AND PERIODICALS

Bray and South Dublin Herald
Catholic Bulletin, The, 1923
Capuchin Annual, The, 1956 and 1965
Éire, the Irish Nation
Evening Herald
Evening Telegraph and Evening Press
Daily News
Dublin Evening Mail
Freeman's Journal
History Ireland, March/April 2009, Vol. 17, No. 2
Irish Times
Irish Independent
Irish Press
Irish News and Belfast Morning News.
Irish Volunteer
Kildare Nationalist
Our Boys 1922
Roscommon Herald
St Michael's GAA club, Ardcarne Park Official Opening, Souvenir Programme
Sunday Press
The Nation
Weekly Freeman
Watchword of Labour

Secondary Sources

Abbott, Richard, *Police Casualties in Ireland 1919–1922* (Mercier Press, 2000)

Andrews, C.S. (Todd), *Dublin Made Me* (Mercier Press, 1979)

Augusteijn, Joost, *From Public Defiance to Guerilla Warfare: the experience of ordinary Volunteers in the Irish War of Independence 1916–1921,* (Irish Academic Press, 1996)

Bowden, Tom, 'Bloody Sunday – a Reappraisal', *European Studies Review,* Vol. 1 (1972)

Breen, Dan, *My Fight for Irish Freedom* (Anvil Press, 1955)

Brennan, Robert, *Allegiance* (Browne and Nolan Limited, 1950)

Brennan Whitmore, W.J., *With the Irish in Frongoch* (Talbot Press, 1917)

Carey, Tim, *Mountjoy: the Story of a Prison* (Collins Press, 2000)

—— *Hanged for Ireland: the forgotten ten, executed 1920–1921* (Blackwater Press, 2001)

Carroll, Denis, *'They have fooled you again': Micheál Ó Flannagáin (1876–1942), priest, republican, social critic* (Columba Press, 1993)

Cronin, Seán, *Kevin Barry,* (National Publications Committee, Cork 1965, reprinted 1971)

Crozier, F.P., *The Men I Killed* (Michael Joseph Ltd, 1937)

Dalton, Charles, *With the Dublin Brigade 1917–1921* (Peter Davies Ltd, 1929)

Dwyer, T. Ryle, *The Squad* (Mercier Press, 2005)

De Búrca, Marcus, *The GAA – A History* (Gill & Macmillan, First Published 1980, Paperback edition 2000)

Ebenezer, Lyn, *Fron-goch and the birth of the IRA* (Gwasg Carreg Gwalch, 2006)

Figgis, Darrell, *A Chronicle of Jails* (The Talbot Press Ltd, 1917)

Forester, Margery, *Michael Collins: The Lost Leader* (Gill & Macmillan, 1989)

Foxrock Local History Club, *Doctor Hermann Goertz. A German Spy in South County Dublin,* text of talk by Brian Kennedy.

Gallagher, Frank, *The Four Glorious Years* (written under *nom de plume,* David Hogan, 2nd edition, Blackwater Press 2005)

Gleeson, James, *Bloody Sunday* (Peter Davies Ltd, 1962)

Hartnett, Noel, *Prison Escapes* (Pillar Publishing County Limited, 1945)

Hopkinson, Michael, *The Irish War of Independence* (Gill & Macmillian, 2002)

—— *Green Against Green, The Irish Civil War* (Gill & Macmillan, 1988)

Horgan, John, *Seán Lemass, The Enigmatic Patriot* (Gill & Macmillan, 1997)

Kerryman, The, *Dublin's Fighting Story 1913–1921 told by the men who made it* (Tralee, 1949)

Killeen, Richard, *A Short History of the Irish Revolution* (Gill & Macmillan, 2007)

Macardle, Dorothy, *The Irish Republic* (Wolfhound Press, 1999)

McConville, Seán, *Irish Political Prisoners, 1848–1922, Theatres of War* (Routledge, 2005)

Meehan, Michael, *In the Front Gate and Out the Back: the story of Frank Teeling* (2007)

Mulcahy, Risteárd, *Richard Mulcahy – A Family Memoir* (Aurelian Press, 1999)

Nolan, William (ed.), *The Gaelic Athletic Association in Dublin 1884–2000*, 3 Vols (Geography Publications, 2005)

O'Callaghan, Micheál, *For Ireland and Freedom, Roscommon's Contribution to the Fight for Independence, 1917–1921* (Roscommon Herald, Boyle 1964)

O'Connor, Ulick, *Michael Collins and the Troubles: the struggle for Irish freedom 1912–1922* (Mainstream, 1975)

O'Doherty, Michael Kevin, *My Parents and Other Rebels – A personal memoir* (Errigal Press, 1999)

O'Donnell, Peadar, *The Gates Flew Open* (Mercier Press, 1965)

O'Malley, Ernie, *On Another Man's Wound* (revised edition, Anvil, 2002)

——, *Rising Out: Seán Connolly of Longford* (edited by Cormac O'Malley, UCD Press, 2007)

Ó Maitiú, Séamus, *W&R Jacob – Celebrating 100 years of Irish Biscuit Making* (Woodfield Press, 2001)

Purdon, Edward, *The War of Independence* (Mercier Press, 2001)

Reilly, Tom, *Joe Stanley: printer to the Rising* (Brandon Press, 2005)

Robbins, Frank, *Under the Starry Plough: Recollections of Irish Citizen Army* (Academy Press, 1977)

Schreibman, Susan, *Collected Poems of Thomas MacGreevy, An annotated edition* (Anna Livia, 1991)

Stephan, Enno, *Spies in Ireland* (McDonald & Co. Publishers, 1963)

Taylor, Rex, *Michael Collins* (Hutchinson & Co. Ltd, 1958, Four Square edition 1961)

Tonra, Reverend Henry, *The Parish of Ardcarne* (self-published, 2001)

Townshend, Charles, 'Bloody Sunday – Michael Collins Speaks', *European studies Review*, Vol. 9 (1979)

Whelan, Irene, *The Bible War in Ireland: the 'Second Reformation' and the polarization of Protestant-Catholic Relations, 1800–1840* (The University of Wisconsin Press, 2005)

Winter, Sir Ormonde, *Winter's Tale – An Autobiography* (Richards Press, 1955)

Villiers-Tuthill, Kathleen, *Beyond the Twelve Bens – A History of Clifden and the District 1860–1923* (Conemara Girl Publications, second edition, 1990)

Yates, Pádraic, *Lockout Dublin 1913* (Gill & Macmillan, 2000)

Acknowledgements

I would like to thank my Aunt B. for preserving so much material relating to her brother, Paddy, and for entrusting it to me. This was the catalyst that compelled me to research my Uncle Paddy's story and that material forms a large part of this book.

I want to acknowledge the assistance given to me by the following libraries and record depositories who allowed me to consult material in their possession: the Roscommon County Library and particularly Patricia O'Flaherty and staff in the Boyle Branch, Leitrim County Library; the Allen Library; the Pearse Street Library; the National Library of Ireland; the Cardinal Ó Fiaich Library, Armagh; the National Archives of Ireland; the British National Archives; the House of Parliament, Westminster, London; the Military Archives, Cathal Brugha Barracks, Dublin; the Dublin County Board, GAA; University College Dublin Archives; Niall Bergin, supervisor, Kilmainham Gaol Museum; Mandate Trade Union General Secretary John Douglas and his staff.

I want to thank the Department of the Taoiseach, the Irish Prison Service, the Defence Forces, the ad hoc committee under the chairmanship of Brian Ó Cléirigh, and all those involved in the careful planning and professional implementation of the state funeral in October 2001. Thanks also to Rosie Nic Cionnaith and Múnla (Midas) Productions for TG4, for the documentary film *The Forgotten Ten, An Deichniúr Dearmadta*, which was made about the ten men in 2001–2002.

Anthony (Tony) Behan, President of the Institute of Legal Cost Accountants and a member of the Dublin Historical Society, alerted me to the acquisition by the National Library of the Noyk Papers at an early stage in my research.

Dr Michael Kennedy, National Archives, Dublin, read and commented on a synopsis of the story and encouraged me to put it into print. Finbar O'Shea, Bantry, County Cork, gave me valuable advice at a critical stage in my work. Both were introduced to me by Kathleen Harte who, through her experience in publishing, was a great help along the way. Kathleen and her sister, Philomena, listened and contributed to many conversations on the writing of this book.

I would like to thank Eoin Purcell, for his encouragement when I began writing this book. Danny and Caitríona Donnelly, Dundrum, Dublin, encouraged and advised me and provided photographs from the state funeral and from a celebration in Crossna in October 2001.

Tommy Whelan, nephew of Tommy Whelan who was executed with Paddy Moran, provided information and directed me to sources of information about his uncle.

Micheál and Betty Hodgins and Páid Hodgins provided information about Margaret Hodgins, née O'Flanagan (Micheál and Páid's mother), and took photographs for me. Micheál took a very keen and personal interest in the project and he researched and found several items of interest relating to Dun Laoghaire and Blackrock for me.

Paddy and Rose Richardson, the family who lived next door to Bea and Mary Farrell in Spencer Villas, Glenageary, County Dublin, invited me into their home and shared their memories of the Farrells with me.

Marie Thérèse West (née Keegan), grandniece of Paddy Moran, did research for me in the British National Archives at an early stage.

Joe Duignan, a nephew of Paddy Moran, recalled for me his associations with the Barmen's Union and their football team.

Patrick Doherty, my cousin from Donegal, forwarded several pieces of relevant information from various sources and introduced me to Francis McKay. Francis showed me his extensive collection of memorabilia from the War of Independence and shared his knowledge of that period with Patrick and me.

I particularly want to thank Kathleen Farry, Micheál Shivnan, Maura Clancy, Anne O'Connor, Anna Sheerin, my sister, and Seán Moran, my brother, for reading the manuscript and making very valuable comments and changes and for their words of encouragement. In addition, Maura Clancy proofread the manuscript and made several very useful suggestions.

My sister, Bridie, and her husband, Albert Plummer, welcomed me to their home on my trips to London to research the story and provided hospitality, friendship and transport.

In Dublin, my sister Rita and her husband, Charles and their family did likewise. Charles sourced information from Tony Behan, he introduced me to Michael Reilly, son of Sergeant Reilly, and to Andy Gibbons, former Patrick Morans player. Charles accompanied me to the headquarters of the Dublin county board to meet Seán O'Mahony and to research Paddy's GAA associations in the minute books.

Michael Reilly kindly drove to meet me in the West County Hotel in July 2009, at the age of eighty-seven, and shared information, photographs and his wisdom during that conversation.

Andy Gibbons, Stillorgan, County Dublin, the last surviving member of the Patrick Morans Football Club, gave me information about that football and hurling club and introduced me to Maureen Flynn, Ballybrack, County Dublin, who gave me copies of items brought from Mountjoy Jail by Warder Wheeler after the executions.

In Armagh, I had the pleasure of spending time with my cousin, Fionnuala Waters (née Fleming), when I went to the Cardinal Ó Fiaich Library to meet Dónal Mac an Ailin. Dónal has collected files of newspaper cuttings from a variety of sources. He was kind enough to arrange for me to access them in the Cardinal Ó Fiaich Library.

Joe McKiernan often recounted his experiences of 'living in' as a grocer's assistant and he generously allowed me to recall and summarise some of those experiences.

Canon Peadar Lavin, PP, Knockcroghery, County Roscommon, shared information he had from his conversations with his father, Andy Lavin, a Sinn Féin TD in the First Dáil, and allowed me to use it.

I would like to acknowledge the support of Fr Brian Conlon and the people of Crossna and their interest in the recording of this piece of history.

I want to thank all my friends for their friendship, for their encouragement, for their support, their interest in this project and for all the good times we have shared together. I especially mention Maura Clancy, whose friendship has stood the test of time; we met when we both arrived in Mount Sackville in September 1958 to begin our secondary education.

Joseph Moran, my youngest brother, took a keen interest in the life of his uncle, Paddy Moran. He discussed with me many of the pieces of research that I unearthed and gave me his candid opinion. Sadly, Joseph died without seeing all those efforts come to fruition. However, I think he has been a guiding light from a higher place. It would have been a source of pleasure to him that his daughter, Claire, took a keen interest in her granduncle and completed a thesis on him at Galway Institute of Technology.

Fr Tommy Moran, RIP, Paddy's nephew, might have been the person writing this book if he had not died so young. Fr Tommy was, during his lifetime, spokesperson for the family on various occasions when Paddy Moran was honoured.

Seán, my brother, was a great help to me and shared the knowledge that he had gained through his conversations with our father, Tom.

I would like to express my sincere thanks to Paddy, my brother, Maureen, his wife, and their family, for their support, hospitality and generosity over the years. To be living beside them in my native Crossna is a great pleasure for me.

Finally, I dedicate this book to all the descendants of Paddy Moran, his nephews and nieces, his grandnephews and grandnieces,

great grandnephews and great grandnieces, his cousins on the Moran
and Sheerin sides and the many in-laws on all sides in the hope that
it will serve to keep his memory alive and enable them to know more
about Paddy Moran than I knew up to now.

INDEX

Also available from Mercier Press

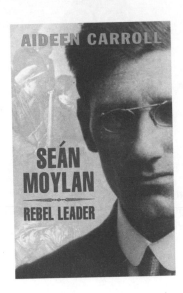

Seán Moylan: Rebel Leader

Aideen Carroll

978 1 85635 669 5

Seán Moylan played a crucial part in the War of Independence as leader of the Newmarket Battalion and later O/C of Cork No. 2 Brigade, masterminding the ambushes at Tureengarriffe and Clonbanin which had such a demoralising effect on the morale of the British forces. Following the Truce he argued vehemently against the Treaty and during the Civil War fought on the republican side.

In 1932 he joined Fianna Fáil and stood for election. He remained a prominent member of the Dáil, as both TD and in various ministerial posts, until his death in 1957. Moylan successfully made the difficult transition from guerrilla leader to constitutional politician and helped lead his country towards peace and prosperity.

www.mercierpress.ie

MERCIER PRESS

IRISH PUBLISHER - IRISH STORY

We hope you enjoyed this book.

Since 1944, Mercier Press has published books that have been critically important to Irish life and culture. Books that dealt with subjects that informed readers about Irish scholars, Irish writers, Irish history and Ireland's rich heritage.

We believe in the importance of providing accessible histories and cultural books for all readers and all who are interested in Irish cultural life.

Our website is the best place to find out more information about Mercier, our books, authors, news and the best deals on a wide variety of books. Mercier track the best prices for our books online and we seek to offer the best value to our customers, offering free delivery within Ireland.

Sign up on our website or complete and return the form below to receive updates and special offers.

www.mercierpress.ie
www.facebook.com/mercier.press
www.twitter.com/irishpublisher

Name:

Email:

Address:

Mercier Press, Unit 3b, Oak House, Bessboro Rd, Blackrock, Cork, Ireland